BUILDING FAITH IN FAMILIES

BUILDING FAITH IN FAMILIES
Using the Sacraments in Pastoral Ministry

FRANK GASQUE DUNN

MOREHOUSE-BARLOW
Wilton, CT

Morehouse-Barlow Co., Inc.
78 Danbury Road
Wilton, Connecticut 06897

Library of Congress Cataloging-in-Publication Data

Dunn, Frank Gasque, 1945-
Building faith in families.

Bibliography: p.
1. Church work with families. 2. Family—Religious life.
3. Sacraments. I. Title.
BV4438.D86   1986   253   86-21818
ISBN 0-8192-1394-2

Printed in the United States of America
2 4 6 8 10 9 7 5 3 1

For Barbara

CONTENTS

Acknowledgments

Building Faith in Families is the work of many people. As will be obvious on page after page, I owe a great debt of gratitude to John Westerhoff, whose workshops I began attending in 1975 in North Carolina. I am grateful, too, for the parishes of St. Martin's, Charlotte, North Carolina; St. Andrew's, Charlotte; and Trinity Church, Newtown, Connecticut, where many of these ideas have been tested and evaluated. I thank those co-workers with whom I have shared parts of this journey: Jim Kowalski, who is responsible for many ideas in the Chapter on Confirmation; Margie Robinson, who has implemented and tested many of the Christian education approaches; Kent Smith for his encouragement, support, and willingness to pick up the slack occasioned by my writing; Marge Cassin, my secretary, for being understanding, as always.

I cannot forget the kindness of the staff at Okemo Mountain Trailside, Ludlow, Vermont, where I wrote much of the manuscript. Nor Sister Lucia, C.H.S., who hosted me while I wrote some chapters at St. Cuthbert's House. Carlynn Reed graciously helped me shape the outline. Ruth Turney assisted me at crucial points, not the least of which was to learn something about the world of religious publishing. Margaret Warner read the manuscript, and, as always, cheered me on. Morehouse-Barlow's Steve Wilburn has been a gift. It is to his vision and enthusiasm that I owe the publication of these ideas.

Margy Harrington improved this book immeasurably with her suggestions for tighter, clearer writing. I am as thankful for her patience and interest as for her expertise.

And, of course, to my own family I owe the deepest thanks. In many ways, this book belongs to them.

F.G.D.
Newtown, Connecticut
The Second Sunday after Pentecost,
June 1, 1986

BUILDING FAITH IN FAMILIES

Introduction

Early Thursday morning found us rushing around more than usual. School lunches half-fixed, cereal boxes out, bagels thawing, and the voice of David Hartman hummed out by the dishwasher. The phone rang. One of our daughter Sarah Marsh Dunn's friends checking what outfit she was wearing to school, I guessed.

"Frank?" My mother-in-law sounded weak. Even more tired than she sounded two nights before. I tensed, fearing the conversation to come. My wife's father, Walter, was in the hospital in Virginia twelve hours away. Nearly a week before, we sat at home and wondered through his operation. We had prayed. A full recovery from massive infection hardly seemed in the realm of answerable prayer. It would not have surprised us if he had not made it through the operation. But he had. And he made it past the critical twenty-four, forty-eight, seventy-two hour periods, with kidneys, heart, lungs all working.

"The hospital called and told me to get over there as quickly as I could . . ." Barely able to hear her, I was straining to get Evelyn's every sound. Barbara and the girls heard me call her name, and one by one the sounds stopped around me. My mind raced ahead to calculate whether we could leave immediately, rather than the next morning as we had planned. Appointments would have to be

1

cancelled, meetings postponed, the noon Eucharist celebrated by Kent. I heard Barbara pick up the study phone.

Her mother repeated what she had just told me. He had had a bad night. A turn for the worse, the doctor said. Breathing was rapid, light. Maybe pneumonia again.

In a few hours we were packed and on the road. So many times we have driven down the east coast on vacation. The routes and scenes are memorized. I wondered if we would get there before he died. The girls, ages 13 and 10, kept asking questions that had no answers. Would he live? Could he live? What happened? Grandaddy Jones was special to them. And they no more than I, his only son-in-law, nor Barbara, his only child, could grasp what it would be like to say good-bye, even though we had rehearsed the possibility. He had gone into the hospital to have what was predicted to be a simple removal of a gallstone in the bile duct. It hadn't worked. One of the two big stones was still lodged in the duct. Several days at home after a five-week hospital stay had seen him get worse and worse; hence the operation. He was gravely sick.

Confound it, I thought. Can't they do anything in this day and age to get rid of infection? Ridiculous. People just don't die of infections in the 1980s. My mind skimmed incidents of unlikely deaths I have known. Yes, people do die of infections. And from less. I prayed.

We rolled into the hospital parking lot at midnight. I wondered if we could get in. What would we find? How would the girls respond? In the midst of these concerns some things are refreshingly stable. As, for instance, a midnight "discussion" about who gets to push the elevator button. And hospital smells, always clean.

Grandmommie roused herself from the couch when we spilled out of the elevator. I expected a feeling of relief, hers and ours, but I had not foreseen the joy of reunion. Hugs, kisses. Some things you can count on.

Barbara, Evelyn, and I went into the Intensive Care Unit, leaving the children to wait. So many tubes that I'd seen on hospital visits before now ran into and out of one I loved. The sucking sound of the respirator punctuated our greetings. Eye movements in response to our words told us he could hear. Only involuntary movements stirred his body. His eyes, swollen and filmy, could not open long enough to focus on us, yet we were there. He knew.

That night I dreamed he and I were going to play golf. I was to meet him at a certain course we had been wanting to play. Something kept me from getting there. I looked out in the middle of a street and saw his tan golf hat. I went over, picked it up, put it on my head. That was the end of the dream.

Friday morning Barbara woke me. The hospital had again called. His blood pressure had dropped drastically, and they couldn't stabilize it. Evelyn was waiting for me to take her from Altavista to Lynchburg. I was not surprised. What I had seen the night before told me death was on the way. The question was whether we could get to the hospital before death did.

"We've tried about everything we can try," the young doctor said to Evelyn and me as he took his seat in the cramped consultation room. "We've got him stabilized now. I thought three times we had lost him. But the blood pressure is up and holding steady." I began to sense the difference between being someone's priest and being someone's son-in-law. I knew what was going on, but didn't know what to say, so I asked questions: How long do you think you can, doctor? What kind, doctor? How much, doctor? He was a very nice man with a very nice red tie. I liked his forthrightness. I was glad he was there.

I heard Barbara and the kids in the hall. Yes, I assured them, he was still alive. The doctor made his comments again for the five of us. He was the first one of many medical people we were to meet in the next week. Every one of them was incredibly sensitive, understanding, patient. We were assured that we could come and go in the Intensive Care Unit. I supposed that they relaxed the visiting policy because they knew it would not be for long. Nurses brought us coffee and tea. The nursing staff took care to include our children in conversations, explaining to them about the tubes, machines, and monitors they would live around in the days to come.

This proved especially important. Though we had tried to prepare them, the children's first visit to their grandfather in ICU shocked them. They last had seen him the previous Thanksgiving, when the six of us gathered at Hershey Park, Pennsylvania. It was like so many other times when we had shopped, toured, posed for his camera. But this Friday was Valentine's Day, and nothing seemed the same. Sarah Marsh described it on paper:

> Grandad is in Virginia Baptist Hospital. He looks sad. He has a tube leading down his throat to assist him in breathing. He really isn't the Grandad I know. I usually see him laughing or at least looking attentive, holding my hand.
>
> Now he is lying still, an occasional unconscious nod of the head. His eyes are grey-green with a filmy shade. I don't think he can focus—but I'm almost sure he senses I'm there. His face is swollen, pushed to the side. Tubes and IVs are leading most of his actions.
>
> Today is Valentine's Day. I touched his limp hand and said, "I love you."
>
> Grandad is going to die. I think I've pretty much accepted that. Every time the phone rings, though, I jump. Grandma says he doesn't want to suffer. I say that's true—I want him to be comfortable.
>
> He just isn't well. His smooth, white hair is matted down. Last night I had a dream. I walked in a dim room. Grandad had a, well, Zip-Loc bag over his head with water, blood, fluid filling it. (I couldn't make out the image of his face.)
>
> Then the scene changed to a brighter room. With a tall boy and a painting, plus the hospital bed. Grandad was wearing a turtleneck, golf sweater, plaid pants, and his Bean shoes (his usual outfit). He got up and hugged me, saying, "Sugar, I love you. I better lie down though because Grandma sure won't like me getting up like this!"
>
> I think that was his good-bye to me. The dream touched me.
>
> I noticed in the Care Unit new slippers. Grandma probably got them for him. She said his old ones "clunked around." I know . . . the three of us liked that sound.

What I witnessed in the next few days was truly remarkable. Every day was spent at the hospital. Walter did not change. The change came in the rest of us. I first noticed it in Evelyn. Though tired, sad, anxious, and drawn, she would brighten, would laugh when the girls were around, or when something funny would happen in the waiting room. They kidded her. She told them stories. The time her brother was riding on the running board of the car and fell off unnoticed, and Evelyn *finally* reported it a mile down the road—a dutiful sister. Other stories—some twice told, some new.

The children changed, too. They did not grow to like Intensive Care, but they grew less afraid of it. They would take turns sitting with their grandmother, holding her hand, talking, sitting in silence, pointing out something or asking a question. Their fears shrank. They could go up to Grandad and hold his hand and talk to him, expecting nothing back. Anne learned how to read the various monitors and what each one of them meant. She insisted on talking to the doctors, and they addressed her as if she were twice her age. Both girls ministered, though they never used the word, nor heard it applied to them. And their grandmother ministered to them. She gave them an image of what it means to have and to hold someone in sickness as in health.

In some sense, Barbara had the most difficult time. All her life she had been "the only child." With almost no warning, some of her major roles began to shift. She became the decision-maker, the mainstay. No matter how much we rehearse for life's crises, they often end up flattening us. It was her turn to be squeezed between two generations: aging parents who needed her and children who depended upon her. The squeeze was tight. Her crossed arms said so.

I knew her instincts would lead her to the basement not long after she got to her parent's home. It was Walter's space, more than any other. His the workshop, his the ten screwdrivers neatly arranged in their rack, his the half-finished doll house. I put my arm around her. "We're going to miss him."

"He has always been here when I needed him." She tightened her lip. "I can't imagine what it will be without him." She picked up a golf shoe and fingered the tassel. Shoes always look like the people who wear them. "Everything reminds us of him, doesn't it?" Her glance surveyed the garden equipment, the neatly stored 1940s croquet set, his shoeshine box. The basement was full of its slightly musty odor. A voice called, "Mom." We put memories on hold.

Next day at the hospital, I felt in my pocket the little round

brass oil stock for anointing and wondered why I had brought it.
I do not routinely carry it with me. On some level I suspect I knew
I would want it. I did not try to be Walter's priest. I did not want
to be. Or need to be. But I did need to give him a gift, to do for
him something that I can do and like to do for others. So, while
Barbara and I were with him, I pressed my thumb into the oil for
the healing of the sick and traced with it the sign of the cross on
his forehead:

> Walter, I lay my hands upon you and anoint you with oil,
> in the Name of the Father, and of the Son, and of the Holy
> Spirit, beseeching our Lord Jesus Christ to sustain you with
> his presence, to drive away all sickness of body and spirit, and
> to give you that victory of life and peace which will enable
> you to serve him both now and evermore.[1]

I turned and embraced Barbara. "I need a priest," I said.

The First Sunday in Lent dawned with snow on the ground and
me not knowing where to go to church. Barbara went to telephone
a church near the hospital to find out times of services. "Guess who's
the Rector of St. John's," she asked me when she returned. "Joel."
Our old friend Joel. Providence had moved him from North
Carolina in time for us! I couldn't wait to see him. I wanted to
weep when I finally did see him.

Over the next several days Joel was in and out of the hospital,
helping us to get through our night. I don't know how he had the
time just to sit and visit at the end of a long day. But I learned
how much it means to a family when someone is there. Not for
long. A little while will do. I had never reckoned that my own
hospital visits were all that important to people. I had found out
a month before, when Walter was in the hospital in Chapel Hill,
what it felt like to call an unknown priest and say, "I know you're
busy, and you probably can't respond, but if you just happen to
be there, could you . . .?" and be told, "I'm just heading that way.
I'll be sure to stop by." And here it was again. Presence. That is
what ministry is. Not what we do but what we are.

God's gifts are sometimes hard, and always good. We had the
gift of a week together as a family as Grandaddy Jones died. We
had time to say good-bye, to remember, to get used to the idea,

to be angry and sad and scared, to hold one another up. We were given the gift to tell him we loved him. We were able to cry, and dry our eyes, and cry some more. And we found the grace that builds faith.

Almost a week to the minute after our arrival, he died. Sarah Marsh, a short while before the end, came to his bedside. "Grandad," she said, "I have a prayer I want to say for you. Now I lay me down to sleep . . ." she began. Blood pressure dropped slowly, steadily. Heartbeats became fainter. Then there was the long solid line on the monitor. We gathered around his bed and prayed. Hearing is the last sense to die.

Phone calls. Visitors. The story of his sickness and dying told and repeated. And then the funeral. We sang "Praise to the Lord, the Almighty, the King of Creation" and "A Mighty Fortress Is Our God." The minister's sermon was brilliant. He ended by re-telling the scene from C.S. Lewis' *The Last Battle* in *The Chronicles of Narnia*, when those who have loved Aslan win the final victory. The service over, we turned and walked toward the west. A glorious sunburst lit the February sky, an outward sign of the Light that had enlightened our darkness all week.

This book was written almost entirely before Walter's death, but that experience was another confirmation of the truth that what I have learned about building faith in families has come not through research, nor even through my work with families as a priest, but through what my family and I have lived through. During this time, we were not only dealing with the loss of a person we loved deeply; we were forever bumping up against things like oil, bread and wine, touch, prayer, memory, and story which help us make sense of our lives. What follows is an attempt to articulate ways that such things can contribute to the building of faith in families, especially as clergy and lay leaders in parishes prepare people for, and use, the Sacraments of the Church.

PART ONE

LAYING THE FOUNDATION

ONE

Does the Church Care?

Louise, a parishioner distinguished by her frankness, came up with
tears in her eyes after the Sunday service. "Don't you ever do that
to me again!" she fumed.

I was thrown off balance. There was more emotion in that
comment than I had grown to expect even from Louise.

"What did I do?" I asked, innocent of any intentional offense.

"You paraded all those married people up there in front of all
the rest of us. You had them stand up there and renew their
marriage vows. How do you think folks like me felt? Albert's been
dead for a little over six months, but I haven't gotten over it. And
this morning didn't help one bit!"

I wilted. It had never once occurred to me, when I was planning
this service including the optional renewal of marriage vows, that
it could in any sense feel like a negative commentary on those in
the congregation who happened not to be married. I indeed had
thought about the presence of unmarried people, but reasoned that
they would feel no more left out than at a baptism of someone else's
child. But I had not thought specifically about widows and
widowers. I knew Louise was not fooling. This had been a painful
experience for her, and probably for others like her.

After mumbling something of an embarrassed apology, I went

to my office and reflected on Louise's comment. After getting through my initial defensiveness, I could see her point. I had even said numberless times that the church ought to be careful how it treats those outside families or marriages. Now I was discovering how very easy it was to be thoughtless of them.

I vowed not to let that happen again. I became not only conscious, but probably compulsive, about including the unmarried in whatever was going on. Parish programming came to reflect an intentional flexibility to give single persons, one-parent families, older persons, the divorced and widowed—everyone—an equal chance to participate in everything possible.

Based on Louise's experience, and of thousands like her, one could assume that the church is, if anything, too oriented to the married and to families. There seems to be little place for single persons, or even for people whose spouses or children do not attend church with them. Does the Church care about families? Quite obviously, yes!

All parish clergy know that families are the lifeblood of parishes. Even the single, the elderly, the childless repeat the folk wisdom that young people are the future of the church. Clergy read statistics. When looking at a prospective new parish, one of the first things many look at is the number of infant baptisms in recent years. And at how many students are enrolled in the church school. We want to know what kind of a youth program there is, and how much money is budgeted for it. Implicit in all this is the dominant role that families, especially those with children, play in the life of a parish. They remain crucial, even though we become more conscious each year of the special needs of the aging, single adult and those who live alone.

Yet there is another side to this story. As family-oriented as the parish church might seem, observe what it does to, with, and for its families. The Joneses arrive at church early on a Sunday morning, and immediately they leave two-year-old Heather screaming in the nursery. After tearful reassurances that Mommy and Daddy will be back for Heather, Mom takes six-year-old Jennifer to the children's choir room, to check to see if her vestments are there, and to inquire of the choirmaster what Jennifer needs to bring to the party Wednesday afternoon. Meanwhile, Dad has a meeting of the education committee, which has been called before church begins. Mom has some altar guild duties to perform, so she hurries off to the sacristy. Tommy Jones goes to the classroom for third-graders, where his teacher will keep him until time for children third-grade and younger to go to church. They will then, of course, go together as a class.

Search the parish church—any church—on any Sunday morning in America, and you will be hard-put to find one that does not manage to split up families. Nor is all this necessarily bad. Women perhaps need the chance to be with other women, or at least with other adults, instead of their children for an hour or so. Men perhaps need the chance to be with other men. Teenagers need a chance to be with each other, to talk about who sat with whom at the basketball game, and what is likely to be on Mr. Clark's history test tomorrow. And clearly our school system has by now acclimated all of us to learning with our own age group. For several generations we have tried nobly to see that all Sunday Schools are set up along age-graded lines, parallel with those of the public schools.[1] So we expect to be separated from family members when we go to the parish church.

Recently while on vacation, I visited a church. In the pew in front of me were a man and his son, who looked about ten. Nothing too awful was going on, yet I could sense the father's annoyance at his son's incessant pleas for attention. When the boy tried for about the third time to climb into his father's lap, the father rather firmly (I thought with great restraint) told the youngster to slide further down the pew. The boy slid. He also looked as if he could bite nails.

Meanwhile, sitting beside me was a lone pregnant woman. I thought, "How lovely of her to come to church. Wonder where her husband is? In the choir? Ushering? Maybe one of the chalice ministers. I'll bet this is her first child." My thoughts went back to the sermon. I forgot about my pregnant pew-mate until halfway through the service when the children were brought in and told to find their parents. Two joined her. A girl, maybe five years old, and a boy, probably three. He screamed. I wondered if he screamed because he had been separated from her or because he had been reunited with her in a situation where she could not give him the attention he wanted. I watched them go to the communion rail, where he staged a first-class tantrum. Finally, she took him out, somehow managed to calm him, and they returned. For the moment he was quiet. How very much she needed communion after all that, I mused.

It is not easy. We try to bring families together at least some of the time at church, but much militates against our efforts. Children get restless. Adults get frustrated. "Intergenerational" is not something that most churches can be or want to be. For the most part, we live in this culture along generational lines, adults with adults and children with children. We have grown to expect it to be that way.

But we have to look more closely at what the church does to families. Examine, for instance, the premium we place on commitment. This is a big word in the Church's vocabulary. We want to get people "involved." We want them to give their time and energies to the parish church. A favorite eulogy Christians make of their dead parents is to say appreciatively that those parents were at church every time the doors were opened. Implication: that is real commitment; *that* is living by the Gospel. In every parish I have served there have been people who obviously operated—consciously or unconsciously, although I suspect the former—on the basis of "the more I do for the parish church, the better Christian I am." I shall have more to say in Chapter Two about grace; but at this point I wish to say that few things undermine a doctrine of grace in our churches quite so much as the idea that "the-more-I-do-the-better-I-am." What that does to the family is terribly damaging.

Many adults absent themselves from the family, night after night, week after week, all in the name of being good Christians. Or, in some cases, they drag their children along to meetings, prayer groups, Bible studies, etc., where the children are miserably bored by adult conversation. I remember a couple who took their eight-year-old son everywhere, and that meant to some different religious affair each night, as they went from group to group, meeting to meeting. I wondered then, and I wonder now, what will be that child's attitude toward Church and toward religion when he is older.

Religion can sometimes be the chief competitor of family life.

My wife once stunned me with the comment that she found it awfully hard not to feel guilty at her anger with my overworking. After all, when she got annoyed she heard "tapes" in her head saying that she was wrong; that all her husband was doing was for God. Who was she to begrudge God? She is not the only one who feels that kind of tension. Many a spouse wants to blow the whistle on a mate who is overly involved in church activities, but caves in to the thought that it is a Christian duty to sacrifice home to church. So marriage and family life suffer because of the great delusion that, when we're out of the house for God, we're out for good reasons. Perhaps the reason more and more church members seem to feel justified in staying away from worship guiltlessly is that they sense the absurdity of being in church all the time.

On the other hand there are parents who commute, or travel, and they miss their families all week long. The weekend comes and they want and need some time together as a family. Church is all right once a month, or maybe every two weeks, but more than that encroaches on family time. When I can get beyond reacting negatively to what I often perceive as a smokescreen for other concerns, I have some sympathy with people like this. We do lead increasingly complex and demanding lives. It takes its toll on family time. Is it right that people must choose between church and family? Church leaders can think of a dozen reasons why this is a false dichotomy; of how the investment in religious activity for a couple of hours once a week is a good thing for families. Yet, the fact remains that choices have to be made. And many modern American families choose to go to the lake, the tennis courts, camping, to the club—anywhere they can be together.

There is no simple solution to all this. The church cannot please everyone: the old woman who does not want to be disturbed in church by the noises of fidgety kids; the mom who wants one hour of peace and quiet; the person who wants to spend some time with his family he has not seen all week; the people who want the teens to be off by themselves having a jolly time; the clergy who want even nursing babies to be present at the liturgy. We cannot have the renewal of marriage vows on a Sunday morning and still make the Louises of the congregation comfortable. Choices have to be made.

There are some things, however, that the church, and particularly
the lay and ordained leadership, can do. First, we can take a good
look at the question of whether we really do care about families.
Are we merely giving verbal support to the idea of the family's
importance, or are we offering ways through the parish ministry
whereby families can be strengthened and supported?

Second, we can test our own definitions of "family" when we
use it as a part of church rhetoric. Many of us are fond of speaking
of the church as the Family of God, or as "our parish family." There
is no problem with that in itself. Yet how inclusive is this "family"?
Can we find a way to include the Louises and the other single
persons in a true family that also includes husbands and wives and
their children? We need to examine the kinds of families we have
in mind when we design programs or ministries for them. Are we
often thinking about the nuclear family—mother, father, kids? Is
there a consciousness that in many of our congregations there is a
substantial number of families with single parents? I think the best
definition of a family is one I learned to use years ago when
beginning to design family enrichment events:

> A family is two or more people who share the same living
> space, a common past, and a common future.

That is wide open. It also covers any kind of family one is going
to meet in the parish church.

Third, we can look carefully and critically at the effect of parish
programming on family life. There must be some balance between
liturgies that include the whole family and those designed with
specific groups in mind. We should provide occasions that bring
whole families and several generations together, and those that give
adults, children, and adolescents opportunities to be with their own
age groups. Above all, church leaders can articulate the point of
view that it is imperative that folks establish a priority of family
time. We are not doing ourselves, God, or the church a favor by
seeing how many tasks we can assume and accomplish, especially
if those tasks compete with time at home. We should set limits and
become examples by spending time with our families. We should
draw the line at two meetings out per week, and encourage others
to do the same. This way, church leaders can practice helping

people give themselves permission not to let parish involvement eat up family time.

FAMILIES OR INDIVIDUALS?

When I first wrote the phrase, "The Pastoral Care of Families" an image came to mind. I saw a cleric—black clad, of course—going in the early evening to call on a family, all of whom were at home. There was once a time when clergy could visit families and assume that they would not be interfering with the family's life. Clergy were welcomed. And they could expect that, at the end of the day, all the family would be inside, chores done, huddling around the fireplace. (I also wonder just how prevalent clergy visits were in those days. My guess is that, before the automobile, most clergy who did any evening visiting were jockeying about a far-flung flock, staying overnight with families hither and yon.) Certainly there was, before the twentieth century, little chance the parson would find the family unoccupied, if indeed at home and not in the fields or shop, were he to come calling during the day. Of course, people expected the priest or parson to call if anyone in the family were ill or in other serious difficulty.

In smalltown America of the nineteenth and early twentieth centuries, it was possible for the parson to wander in and out among places of business, greeting people and speaking to parishioners. It was also possible for him to move around neighborhoods in the afternoon ringing doorbells, with a fair chance of finding women, and perhaps children, at home.

We maintain that image, or at least a good many lay people do. We forget, however, that pressures have been steadily mounting to change radically both parishioners' and pastors' time. For example, in former days there was no hospital calling because there were few or no hospitals. Women were at home because they had to be; today, most have to work. Liturgical revision was unknown: no one was introducing new hymnals and Prayer Books. There were few study courses. And no demand for pastoral counseling on the scale now existing. Parish clergy had no users of hard drugs to cope with. Sexual abuse, child abuse, abortions, even alcoholism are much more readily dealt with today. We pay in time the price for their being out of the closet.

Society has changed. The family has changed. Have our modes of pastoral care *of the family* changed? Certainly, many parishes keep alive the expectation that clergy will call in homes regularly. Yet, when they "drop by for a friendly chat," as one parish handbook advertises, they often find no one at home. Try calling to arrange a suitable time to visit a family. I have scheduled visits three months in advance, because no available Saturdays, Sundays, or evenings came any sooner. Those, of course, are the only times one can reasonably expect to find whole families at home. It is time we re-thought the pastoral call as an effective means of caring for families. I am not advocating abandoning it, just stating the need to come clean about its limitations.

In recent years, family counseling has come into prominence as a natural outgrowth of marriage counseling, which has been increasing in popularity and demand since World War II. People— families are no exception—do not go "for counseling" unless there are problems, however, and fairly grave ones at that. As with individuals, families will let life slide until they no longer can stand the pressures, and feel constrained to do something about them. Then they seek a counselor. And, more accurately, *families* do not seek help; parents usually do because of trouble they perceive one of the children to be causing.

Mike and Mary were preparing for marriage. It was to be a second marriage for both of them. Mike's son lived with his mother in another part of the country. Mary's two children, a son and a daughter, lived with her. As they talked about their lives, their hopes, their concerns about the blended family they proposed to form, it became clear to the pastor that there were some problems with Mary's children. They were, he reasoned, probably grieving and "acting out" as a result of the recent divorce (Mary's divorce had become final within the previous several months). The pastor thought it wise to drop by and visit Mary's children, with Mike present. He found that he had seriously underestimated the hostility the children, particularly Joyce, the daughter, felt toward Mike. She was angry, fiercely combative, and uncooperative towards him, and to a lesser extent towards her mother. The pastor found her somewhat receptive to him, and offered to see her at some time of her choosing to talk over her feelings about the upcoming wedding.

Joyce never came. Mike and Mary grew increasingly disturbed and frustrated by Joyce's behavior: she became truant, ran away several times, and got into some minor scrapes with the police, having to do with petty larceny and marijuana use. The pastor was candid with Mike and Mary, telling them that he believed they would have to work diligently and long to incorporate Joyce into the family circle, and committed himself to work with them. But, it took nearly a year for Mike and Mary to be convinced that the *family* had a problem. Every conversation found them saying with deep conviction that Joyce was the one who was the problem. And, of course, the more Joyce became identified as "the problem," the more she acted the part. It was a vicious spiral to nowhere.

At length, the pastor was able to persuade Mike and Mary to bring the children with them to some of their sessions. Joyce continued to be hostile or noncommunicative. Her younger brother was bored and somewhat angry at being "forced" to be present. Mike's strategy was to put Joyce down. Mary felt caught in the middle. The most important thing that the family sessions accomplished was that special help was sought from another counselor for Joyce. She began to find ways of feeling better about herself, and gradually the whole family began to experience some healing. They are still traveling a hard road, however.

This experience is not atypical of families in counseling. Add to the difficulty of the dynamics the problems of scheduling with a heavy calendar on the pastor's desk, possibly travel on one or both parents' part, and the children's various obligations, and simply finding time when everyone can be together. Only when a situation has reached crisis proportions are those involved usually ready to make it an absolute priority. The conclusion I arrive at is that, while family therapy may be important and even rewarding, it is hardly a way to reach many families.

Another model for the pastoral care of families is family enrichment. The immediate value of this approach is that it is not problem-oriented, as is family counseling. Many family enrichment events bring together different sorts of families in a Sunday, weekend, or evening event. These can be great fun, and are probably the best thing in our current repertoire of structured support for families. Yet, this too has its limitations. Families who tend to participate in this kind of event are often extraverted. Many families shy away from this type of activity, afraid their weaknesses will be on display, despite the reassurances they are offered before-hand. Or, on the contrary, some families with distinct problems are drawn to the family enrichment event hoping that they will find ways of muddling through their problems more creatively. Usually they go away disappointed.

Family enrichment events, family clusters, intergenerational programs are exciting, energizing, and sometimes remarkably successful. Yet they consume an enormous amount of planning. Church leaders often become discouraged not only at the amount of time and energy such programs demand, but at the lack of skilled people needed to put them together and lead them. Again, I conclude that the model of family enrichment is not a way to offer sustained pastoral care to large numbers of families effectively.

What remains are models of pastoral care that are generally individual-oriented. There is the variety of one-on-one relationships found in the penitent/confessor, pastoral counselor/counselee, spiritual guide-director-friend models. All of these are valuable. Yet none of them seems suited to the care of families, as such. We are left with having to re-think the relationship of the family unit to the larger parish community and the position of the family within the church.

The pastoral care of families must begin, I believe, with the datum that in Christianity the church—the congregation of the faithful—is primary. The home is not. The family is significant, important, but not primary. This has been true from the begin-ning. It is clear from Mark's Gospel that Jesus himself had to make a break with his family. "Who are my mother and brothers?" he asked when Mary and her other sons stood outside, hoping to persuade him to give up his career and take an early retirement in Nazareth.

And a crowd was sitting about him; and they said to him, "Your mother and your brothers are outside, asking for you." And he replied, "Who are my mother and my brothers?" And looking around on those who sat about him, he said, "Here are my mother and my brothers! Whoever does the will of God is my brother, and sister and mother."[2]

There was a reason the Church preserved that story. Just as there was a reason that the Church remembered Peter's saying, "Lo, we have left everything and followed you."[3] Family ties were secondary to the relationships of the Kingdom. All that we know about the Early Church suggests that this remained the case for some centuries. When Clement of Alexandria and Cyprian referred to religious ritual in family life, they took for granted that the family extended the liturgy of the church into the home. There was never any suggestion that the family took pre-eminence over the larger Christian community.[4]

All of this is to say that we need to be centered on what the Church must do to produce people who are growing in the faith. As simple as that sounds, it stands in serious contrast to much of the agenda of the contemporary parish. Expressed or unexpressed, that agenda is shaped by a consumer mentality which sees the church in business to "serve" various clientele: the elderly who need companionship, the young who need togetherness, children who need a sense of belonging and a religious education, and families who need some reprieve from the stress they are under—to name just a few. The pastoral care of families must not arise out of this conglomeration, but rather from an understanding on the Church's part that its primary task is to equip people to live a life of union with God.

This is precisely the place where the Church's sacraments become pivotal. The purpose of the sacraments, beginning with Holy Baptism, is to bring the life of God in Christ, through the power of the Holy Spirit, together with our lives. The sacraments are meant to transform our lives so completely that we can say with St. Paul, "It is no more I who live, but Christ who lives in me." If one looks at a list of the sacraments, it becomes clear that the implicit goal of the whole series of sacraments is to sanctify ordinary life—to make it holy, to bring it into conjunction with Divine reality. This view will be spelled out more fully in the next chapter. At this juncture, let it suffice for us to connect this sanctification process to the family's primary goal: getting people safely through the life cycle.

THE FAMILY'S FUNCTION

To some extent, the family's function has always been to get people through life. Yet, in earlier cultures that goal was often realized by having *family* become so large and include so many people that it became tribe or clan. Ties of kinship were important for defense and for economic well-being, and for safeguarding the latter by means of the former. In the Middle Ages, family was important for the orderly transmission of property from one generation to the next. Even two hundred years ago, the family's job was to keep its members alive from one day to the next. Until recently, no one understood families as the context in which individuals would be nurtured to "reach their potential," or even to reach maturity. In former times (and still in much of the world), people had babies hoping that enough of them might survive that there would be hands aplenty on the farm to scratch out a living. The weight we in the western world place on the affective relationships in a family is a new thing. The idea of bringing children into the world to complete the happiness of a couple is a recently hatched sentiment that only in this day of economic prosperity could have any meaning. (It bears pointing out that that economic prosperity is restricted to a very small portion of the world, and to a very minor sliver of the population in that portion!)[5]

But today, the family in America and in most of the Western world can view as its task getting people safely through the life cycle. We have still inherited from our ancient nomadic past the need for the family to provide a certain amount of security against the elements, against enemies, and against starvation. And we have inherited a certain amount of concern from our medieval forebears that we need to transmit property—or, if not valuables, then values —from one generation to the next. But the nuclear family today has the goal of making children sufficiently independent when they reach adulthood to earn their own living and to start their own families. And in very few families of suburban middle-class America are children viewed as a means of increasing the family's economic efficiency. The general pattern that has emerged is one wherein children reach maturity; spend some time experimenting with education, sexual alliances, and vocational options; and eventually

marry and form families of their own. (Part of the problem with
our handling of an increasing elderly population, incidentally, is
that the nuclear family is ill-equipped to take care of aging persons.
The American public has yet to buy emotionally the necessity of
nursing homes and other institutions devoted to caring for the aging,
but it is a fact that this society has to have some context other than
a nuclear family in which to provide for the needs of old people.
This was not the case before the complete advent of the stripped-
down nuclear family, and it is still not the case in those areas where
some form of extended family prevails.)

Whether we live in our families of origin or in the families we
have created through marriage, we confront the same passages and
the same issues. Who am I? What am I going to be when I reach
adulthood? Where am I going with my life? What about my inner
self, my soul—what is happening to that part of me as I make my
external choices of mate and vocation? With whom do I wish to
spend my life? How am I going to deal with my aging body, the
crises of sickness, the death of family members, my own death?
What about my relationships with the larger community? Do I have
any obligations other than to myself and my immediate family?
Do I have any accountability before God? These are basic, and in
some cases ultimate, questions. Not all of us, but most of us, ask
and answer them in the context of lives lived in families. The extent
to which the family helps us to deal with them is the extent to which
the family is fulfilling its function of aiding the individual in getting
through life.

I used the phrase above, "getting safely through life." Why
"safely"? This is an important qualifier. It implies that the family
has some kind of protective, perhaps even a salvific, function. The
job my parents had in rearing me to adulthood was not just physical
and economic. It included seeing that I reached adulthood as whole
an individual as I could be. This may or may not have been
consciously expressed; but it underlay everything that my parents
did for me during my growth to adulthood. Now I am a parent.
My family still has some responsibility for helping me to grow, to
address those basic questions of life. To put it bluntly, the job of
my family will be well accomplished if I come to the grave having
lived life as fully as possible, and having died as whole a person

as I could have become. The task of the family is never done perfectly. None of us arrives at adulthood without in some way being damaged, often by what our parents do or don't do to and for us. And our families can never ensure that we shall reach the end of our earthly pilgrimages without scars, without missing pieces. But to see that we get to our destination with as much intact as possible—that is the family's task. That is getting us through life as *safely* as possible.

What the Church needs is to find a way of lacing together its purpose and the purpose of the family. There must be a connection between the life of growing into ever-deepening union with God provided through the sacraments, and the ordinary stuff of life that we are living in the context of our families. These two have to become one. "Ordinary" life is the only life there is to sanctify, to make holy. We can put the question in either of two ways, which amount to the same thing. Either we can ask how the family can support the process of transformation into the image and life of Christ; or we can ask how the Church can support the family in getting its members through life as safely as possible—so that they arrive at their deaths as whole as they can be.

A "NEW" WAY OF CARING

There is nothing very new about this "new" way of caring. The "new" way of building faith in families is for the Church to take its sacramental life seriously and to prepare its people diligently to receive the sacraments faithfully. As simple as that may sound, it will bring about a major revolution in the way many parish churches operate. To name just a few things:

> We shall have to say goodbye, once and for all, to private baptisms.

> We shall have to say to couples who come to the church for the first time only a month or so before their wedding that we are as sorry as we can be, but preparation for marriage is considerably more involved than something that can be done in a few hours over a few weeks.

> We shall have to come to terms with confession as an integral part of the Christian life. If we are Roman Catholic, that

means we shall have to take confession with a seriousness that far exceeds perfunctory confession. If we are Anglican, that means we have to begin doing a good deal of teaching about the dynamic of confession as a part of corporate responsibility as well as individual growth. If we are Protestant, that means we are going to have to search our traditions to come up with suitable ways for dealing with the individual's accountability to the Christian community for behavior and decisions.

We must look carefully at the ways we approach sickness and death. We can no longer be content to stand by and watch while people get sick and either mend or die. We have to take the Sacrament of Healing as a vital, effective expression of the wholeness of Christ and bring it into homes. We shall have to learn to talk about healing *and* dying with parents and children.

We shall have to learn, all over again, how to use language about the state of the soul: its growth and its potential.

All of this will not be easy. We shall need a radically renewed view of the power of these sacraments that we have been, in many places, administering perfunctorily over the years, and taking for granted. Our culture, which is so thoroughly organized and rational in its outlook, is going to pull very hard against our attempt to live more deeply out of the context of mystery.

One thing that stands in our favor is that the general population still expects, as one wag put it, "to be hatched, matched, and dispatched" with the help of the church. People already come to the parish church for baptisms, marriages and funerals, and many times for support in dealing with illness and other difficulties. It is true that many who come do so with a set of expectations foreign to anything that the church wants to achieve. However, my plea is that clergy and other church leaders not react to this by turning people away. Many well-meaning clergy seem to be opting for a hard-nosed approach to all but the very faithful. I was recently with a priest who commented that she had been ordained for two years and had not yet performed a marriage. She simply couldn't find people willing to accept her requirements for marital preparation. Let us uphold the necessity and desirability of having meaningful standards; but standards must be applied in a way that will draw people, and families, more deeply into the sacramental life of the church. I believe one can uphold high standards without being rigid. Let me illustrate with two stories, one of a marriage and one of a baptism.

One Sunday after the service, a parishioner who was home from college introduced me to two friends, Fred and Cecile. They both said complimentary things about the service, and about the church. They told me that they were both students at the state university, and that they hoped to be married. In fact, they wondered if they could come by some time and talk with me about that. Red flags went up for me. Was this another couple who wanted to be married in a few weeks or a month? Were they simply looking for a pretty building in which to be married? I replied with my stock answer: that I would be happy to schedule a time to see them, and to explain to them the approach used in our parish for marriage preparation. It was agreed that they would call and set up an appointment.

When they came, I half expected that they would, like many other couples, fade away from the scene once they learned what we expect in premarital counseling: to attend a number of sessions, do considerable homework in reflection upon some issues important to marriage, and attend church as actively as possible. They had told me that neither of them was affiliated in any active way with another congregation, so I encouraged them to attend our church when they were in town, and to look up the chaplain at the university when they were back on campus. To my surprise, they agreed exceedingly quickly to all that was asked.

Like many clergy, I had come to be skeptical about people suddenly coming to church who have little experience in regular attendance. When I was first ordained, I would go to parties on Saturday nights, and often meet unchurched people who, when they found out I was a priest, would engage me in interesting conversation, and end by telling me that they would come to church. I believed them! Rarely did I ever see them again. So I have come to distrust the quickly made vow or agreement to attend church. Nevertheless, I do ask, and expect, premarital counselees to attend church, on the theory that they ought to get to know the community they are asking to bless their marriage, and, of course, in the hope that if they are not actively involved in a congregation, they will get a taste of what the church can mean to them. All the same, I am geared to be unsurprised if they attend less than weekly.

Fred and Cecile amazed me. Our initial interview took place in the early summer. When they were in town—which was most of the summer—they indeed attended church. They participated with enthusiasm in our sessions. They began to share with me and with each other their journey of growth in faith, including some of its spiritual dimensions. When they returned home for vacation the following academic year, they always came to church.

As I shall relate in Chapter Three, I require of those preparing for marriage a sizable commitment of time and reflection. Often I am told by couples, after they have completed the process, that they initially doubted the value of the things they were asked to do. Yet through the process they had come to understand more about themselves, about the Sacrament of Marriage, and about their relationship. Usually, I feel very positive when I stand at the altar to witness and to bless the joining together of a man and a woman within the Covenant of Marriage. Never have I felt happier or more "right" about a couple than I did with Fred and Cecile. It *is* possible for a couple with little experience in the Church to come to a fuller understanding of the sacraments, and to build their home and their marriage on the foundation of faith in Christ.

My second story is of a couple who, like many others in our parish, had recently moved into town, had a new baby (in this case about 18 months old), and wished to have the baby baptized. One of the priests went to call on this family, our standard response to requests for baptism from people who have no active relationship with the parish. (Incidentally, it is rarely people who are new to the parish who will resist what the Church asks of them; it is normally those who are inactive, but tangentially related to the parish, who will wonder why the clergy don't understand that this is their church and they have as much right as anybody to baptism, etc., etc.) The priest found, when visiting this family, that the wife had grown up in our tradition. Her husband, however, while not hostile to the idea of baptism, was certainly unenthusiastic about religion, church, and most of all the suggestion that he would have to attend three(!) prebaptismal sessions. After all, an older child had been "done" on a Saturday in the grandparents' home. Why were we so insistent that the baptism had to take place on a Sunday during a service, with all this preparation? The priest explained what we were trying to accomplish in baptismal preparation, and how we feel that what we ask is in line with what the Church teaches Holy Baptism to be about. The response, phoned later to the priest by the wife, was that they would plan for a baptism somewhat later.

We did not expect to see them again. But one Sunday, for no particular reason we could discern, they showed up in church. Afterward, they told the priest who had called on them that they would be in touch, and planned to join the next series of baptismal preparations. Time passed, and no one called. Finally, they did enroll and came with some degree of commitment, if not enthusiasm. Their baby was baptized. They got to know the parish sponsors who were selected to get to know them and to develop a relationship with them and their family. And they stayed. They have become actively involved—though in no flashy ways—in the life of the parish. Somehow, in preparing them for the reception of this basic Sacrament of Holy Baptism, we were able to reach out and to bring into the fellowship of the church a family who otherwise would still be sitting at home with two baptized children. Period. Now the challenge is to help them grow and to develop in this faith into which they have brought their children.

The following chapters will go more thoroughly into ways in which the fabric of community can be strengthened while families are themselves supported and nurtured in developing faith. It will be obvious throughout that there are no foolproof ways of doing this. But it will be apparent that the pastoral care of families means the diligent and gentle care of individuals as they advance from stage to stage on their life's journey—care that needs to involve the concern, energy, and support of fellow family members. When we prepare people to participate fully in the life of the Risen Lord, we are doing the very best thing we can do to help families do their job effectively.

BEYOND FIXING FAMILIES IN CRISIS

This model for using the sacraments in the pastoral care of the church's families is an approach which is continuous, life-long, and systematic. Unlike various kinds of family counseling, it is not problem-centered or explicitly therapeutic. Unlike family enrichment events, it is not limited to families, but takes all persons, even those not living in families, into account. We shall continue to need both the therapeutic values of family counseling and the renewal, fun, and promise that family enrichment enterprises can afford. Meanwhile, we can move towards the building of faith among all persons and all families, wherever they are, and in whatever state of healthiness they happen to be.

Sacrament-based pastoral care of families is not the same as dispensing sacraments through the parish as if they were panaceas. The following chapters will examine the manifold dimensions of these central rites and rituals of church life, showing them to be, in the largest sense, life-shaping. Ministry focused on the sacraments emerges as total, organic, coherent; it addresses literally every stage, passage, and issue that life turns up. Hence, the Sacrament of Holy Eucharist figures in family ministry not just as the occasional home celebration of communion, but as the ground on which the family builds a ritual life related to the parish communion. Likewise, the Sacrament of Unction is far more than the occasional anointing of the sick with family members present. It is a sweeping background against which the family continues to work out its experiences with sickness, death, and grief. Sacraments are not delimited, esoteric rites that belong only to certain Christians; they are patterns of innumerable ways in which God pours the abundance of his grace into every crevice of our lives.

Families need that grace, so it is towards understanding grace that we now turn.

TWO

Families Need Grace

It was that time of afternoon when the sun is the enemy of productivity. I was about through shuffling the papers on my desk and thought it would be good to get out and drive to the hospital. Only one parishioner was there, and it wouldn't take long.

The phone rang. The nervous voice on the other end was one I knew well. Jenny was telling me that she had that minute learned that her elderly father had died. She guessed it was a heart attack. It must have happened at work. She didn't know. The hospital had called. They couldn't find Laura, her sister-in-law. Would I meet her at her brother's house and tell them?

Before I could get out of my chair, the phone rang. Jenny's voice again, this time full of fright. It wasn't her father; it was her brother! Apparently he had had a heart attack while away on a fishing trip. She didn't know anything, but we had both better get over to Laura's quickly. She wasn't sure Laura was there. She hadn't been able to get an answer. Maybe Laura didn't even know.

Judd was not much older than forty. He and Laura had three children: Allison, in college; Bob, in a technical high school; and Shelley, six. This was going to be bad. And what if Laura wasn't there? Maybe caught in afternoon traffic, or at the grocery store, who knows? And maybe Bob would be home. Oh, God, could he be alone? All of this flew through my mind before I was out of the office door, pulling on my coat as I sailed down the stairs.

All outdoors was September orange. Leaves, just turning, trembled in a breeze. When would the light change? Oh, God, what if? "Help me, Lord. Help! Help!" I couldn't get another word out of my dry throat. Help. And should I be praying for me and not this family? "Help them, Lord, too. But help *me.*"

In all my years as a priest, I had never once been called upon to "break the news" to anyone. I had been there before death, at the time of death, after death. I had been called in the middle of the night to come to the hospital. Shades of Eleanor calling me about Jack years ago. "Frank, can you come over to the cardiac unit? He . . . he didn't make it, Frank." And Kate, as she lay dying. Freda's face. Mildred.

Why did I always get behind an eighty-seven-year-old man driving a 1956 Nash Rambler at 25 miles an hour? Walnut Tree Hill seemed ten miles long. And yet not long enough. I saw Judd's house; when I saw two other cars in the driveway, I knew that news had already come. They had heard.

I pulled out of the driveway two hours later. "Lord, be with them. Let them feel your presence. Help them, Lord. They need you. Help." The last word stopped at my teeth. Help had indeed come. The Presence was there. I had been what I needed to be. Sheer grace, I thought. Thank the Lord.

Grace: the help, the presence of God when nothing and no one but God can help. When the world flies out of control, when you are called on to do something that you know you cannot do, or at least you know you are scared stiff at the thought of having to do: you scream "Help!" and hope to God that someone somewhere in the universe who knows more about it than you will hear and get you off the hook. Help! It is not often that we cry for it. It's like crying "Wolf!" Better save it because one day we'll really need help and we'll need some credibility to get it. Meanwhile we think we can manage.

The odd thing about grace is that it is not grace if you can expect it. Earl Brill once said that for anything to qualify as grace, it has to be something of a surprise. Not only that, but grace rarely (I would say never) comes to one who is "managing very well." The

strange thing about the grace of God is that it seems to materialize
when we are up against the wall. Nowhere to go and nowhere to
hide.

Though it is true that grace is often easier to discern in instances
such as Judd's death, when we are in crisis, God's help and healing
power—which we call "grace"—is in fact present everywhere,
available all the time. The truth is that we are no more helpless
when we are in crisis than when we are not. Perhaps, to say the
same thing more clearly, we do not usually recognize our continuous
need of God's presence and power.

Judd died on Holy Cross Day. I learned something about grace
that day. Grace is God present for me because I can *never* go it
on my own. Paul wrote to the Romans,

> "Through [Jesus] we have obtained access to this grace in
> which we stand, and we rejoice in our hope of sharing the
> glory of God. More than that, we rejoice in our sufferings,
> knowing that suffering produces endurance, and endurance
> produces character, and character produces hope, and hope
> does not disappoint us, because God's love has been poured
> into our hearts through the Holy Spirit which has been given
> to us."[1]

That is the meaning of the Cross for Paul. It is the free gift of
God, given through the willing obedience of Jesus to death, which
does for us what we could never do on our own: it justifies us—it
makes us right—with God. *Grace is the free gift of ultimate help.*

One of those monosyllables in the Christian vocabulary, grace
tastes rather dry to many people. Perhaps moreso because, unlike
some of the other monosyllables, it goes against the grain of many
things that we middle-class Americans cherish. I participated in
a discussion several years ago about encouraging Sunday-school
attendance. One person remembered how in his own youth he had
received attendance awards (those little pins which say "First Year,"
"Second Year," etc. I think I got up to seven or eight when I was
in Sunday school). The idea excited everybody. They were all ready
to order the pins when I asked, "Should we reward people for doing
what we teach is their duty? Do we want to convey the idea that
we value people more if they keep the rules, such as attending

church? If so, what we are teaching undercuts the idea of grace, God's *free*, unmerited love." They had no idea what I meant.

Despite what we preach and teach, we still live in a system of reward and punishment. Do the right thing and you'll win the favor of the Church (and by extension, the favor of God). You'll win enough points that you'll be saved by and by. Though in our day we are loathe to articulate it, there is subtly implied a converse program of punishment—though not necessarily severe. Do *not* do the right thing, and you'll incur the disfavor of the community, the religious authorities, and—who knows—even God and Jesus.

Punishment might be in the form of being ignored, passed over, or even ostracized. A man who had become very active in the parish telephoned me. Why had I not chosen him to administer a chalice at Holy Communion? Had he not done something he should have done? Had he somehow failed my expectations? I was flabbergasted. My choice of someone else had nothing to do with him whatever. He was a person who, though fairly thoroughly immersed in the language of the Church and certainly in its organizational life, was living out of a context of merits and punishments. To be passed over was to him a punishment that he could not understand. To have been chosen for that particular role would have been a reward for his faithful service. He had been, in his own words, "working for that" for three years. It represented to him the ultimate status for lay persons.

The Church is full of that kind of thinking. Instead of teaching our people more about grace, we clergy comply with the system of salvation through merit, passing out our "pins" to those who have measured up to our expectations. We underscore the attitude that if one tries hard enough, one will (maybe) make it into the Kingdom.

Before we can use, or even talk about, the sacraments as a means of building faith in families, we need a clear language of grace. That is what sacraments are—a means of grace. In the following sections, I shall lay out a way of understanding and talking about grace. First, we shall examine the theology that underpins the sacraments. Next, we shall see how Jesus' life and work is sacramental. A third section will examine how the Church as a sacramental community extends the life and work of Jesus. Finally, we shall survey the ways each of the sacraments, and all of them together, sanctify the human life cycle, supplying the grace that families need for forming and nurturing persons for life.

THE LANGUAGE OF GRACE

The language of grace begins with the concept that God is the only reality. We are not used to thinking that way, not even in theological circles. We think in the categories of God, humanity, and world. We need to recover in Christianity the basic oneness of the universe, so that we see personal salvation, social responsibility, the treatment of the environment, all woven together into a single whole. That whole is the life of God. Even our ideas of God, partial and fragmented by necessity, are contained in the One who encompasses everything.

It is possible to do this without denying that in some sense God is totally "other than" the world. God gives the world its reality by bringing it into being. The biblical doctrine of creation holds two things in tension: the Creator-God is in every way distinct from his creation, and yet He also expresses himself through his creation. To say, as Genesis 1 does, that all comes from God is to say that all was contained in him until, at creation, it was given existence through God's speech—His Word. This grounds the understanding of creation in a fundamental and primal oneness.

God creates everything that is. Well, almost everything. The priestly writer says in Genesis 1 that "the darkness was upon the face of the deep. . . ." And later, having created light, "God separated the light from the darkness. . . . and the darkness he called Night."[2] What God did not make from scratch, he named, and thus brought under his control. The writer is expressing God's absolute sovereignty over everything in creation, including the forces of chaos and darkness.

As we shall see, this doctrine of creation is essential to sacramental theology. Everything material is good because God brings it into existence by his Word. Bede Griffiths writes, "Every material thing is a kind of incarnation, an expression in terms of matter and energy and life of the one supreme reality."[3] The writer of St. John's Gospel put into the language of poetry the identification of the Word and the Incarnation of God in Jesus Christ. Without the Word of God,

him whom we know as Jesus, "nothing was made that was made."[4]
It is amazing how many folks recite the Nicene Creed week after
week and never connect the phrase "through him all things were
made" with Christ. This is a foundational idea in understanding
the sacraments, because it links the one we call Lord and Christ
and Word to the material world which God made through him,
the *Dabar*, the *Logos*. Long before the writer of John and the
fathers of the Early Church made this connection, the priestly writer
of Genesis 1 was telling a *mythos*, a story in images, saying the same
thing: that behind everything there is a fundamental Unity, and
that Unity is God.

The next development of the language of grace coincides with
the next stage in the development of the doctrine of creation.
God blesses creation. Specifically, he sees that it is good. What
does this mean? The author is saying that God not only expresses
himself through his creation, but is pleased with it. There is
thus a basic goodness to all that is. Yet the story presses further.
When God creates man and woman, he blesses them, and says
to them, "Be fruitful and multiply, and fill the earth and subdue
it; and have dominion over the fish of the sea and over the
birds of the air and over every living thing that moves upon
the earth."[5] Out of this comes an understanding that God gives
to creation all it needs. And he gives it freely. The Psalmist
writes,

> The eyes of all look to thee, and thou givest them their meat
> in due season. Thou openest thy hand, thou satisfiest the desire
> of every living thing.[6]

The person of faith does not look at creation as simply a collection
of things, let alone as a field ripe for exploitation, but as exquisite
work of the Ultimate Artist. Addison heard the music of the spheres,
silent to all but Reason's ear, uttering forth a glorious voice,

> For ever singing as they shine,
> The hand that made us is divine.[7]

All creation is blessed by the God who made it so that it not only
enjoys the sustenance of the Creator, but manifests his life. In the
words of Gerard Manley Hopkins,

The world is charged with the grandeur of
   God.
It will flame out, like the shining from
shook foil;
It gathers to a greatness like the
    ooze of oil
Crushed.[8]

Parallel with this blessedness of creation is the idea that God has placed his limits on it. For this we have to look at the other creation story, Genesis 2. The Tree of the Knowledge of Good and Evil and the Tree of Life are definitely off limits to the Man and the Woman. He remains in charge, and his creation, including humanity, are subordinate. It is when this natural subordination is transgressed that the order is upset and wholeness is threatened. It is interesting to note that the story itself links this "fall" of Adam and Eve with the coming of consciousness. After they have eaten the forbidden fruit, "their eyes are opened."[9] The fall, therefore, is a *felix culpa*, an upward fall, into consciousness. Creation has progressed to the point where nature itself becomes conscious in humanity, and the man and the woman are in a position of standing over against God and over against the rest of the created order.

Both these dimensions of the story of creation—the blessing God gives to what he has made and the limits drawn and then transgressed—are important to the understanding of grace. Grace is on the one hand all that God freely gives, including life itself. Grace, on the other hand, includes the proper dependence of the creation upon the Creator. Grace implies a harmony, which takes shape in human awareness as appropriate thankfulness, which we see as the creation story continues. In the story of Cain and Abel, we see the two brothers making sacrifices, the chief way that humanity develops to express its dependence upon the Creator. Sacrifices may be seen as attempts to placate the divine will so that it will be benevolent rather than destructive. Or they may be seen as rightfully giving to the Creator what belongs to him. They also come to be seen as ways of atoning for sins and as means of making peace with the moral God to whom humanity owes its deepest apologies. In any case, sacrifices are expressions of this *dependence of humanity upon the Creator.* Sacrifice is intricately tied to the offering of thanks and praise. One giving thanks has to confess one's subordination (indebtedness) to the One thanked. And this offering of thanks is appropriate *grace* on our part. (We refer to the thanksgiving before meals as "grace," and some languages express the idea of thanks with the words *gratia, gracias, action de grace.*

Grace, then, reflects a deep harmony between Creator and creation. The Bible goes on to tell us that, ideally, there is no duality in the fabric of the universe. It is significant that it was not the mind of primitive man that first imagined Satan, or evil. The Old Testament knows no essential evil until very late in its development. The serpent in the creation story is just that: a serpent, who is a beguiling creature, but nothing like a demon. Indeed demonic powers are ascribed to Yahweh himself, as in the story of his seeking to kill Moses on the way back from Midian to Egypt.[10] It is only much later in the development of Judaism that the primal unity is conceived to be broken into good and evil components. Once a struggle between good and evil begins to take shape, then the echoes of the old harmony fade away, and the goal becomes the reunion of opposites and the restoration of wholeness. To put it in terms of the creation-salvation story, once the man and woman are driven from the Garden, the rest of their lives are spent trying to find it. It is to be found only through Christ, and then not as a *fait accompli*, but in the form of a promise, a direction that will be pursued until the end of history. This end towards which all things are moving is imaged in the Book of Revelation not as a garden, but as a holy city. The city has, however, a river of the water of life, flowing through its middle. The river is symbolic of the blessings that flow from the throne of God, and suggests that the creation has been restored to the Oneness that was lost in Eden. The banks of the river are lined with the tree of life,

> with its twelve kinds of fruit, yielding its fruit each month;
> and the leaves of the tree were for the healing of the nations.[11]

Thus the Tree of Life symbolizes the powers that are needed to bring creation back to God. It might well be said that the Tree of Life is indeed a Tree of Grace, just as the River of the water of life is a river of blessings streaming from the open-handed God of Grace.

This vision of unity is something so deep within the human psyche that it finds nearly universal expression. We hear Thales saying in ancient Greece that there is a unity which embraces everything. Likewise, as Bede Griffiths shows with great clarity, the Vedic tradition of India points to the same truth:

> There are monist and pantheist and poly-theistic interpretations of the Veds, but the Vedic doctrine itself, the doctrine of the Vedas, the Upanishads, and the Bhagavad Gita, is none of these things. It is a doctrine of supreme wisdom, coming down from remote antiquity in the form of a divine revelation, expressed originally in myth and symbol, and developed through profound meditation, so as to give a unique insight into ultimate reality, that is, the ultimate nature of man and the universe.[12]

That reality is understood as a basic unity. This is parallel to the Judaeo-Christian view that the process of creation itself produces a nature that becomes conscious in humanity. The Christian view is that God will not rest until his creation is brought back into oneness with himself.

The program to bring humanity back is the beginning of the historical movement of grace. The fall results from disobedience, which in Hebrew understanding is never the simple breaking of a law or commandment, but a more profound failure *to hear*. Henri Nouwen has pointed out that our word *obey* comes from the Latin *ob* + *audire* = from + to hear. And Wayne Oates, outlining the various understandings of sin in the Judaeo-Christian tradition,[13] reminds us that one of these is self-elevation, which is certainly the sin most explicitly shown in the story of the fall. Adam and Eve, in effect, say that they do not need to obey God; they are perfectly capable of deciding things for themselves. Deciding to eat the fruit of the Tree of Knowledge results not only in the birth of self-consciousness, but in a concommitant split from God. When the moment of confrontation with God comes,

> . . . they heard the sound of the Lord God walking in the garden in the cool of the day, and the man and his wife hid

themselves from the presence of the Lord God among the trees of the garden.[14]

What this story gives us in image is the alienation which becomes manifest in the divorce of reason from intuition, the split between masculine and feminine, the split between man and nature, the split between body and spirit. It is the story of how the primeval unity of the Garden is fractured. This sets in motion the rest of the story to follow: God's response to the breakup.

That response is, quite simply, to heal the breach. To tell it in story form: even for Yahweh that is not easily done. But the healing begins when compassionately Yahweh Elohim makes for Adam and Eve garments of skins and clothes them. This protective care on the part of God is laid over the presupposition that *something had to die in order for atonement to be made.* Animals die; their skins become the instrument of healing and protection. As the story continues, however, we see how at each stage of healing, a price must be paid. Sodom and Gommorah are destroyed; the first-born of Egypt are struck down; the Canaanites are defeated; Saul is supplanted by David; Jesus is crucified. Always something dies before new life can form.

Sin multiplies with such force and effect that the Lord despairs of the whole project of creation. Violence increases geometrically, as the brief story of Lamech shows:

> Lamech said to his wives; "Adah and Zillah, hear my voice; you wives of Lamech, hearken to what I say: I have slain a man for wounding me, a young man for striking me. If Cain is avenged sevenfold, truly Lamech seventy-sevenfold.[15]

Finally there seems nothing left to do but for God to destroy his creation, since he

> . . . saw that the wickedness of man was great in the earth, and that every imagination of the thoughts of his heart was only evil continually. And the Lord was sorry that he had made man on the earth, and it grieved him to his heart. So the Lord said, 'I will blot out man whom I have created from the face of the ground, man and beast and creeping thing and birds of the air, for I am sorry that I have made them.'[16]

The experiment with Noah is an attempt to save something of creation. God does not give up totally. Since Noah is the *one* person he can find who is righteous, i.e., who stands in a right relation to him, God is willing to find a way to redeem creation through Noah and his family. They can begin the order all over. Maybe the second time it will work. But first, judgment must come in the flood-waters, which will purge creation of all its wickedness.

The flood is scarcely over when Noah begins to farm, grows a vineyard, drinks wine, gets drunk. The experiment succeeded in saving some to begin the human family again. But it failed as an attempt to bring about the restoration of humanity's relationship with God.

The flood having failed to bring about the re-union God desired, he turns his attention to Abram. God calls Abram against the chaotic background of a splintered humanity. Since God has been unsuccessful in finding anyone righteous by nature like Noah, he will opt for faithfulness from Abraham. Faithfulness is the key. Abraham is not righteous by nature, but by faith. And that faith, as Paul says, "was reckoned to him as righteousness."[17] By calling Abram, God intends to create a people to whom he can reveal himself and whom he can use to bring the rest of humanity to himself. Unfortunately, this vision will be lost time and again, as the global vocation of Israel narrows into a provincial ethnocentricity. But the point of the story is that God will not stop until he has healed all the splits. The Christian tradition takes up the story and shows how, through Jesus and specifically through the Sacrament of Holy Baptism, the house of Abraham is opened up to include literally all the nations of the earth.

In summary: God is the only reality. Creation itself is a part of a large whole. When that whole is fractured by the disobedience and fall of humanity, God sets about healing the breach. That healing is the work of Grace.

THE LIFE OF CHRIST AS THE PRIMARY SACRAMENT

It is against the backdrop of the stories of creation and fall that we can bring the story of Christ into focus. We have said thus far that sacraments are a means of grace. The language of grace is a language of story and image about the reunification of what has been separated and estranged. The central story and image in the epic of grace is the story of Jesus Christ and the image of his cross, supreme symbol of atonement.

To speak of Jesus as "sacrament" means that the moment has arrived to define *sacrament* more fully. The fundamental idea of sacrament is that it is not so much a *thing* as an *event*. It is a moment of conjunction, of the bringing together of things that have been separated. It is a moment when something material comes into conjunction with Spirit. The necessity of firmly holding that the material world is essentially good becomes clearer now. First, matter is not opposed to Spirit (the divine reality), merely separated from it. Second, the material world, including human life, becomes the means by which God expresses himself again and again. To use the language of Christology, "the Word becomes flesh." Body (corporeal reality) and Spirit (the reality of God), form sacrament. The material becomes transcendent, pointing beyond itself and embodying divine energy and presence.

Bringing together divinity and humanity is the whole idea of the salvation process. Hence, the focus of salvation is where this becomes most real and apparent—in the life of Jesus of Nazareth. The Incarnation is itself a healing event. In Jesus, the ultimately graceful life is manifest and lived to the fullest. It is a balanced life. To use the categories of Carl Jung's personality theory, in Jesus there is the perfect balance between introvert and extrovert, between reason and intuition, between thinking and feeling. His life is a sacrament —an occasion—of true freedom. He puts to rest all notion that life lived in union with God is restrictive, though such life is costly in human terms. Paul grasped that Christ lived a perfectly free life. He consistently envisions the Christian life as being the paradox of true freedom that comes from being "enslaved" to God. In describing the two Covenants, his image of the New Covenant in Christ is a relationship to God characterized by the freedom of the Spirit:

> For it is written that Abraham had two sons, one by a slave and one by a free woman. But the son of the slave was born according to the flesh, the son of the free woman through

promise. Now this is an allegory: these women are two
covenants. One is from Mount Sinai, bearing children for
slavery; she is Hagar. Now Hagar is Mount Sinai in Arabia;
she corresponds to the present Jerusalem, for she is in slavery
with her children. But the Jerusalem above is free, and she
is our mother. . . . Now we, brethren, like Isaac, are children
of promise. . . . So we are not children of the slave but of
the free woman.[18]

Christ's was a totally free life. Only when God and humanity, Spirit
and body are united, can there be true freedom. Christ's freedom
is extended to all who live in him, and who through their baptism
have been brought into the life of the Spirit. So Paul goes on to say:

For freedom Christ has set us free; stand fast therefore, and
do not submit again to a yoke of slavery.[19]

The price of this freedom, if it can be said to be a price, is that
we not gratify the desires of the flesh. We relinquish that center
of desire which came to the fore in Eve when she noticed that the
taboo fruit was "good to eat, a delight to the eyes, and desirable
to make one wise."[20] The flesh-centered life, not to be identified
with the body as such, is understood as bodily life not connected
with the life of the Spirit. When Paul lists the fruits of the Spirit,
he could as well be describing the life of Jesus portrayed in the
Gospels: love, joy, peace, patience, kindness, goodness, faithfulness,
gentleness, self-control. His life was a sacrament in which all of
those things were expressed, manifested, communicated, signified.

Jesus was not only perfectly free; he used his freedom for
righteousness. Ironically, he was, as the ancient hymn in Philippians
2 suggests, the one who, being God, did not "count equality with
God a thing to be grasped, but emptied himself . . ." That is to
say he chose to stand, as man, in a right relationship with God.
He *heard* correctly, and therefore obeyed. Obedience took him
through humility to death, "even death on a cross."[21] It was this
obedience which was the act of righteousness which leads us to
life:

. . . as one man's trespass led to condemnation for all men,
so one man's act of righteousness leads to acquittal and life

for all men. For as by one man's disobedience many were made sinners, so by one man's obedience many will be made righteous.[22]

Through this obedience, Jesus became the one to "listen to the Spirit" and to bring about the restoration of the primary oneness with God which had been lost to human consciousness.

Finally, Jesus' life is totally given to reconciliation. In the New Testament we see the dawn of awareness that reconciling people with each other, with themselves, and with God was the central significance of Jesus. Everything he did was directed to that end: reconciling the things that were pulling against one another. Certainly, the healing miracles can be understood as the reconciliation of body and psyche, the unleashing of power to restore persons to wholeness. But healing is seen consistently in the New Testament as a restoration or a right relationship with God. Thus, Jesus often says, "Your faith has made you well." This does not mean, "You believed hard enough and therefore I responded." It is clear that many of the people healed had very fragile faith in that sense; for example, the woman with a hemorrhage (Mark 5:24-34), the man at the Pool of Bethesda (John 5:2-9), and the man with an epileptic son (Mark 9:24). It does mean, "When one stands in a proper relationship with God, characterized by dependence and trust, then the whole life, including the body, can reflect that which is the essence of wholeness." The work of Jesus is to bring about this union with God, both now and ultimately. He is the Primal Sacrament.

The writer to the Ephesians perhaps articulates this idea most completely when he writes that Jesus brought together Jew and Gentile in his body on the cross:

For he is our peace, who has made us both one, and has broken down the dividing wall of hostility, by abolishing in his flesh the law of commandments and ordinances that he might create in himself one new man in place of the two, so making peace, and might reconcile us both to God in one body through the cross, thereby bringing the hostility to an end.[23]

The hostility which he brought to an end was not only that between Jew and Gentile but that between God and humanity. Or is this what the writer to Ephesians means in the first place? It is significant that the passage above is preceded by the very idea of salvation which we have been working with in this chapter. His argument is that God has, through Christ, made us alive, even though we were dead through the consequences of our disobedience. No longer do we have to follow the leading of the "prince of this world," who is the spirit at work in disobedience. But we can respond to God, who, through the riches of his mercy, has raised us up to himself just as he raised Christ. Indeed he has raised us to his life through grace *by* Christ—through faith in Christ. The uniqueness of Jesus is that he is the one who heals the breach; but his destiny is exactly our own: to "sit with Christ in the heavenly places and enjoy the immeasurable riches of God's kindness." This is a glorious vision which supercedes even the re-establishment of Eden! This reunion is our salvation by grace through faith.

The sacraments of the Church are ways in which that same salvation, that basic wholeness, that long-lost unity, is restored.

THE LIFE OF THE CHURCH AS SACRAMENT

The Church is an extension of the Incarnation. Everything which is true of Christ must be true of the Church. It is surprising and disappointing how few people realize this, the best-kept secret in all Christianity. It makes little sense to talk of sacraments unless we see that the Church who ministers the sacraments is not only a human community but a community which by those very sacraments has been, and is being constantly, infused with the life of God. The Spirit which indwells the Church is a powerful reality, and indeed is the energy and activity of God *in the present* seeking to restore us and all the parts of our lives to union with the Godhead. The Church's mission as the Prayer Book says, is "to restore all people to unity with God and each other in Christ."[24] This does not mean establishing a convivial fellowship of like-minded yuppies, however. It means, in the words of St. Maximus, that "what Christ is by nature, that we become by grace." As he is by nature the child of God of God who perfectly obeys his Father's will, so by grace we are children of God, who can obey His will.

All that can be said about Christ's vocation to reconcile the world to God is what must be said about the Church. Our destiny, realized only in part in this life, is to be fully united with God—as the Fathers said, "divinized." But it is not ours alone. It is the desire of God that the project He began with the call of Abraham be completed—that all the nations of the earth may be brought into union with Him. This is the guiding principle behind all evangelism. Would that we saw it more clearly! The reason for bringing people into the Church is not so that they can become better people, but so that they can realize the destiny of each individual: to be raised with Christ to the life of God. Thus, through baptism, we are made members of God's community, and given the mission of that community to be his ambassadors to the rest of the world. We are, by identification with Christ's death, burial, and resurrection, remade, reborn, transformed. The other sacraments amplify and augment that new life which begins at baptism. So, Paul, writing to the Corinthians, puts it together this way:

> . . . If any one is in Christ, he is a new creation. The old has passed away, behold, the new has come. All this is from God, who through Christ reconciled us to himself and gave us the ministry of reconciliation. . . . So we are ambassadors for Christ, God making his appeal through us. We beseech you on behalf of Christ, be reconciled to God. For our sake he made him to be sin who knew no sin, so that in him we might become the righteousness of God.[25]

The life of the Church is measured by the life of Christ. That is why it is absolutely essential for the Christian community to read the gospels over and over again, to become immersed in the story and spirit of Christ. There is where we find what it is like to be indwelt by the Holy Spirit. The gospels are the texts *par excellence* on life in the Spirit. The life of Christ is the model of the life of any who are or would be reconciled to God. That life is a life of prayer, of healing, of teaching, of feeding, of preaching, of raising the dead, of setting free those who are bound in any way. Whatever he is by nature, and whatever he does by the power of love, that is what by grace the Christian community is to be and to do.

Of course, there is the irony that while we are called to be that as a community, as individual members of it we are always in the process of being reoriented, transformed, refashioned, restored. The process goes on continually. That is part of the work of the sacraments: to ensure that individual members of the community are "grown" more and more in the knowledge and love of God, so that they live life in union with him more and more deeply and completely now, and in the age to come, perfectly.

To speak of the Church as Christ's Body, as Paul does in Romans and 1 Corinthians, is to speak of the community as an embodiment of the Spirit of God. Paul consistently shows that "walking by the Spirit" is to work out the meaning of baptism in very ordinary, everyday, ethical terms. It means making choices for those things that characterize the life of Christ, and putting to death those things that belong to the self-centered life. To translate the same thing into Jesus' language: we are called upon to deny ourselves, to take up our cross, and to follow him.[26] He promises that when we do this, we shall be in touch with the true Self—which is to say with the life of the Spirit: God. The "works of the flesh" in Paul[27] are all things which pull us away from God, away from other people, or create strife within our own psyches: idolatry, sorcery, enmity, dissention, party spirit, envy, drunkenness, carousing, and the like. "If we live by the Spirit, let us also walk by the Spirit," he says, anchoring that "walk" in an absence of self-conceit, provocations, and envy.

When we view the work of the Church to be the work of Christ, we begin to see that reconciliation means not only the restoration of a cosmic relationship of unity with God but also the healings, large and small, that are needed by ourselves and our neighbors. These healings are physical, emotional, psychical, relational. Agnes Sanford, one of the great forces for the rediscovery of the Church's ministry of healing in recent times, used to say in her workshops on pastoral care, "The job of the clergy is to preach, to teach, and to heal. Why are you only doing two-thirds of your job?" The job not only of the clergy, but of the whole Christian community, is to heal—to bring this wholeness on all levels to all who are broken, distressed, troubled, ill, fragmented in a myriad of ways. The Church's sacraments are means of grace, of healing the breach. Not only the big gulf that separates us from our Creator, but the dozens of fissures in the fabric of our souls and that of our common life. Charles Wesley wrote:

> The Son of God for me hast died:
> My Lord, my love is crucified. . . .
> Is crucified for me and you
> To bring us rebels back to God.[28]

To bring us rebels back to God is the work of the Church. The sacraments, along with the proclamation of the Word himself, are the power that the Church has for carrying on the mission and ministry of Christ.

HOW THE SACRAMENTS OPERATE

The classical definition of a sacrament is "an outward and visible sign of inward and spiritual grace, given by Christ as sure and certain means by which we receive that grace."[29] Each of the sacraments is an occasion or event in which something in the material world—something that is open to sense perception— becomes the means by which grace is given. The outward *materia* is both the sign of this giving and the form in which the gift is received.

Our detailed look at the doctrine of creation yields the essential datum that the material world is good. Everything which was brought into being by God, or named by God, bears the impress of God's own integrity. Taking this far enough leads naturally to the conclusion that the whole world and everything in it is sacramental. The seventeenth-century English poet and priest George Herbert was one who articulated this sacramental view of the world. To Herbert, even the most ordinary things were pregnant with possibilities for bearing the divine reality. Mundane human work could become a means by which grace is conveyed by God, and grace ("thanks") for it could be given by men and women to God. In one of Herbert's poems, he prays:

Teach me, my God and King,
In all things thee to see;
And what I do in anything
To do it as for thee.

All may of thee partake;
Nothing can be so mean,
Which with this tincture, 'for thy sake,'
Will not grow bright and clean.[30]

Herbert extends the integrity—the value—of the created order into the realm of human behavior. Creation can be redeemed; so can seemingly meaningless human actions.

The Orthodox hold a similar view in the theology of icons. What seems to the uninitiated eye for all the world like a simple stylized religious painting is understood by the faithful to be a window, through which the pictured holy one looks into the world. The icon becomes a point of contact. The holy person portrayed in the icon and the viewer stand face to face. This is a sacramental event: a moment when spirit and body, the holy and the ordinary are joined.

Each of the Church's sacraments is such a moment. Something ordinary, like water, is taken from the created order. This bit of material becomes the means by which Spirit is conveyed. The power of God is communicated through the water of baptism so that the person washed in that water becomes united to God's people—the Church; becomes united to Christ in his death and resurrection; and becomes united to the Holy Trinity, into whose Name the person is baptized. Ever thereafter, the baptized person journeys more and more deeply into the Godhead itself.

That kind of claim is audacious piety, foolishness, or God's honest truth. Which? I have argued that the whole meaning of creation is God's own self-expression, and that the goal of all human history is the reunion of ourselves with the Self of the whole universe, which is God's Self. God's nature is to give himself. All that the Christian tradition knows about God—as Father, Son, Holy Spirit, or as Creator, Redeemer, Sanctifier—amounts to the assertion that God is always giving himself away. He gives Himself in bringing the world into being. He gives his power away when he voluntarily allows himself to be limited by the free choice which he makes possible in the world. He gives his blessings, his mercy, his love, endlessly. That is the meaning of Jesus. He is God's free gift to humanity "to bring us rebels back to God." And the symbol of the cross says that the nature of Christ was to give, and give, and give again, so much that when he had nothing else to give he literally gave himself.

The reason that giving plays such a large role in Christian worship is that it is understood to be a response of humans to the gift of Christ. This is the foundation of all Christian stewardship. And to the extent that persons give to the Church or to Christian causes without understanding this, they miss the point. An old Greek verse says

Thou didst give thyself for me,
Now I give myself to thee.[31]

Giving is the only way we can symbolize the oblation of ourselves to the Creator. And ourselves, after all, is what the Great Self deeply desires. Behind all this is the shadow of ancient sacrifice:

Wilt thou own the gift I bring?
All my penitence I give thee;
Thou art my exalted King,
Of thy matchless love forgive me.[32]

In the Holy Eucharist, the richest imagery surrounds the bread and wine. They are, first, the oblations of the people. They are the gifts of our life and labor. If we were to get back to our village origins, each worshiper would bring a little bread and wine (and other gifts) to the church. They would be collected at the time of the offertory and brought to the altar. That is why it is essential to have worshipers symbolically bring to the altar the bread and wine to be blessed. We must be conscious that those things are our life-substance, as much so as the money which should be placed on the altar during the consecration. Then those gifts by which we have given ourselves to him become the gifts by which he gives himself to us. This is essential to the psychology of the sacraments. If we are only receiving, not giving ourselves in some sense in faith, opening ourselves to the presence of the Spirit of God, the sacraments are robbed of half their meaning. They degenerate into magic, or get rarefied into "mere symbols."

Central to sacramental theology is the understanding that *God*, through the sacraments, is giving himself to us *here and now*. We grossly misrepresent the sacraments if overemphasis is placed upon their status as pledges, as the early Latin fathers spoke of them (the word means "pledge," or "oath.") Sacraments are not just a way of acting out something that is going to come to pass by and by, though nearly each of them has a futuristic dimension. They are the means by which grace is conveyed *at this moment and at this place*. The phrase in the Christian vocabulary that always denotes this aspect of God is "Holy Spirit." By Holy Spirit we mean God in our midst. Of course, all Trinitarian theology insists that where the Spirit is, there is the Son, and where the Son is there is the Father. Yet, in an important sense God is never totally present in his entire being at any one moment in time. God manifests himself in his energies, as Gregory of Nyssa said, and those energies are scattered throughout the dimensions of space and time. Christian experience is insistent however, that just as God was truly present in Jesus, so by the Holy Spirit, God is present in the Church. Thus, one way of looking at the sacraments is to see the Holy Spirit as the *constant*, and the material form of the sacrament the *variable*.

The sacraments are moments when human life comes into contact with the presence, the gift, the self, of God. This first happens in the *Sacrament of Holy Baptism*. Infant baptism will always be a bone of contention in the Church, because at least the western rational mind will always have trouble seeing how anyone without a fully developed consciousness will be able to appropriate rationally the meaning of baptism. (We often confuse meaning with reality.) But infant baptism is an important underscoring of the absolute centrality of grace—the presence of God unmerited, unearned, and undeserved. The moment we present any qualifications for grace, we have registered for something other than grace. Baptism is a way, moreover, in which parents hand over a child to the larger Christian community, and to the life of God proclaimed, witnessed, and experienced by that community. They are saying in effect, "This child which we have been given is no longer ours to do with as we please; we give him to you." The theology of baptism holds that God's response to this is to accept the child that is offered, and to incorporate him or her into his family (the people of Abraham and of Christ) by *water*. Baptism is birth into this family. It is the initiation of a lifelong journey into wholeness and to the ultimate Oneness of the cosmos. [Meanwhile, the very Self that seeks that Oneness has been given to the newly baptized.]

Herbert Anderson, in his book *Christian Baptism and the Human Life Cycle*, has shown that baptism is the primary sacrament, because here the santification of the human life cycle begins. All other sacraments are ways in which the baptismal reality is lived out. After birth into God's family, the next job is feeding. The newly baptized is given the food of the heavenly kingdom, either immediately (as in the Eastern tradition) or within a few years (as in most of the Western Church). Eating at the family table signals that a new phase in socialization has taken place for the young child. Learning to eat solid food, learning table manners, being taught how to interact appropriately both with the food and with others at the table—all are important in the life of the child and the family. Sometime in the preschool or early school years, the child in the Christian community will be learning about the eucharist, either in preparation for first communion or in reflection upon the communion which he has been receiving for some time. It is significant that this takes place in many churches around school age. This is the first major foray outside the home into the wider community. It prefigures a time in several years when peers will become all-important in a child's life.

Learning how to handle oneself socially is what the rituals of the table are largely about. Admission to the Holy Communion sanctifies this time if it takes place in close conjunction with it. In any case, participation in Holy Communion is never a private affair, no matter how intensely personal. It is a corporate activity. Coming to the communion table with others; learning to make peace with one's enemies as well as to eat with one's friends; learning to claim one's hungers as well as one's strengths: these are the things that participation in the Holy Eucharist sanctifies.

In the *Holy Eucharist*, the bread and wine become the means by which the faithful receive the life of Christ. They are the outward, visible sign of his body and blood. It is almost impossible to cut through twenty centuries of eucharistic doctrine to find answers to the question of how the eucharist operates. It seems to me the heart of the matter is that the eucharist is a feeding. Christ gave himself to as many as would receive him as the bread of life. As the bread and wine are nourishment for the body, so by the power of the Holy Spirit, they are the means by which the grace of God feeds the soul with the reality of Christ. All the battles about the nature of the eucharistic food have raged around how it is that this can be. All the arguments, both Catholic and Protestant, are snagged on rational categories. Among the wisest exegetes of eucharistic doctrine was Elizabeth I, who put it succinctly:

'Twas God the Word that spake it;
He took the bread and brake it;
And what the Word did make it,
That I believe, and take it.[33]

The Word made it, and makes it, his body and blood. It has been said that the purpose of all bread is to become the body of Christ. When a child of God, indwelt by his holy and life-giving Spirit, eats anything, that "bread" does indeed become the body of Christ. Thus, all meals are eucharists, sanctified and blessed by that one who has brought us into his family and is bringing us more and more to himself.

Confirmation is a strengthening of this Life. As the eucharist is food for the journey, confirmation is the supernatural strength needed to combat the enemies along the way. (I pause to marvel at that. Does the imagery of combating evil make any sense at all to twentieth-century people, as it did to Bunyan?) There are indeed enemies that pull us away from our destination. Nor are all these enemies demonic or satanic. There are forces of evil on a cosmic scale, "spiritual forces of wickedness that rebel against God,"[34] and "principalities, powers, spiritual hosts of wickedness in the heavenly places."[35] But more often than not, we project onto the Devil and his associates the personal evil in ourselves which we have not learned to acknowledge. And there are evil powers in this world's political and economic systems that corrupt and destroy us.[36] We are, whether we like it or not, on a journey where there is great treachery to the soul. The ancients knew this well, and understood the danger of the journey. Odysseus, Anaeus, Jason, Perseus had to reckon with deadly enemies along the journey. We neglect the

truth of these stories to our own peril. Jesus had to do battle with
evil and so do we. This is what confirmation is about: the strengthening for the battle.

Our problem is complicated by the fact that many of us do not
recognize that we are on a journey, let alone one which is fraught
with perils. The imagery of confirmation is very clearly the imagery
of dispatching people on a journey or voyage. In traditions where
the bishop is the confirming minister, this is demonstrated powerfully. The bishop is the apostolic person, identified as the successor
in the present day to the apostles themselves. One is not even
constrained to accept the literalness of apostolic succession in order
to grant that the bishop is the guardian of and representative of
the Apostolic Faith. This is crucial. It is *this* faith which is being
affirmed and confirmed. The service of confirmation in the Book
of Common Prayer heavily underscores the dynamic of sending and
being sent. That is what apostolic means (from *apostello*—I send;
the equivalent of the Latin *mitto, mittere*). To be confirmed in the
apostolic faith, to share it, means to be sent into the world on a
mission. The representative of this apostolic community lays hands
on the head of the person being confirmed and prays that he or
she may be strengthened by the Holy Spirit for the journey:

> Strengthen, O Lord, your servant *N.* with your Holy Spirit;
> empower *him* for your service; and sustain *him* all the days
> of his life. Amen.

> *or*

> Defend, O Lord, your servant *N.* with your heavenly grace,
> that *he* may continue yours for ever, and daily increase in your
> Holy Spirit more and more, until *he* comes to your everlasting
> kingdom. *Amen.*[37]

As the life cycle progresses into adulthood, and consciousness
grows, the journey becomes more treacherous. With the arrival of
adulthood, there comes the expectation of leaving home. Protection
and support of parents do not cease, but change form. The crises
of vocation and marriage are to be faced. The person of faith
becomes adept at delving into the intellectual subtleties of the
tradition. One must also learn to relate personal experience to the

tradition, and to examine the tensions between that tradition and the particular pressures the culture exerts on one's faith. There are many places where culture will pull against the tradition, and still other places where a person's own beliefs and values, shaped by many sources including family, will be in tension with either tradition or culture or both. All of this spells great difficulty for navigating through adulthood. Only recently have we begun to take seriously that the pilgrimage continues after adolescence. Gail Sheehy,[38] Theodore Lidz,[39] and Daniel Levinson[40] have all given us a heightened awareness of the complications of the adult phase of the life cycle.

The first crisis many young adults face is the issue of whether to marry or not. Also, the choice of a mate is one of the biggest life-shaping dynamics for most young adults. It is necessary for the church as well as the family to take seriously what often is dismissed as adolescent puppy-love. Unfortunately, with the collapse of a social network which once supervised the process of dating and mating,[44] the church and family are adrift, often feeling incapable of giving any shape to the sexual-social development of their young. This is one of the reasons why the church must take the *Sacrament of Holy Matrimony* with utmost seriousness, using it to address *some* of the issues inherent in the choice of a lifemate. Of course, neither the church nor the family should wait until marriage is about to occur and people have already selected their mates before responding to sexual development. Ideally, the Sacrament of Marriage should be preceded not by a limited number of sessions with the prospective bride and groom, but by years of systematic reflection upon the meaning of human sexuality, and how it is elucidated by the faith of the Church. The point is that this sacrament sanctifies a powerful and vital aspect of life.

In close conjunction with the choice of a mate is the issue of the choice of work. In our society, this is often treated with intense interest, investment, and careful preparation. Nonetheless, many young Americans are in the position of the hero of the film, *All the Right Moves*. The protagonist is a young man who knows that he is trapped in a Pennsylvania steel mill town, where his family has lived and worked for generations. His only ticket to becoming an engineer is his ability to play football. Through a series of misunderstandings and a single misfired communication, the youth's coach blackballs him from a succession of college recruiters. The boy's girlfriend is finally able to exert some influence over the situation by talking to the coach's wife, and the happy ending of the story is that the young man is given a football scholarship to the college where his coach will be on the athletic faculty. This is a story out of the center of the American mind. We want reassurance that there is a way to success for those who aspire to fulfillment through a lifework.

The Church has no sacrament to offer the laity for sanctifying work, or even the vocational choice as such. The Sacrament of Holy Orders is limited to those whose vocation lies within the Church itself. This is a serious deficiency. The solution may be to devise rites that will coincide with a choice of work. This is the direction that the Book of Common Prayer timidly goes in by offering "A Form of Commitment to Christian Service." The design has in mind a special work undertaken either in general terms or in a specific form. It is mandated that the brief service include an Act of Commitment which "should include a reaffirmation of baptismal promises."[42] This idea could be developed so that increasingly our ordinary work would be seen as an elaboration of our baptism, and a means of expressing it.

Holy Orders, of course, are for those on whom they are conferred a specific authority and grace to exercise the ministry of particular offices in the Church: bishop, priest, deacon. The outward, visible component of the Sacrament of Ordination is the laying on of hands by bishops with prayer.

The Sacrament of Reconciliation of a Penitent, or Penance, can be thought of as the working out of relationships within the community of the baptized. In Chapter Six, we shall see how reconciliation is the way a baptized person maintains accountability to the community. It is also a way that the soul is continually groomed for the ultimate union with God, and meanwhile is purged of those things which stand in the way of that union. Its outward, visible sign is the confession of sins in the presence of a priest,[43] and the words or form of absolution that is offered, often with the laying-on-of-hands. The inward, spiritual grace is, of course, the forgiveness of sins—the grace of absolution itself.

Holy Unction is the blessing of the baptized so that they may be healed in spirit, mind and body. The outward, visible sign is the laying on of hands with prayer, with or without the anointing with oil. The Sacrament of Unction is the sanctification of illness— but that is definitely not to be understood (as it often has been) as a way of saying that sickness is good for us. Many people have thought of sickness, and still do, as a form of God's will. That is a troublesome issue, perhaps addressed best by Leslie Weatherhead in his little classic, *The Will of God*. Unction releases the grace of the Holy Spirit to bring about wholeness on a personal level. It brings into the present the eschatalogical wholeness which we shall know fully only at the end of this life, and which the world will know fully only when its journey into Oneness is finally accomplished. The grace of God—God's Self—is not withheld until we die, however, or until the end of the world as we know it. His grace is present to help us in our need this very moment.

The *burial rites* of the Church, while not understood to be sacramental, indeed function much as the sacraments do. They help us along our journey, and are best understood not only as rites whereby the living are strengthened and afforded the opportunity to celebrate, but also as climactic representations of the end of life and the translation of the person to a fuller life beyond death.

In each of the sacraments, then, God's power touches our ordinary life. Hands are laid on. Prayer is offered. The Holy Spirit is invoked. Material from the created order—water, bread, wine, hands, oil, a man and a woman—becomes the means by which grace is conveyed. In these simple things, there is a manifestation of power incredible in its dimensions. To take sacraments seriously is to believe and to experience the availability of the Most High God in the midst of this workaday world. The God who is immanent in us and in all creation is also transcendent—"wholly other," in the phrase of Rudolf Otto.[44] Sacraments make palpable the Grace of the One who is behind and beyond the whole cosmos, yet pervading it entirely with his presence. Someone has compared the sacraments to a magnifying glass held over dry leaves. Sunlight, though present everywhere, is concentrated through the magnifying glass so powerfully that in a few seconds they will ignite. God is present everywhere, and his power is available in myriads of ways. The sacraments make that presence and that power felt and experienced uniquely.

On that Holy Cross Day when Judd died, I learned something new about the power of God. It was not a sacrament that taught me. I neither gave nor received sacraments as such. And yet the power was there, the presence was felt. It is important to recognize that God does not limit himself to those things which the Church singles out and calls "sacraments." As the Prayer Book catechism says, "They are patterns of countless ways by which God uses material things to reach out to us."[45]

Sacraments, in addition to strengthening us and nourishing us with the life of God in the present, also keep pointing us to the destination of the journey. Each meal at the altar anticipates the heavenly banquet, when the Messiah will invite us to be seated at his table. Each person confirmed is sent on a mission which will be accomplished when the Kingdom of God comes in its fullness. Each body, mind, spirit strengthened with the anointing of oil is made stronger for the next leg of the journey, even if that is the final lap which will take us through death. The sacraments lead us into the future, which belongs to the One who "ever shall be, world without end." All the power of God, focused in the sacraments, but filling the world with boundless grace, is directed towards bringing the world to himself. Each of the sacraments points to the consummation of the human journey in Him who is the End as well as the Beginning.

WHERE FAMILIES NEED THE CHURCH

We have arrived at the point where we can begin to put the Christian family into a right perspective. What has the family to do with the process of salvation? It is the vocation of Christian parents to bring up sons and daughters to know, to love, and to serve God. It is their task to give their children the clues they need to find their way along the path that leads to God, which often will be obscure and quite frequently treacherous. Parents are not necessarily the directors of their children's journeys, any more than they are directors of their own. They are, however, the ones who are given the task of guiding the most intimate parts of the formation process. Everything that is done within the family is a matter of helping the individual to become increasingly aware of the image of Christ that is borne within. Every decision made in the family is one which counts for or against life lived in consonance with that image.

There was a time when community—not necessarily Christian community, but village life—was the shaping force of the individual. The annual cycle of festivities drew family members into the larger community. Folklore, celebrations, meals, and carnivals were among the things that this web of human relationships provided. It was here, and not at home, that identity was forged.[46] The disintegration of community life which began in the eighteenth century has left the family without much outside support at all. In America, there is no longer even a pretense of a homogeneous society. There is, in most localities, no larger community that can be depended upon to help the family to inculcate values, to mold character, to inform behavior. And even when there is, for example, in small towns or rural communities, there are few if any ritual links which bind the family to that larger matrix.

So the nuclear family finds itself very much alone, in the words of Edward Shorter, "huddled together into a cozy circle about the fire."[47] Although that may be an exaggeration in some ways, it certainly is descriptive of where the family stands in relationship to the formation of the souls of its individual members. If the family were once to become aware of the monumental task of image formation that is left to it, one can imagine screen doors all over the country flying open and people pouring to churches and synagogues pleading for help.

Consciousness has not progressed that far, alas. What is more apt to happen is a few of those doors do open, and people in their late twenties and early thirties who grew up in the church and have now become parents turn back to the church, hoping that there will be "a religious education" for their children. Little do they realize the strength of the illusion that the Church alone can form its young. But the Church and the family *can* forge an alliance so that the job can be done. By getting in touch with the power available in word and sacrament, parents have a fighting chance of giving their young what they truly need to "get through life": the spirit of truth which leads to peace and wholeness. And the Christian community can find in the family the most effective ally in shepherding people along the journey into deepening union with God.

Ask most families what they need of the Church and one way or another they will say they need help in staying together. That is why that indomitable slogan still appeals: "families that pray together stay together." They hope to heaven that it will work. The family knows it is under seige. The idea of domesticity which brought women out of the fields and shops and into the home to create secure nests where they could raise their young has given way now to the desire of mothers to get out of that sentimental nest and back into the surrounding world. Parents have no real control over the dating habits of their young. Courtship is a completely privatized affair.[48] More important than all this, family members know that they have trouble understanding each other. Nearly everyone seen in marriage counseling talks about "communication" as the problem. Families need help in getting beyond superficial diagnoses like "communication" and down to the business of value-formation, decision-making, and the nurturing of self-esteem. What families need goes deeper than the flare-ups between adolescents and parents. It goes beyond toilet-training and mid-life crises and frustration with elderly parents. They need *shalom*: peace, healing, wholeness. The Church cannot bring *shalom* to them by packaging programs for families or by packing families into church.

The rest of this book is about a way that the Church *can* bring about that healing and wholeness families need. We can make the preparations for, and experience of, the sacraments, the way to build faith in families. By preparing persons thoroughly to live the life made real and present to us in the sacraments, the Church can transform their lives. In the following chapters, we shall call on nearly everything in the Church's repertory to accomplish this: counseling, family enrichment, educational programs for multi-generational groups, liturgy. The goal of everything will be to carry on a kind of pastoral ministry that always has the *shalom*, peace wholeness, oneness of God's Kingdom as its goal and motivation.

I have spoken in depth about this grace which is totally unmerited and undeserved and unearned love, mercy, kindness. I may well be asked, "If it is all those things, why so much emphasis on preparing for the sacraments? Isn't your whole program based on preparing people for something for which there can be no adequate preparation? Grace, while free, is not, in Bonhoeffer's phrase, "cheap." It is neither magic nor automatic. The gift must be picked up, opened, used in order to become effective. That is the whole point. My mother used to have a way of stashing away her most beautiful presents. They were too good to be used. So they would be stored in the trunk or the cedar chest for years. We have that choice with some gifts, but not with God's present of Himself in the sacraments. We walk away from that reality, and we walk away from the only light there is. One does not light a candle and put it under a bushel.[49] What the Church has been lacking is neither power nor rituals; but rituals that are understood adequately so that their power can be released. The power of the sacraments will make lives new only when people open themselves to the life of God released in them.

Few of us and few of our families realize that we need to grow not simply in rational comprehension of the Gospel, but in holiness. We have to come to see holiness not as spiritual smugness, but as true wholeness, an authentic sanctity which embraces everything about our lives. Families need ways to become not only happy, but whole; not only fully functional in the psychological sense, but truly open and free in the exhilarating life of God.

PART TWO

FRAMING A LIFE-LONG STRUCTURE

THREE

Holy Matrimony: Beginning

Seldom do we list Holy Matrimony first among the sacraments.
Indeed, it took twelve centuries for the Church finally to number
marriage among the sacraments at all. Our ideas and emotions
about marriage have always been somewhat mixed. St. Paul, who
has come in for some hard knocks for what he supposedly thought
about marriage, was apparently not so much against it as he was
unconcerned with it. If the Letter to the Ephesians is assumed to
be non-Pauline, as it almost certainly should be, then the apostle
has little to say about marriage. From all appearances, Jesus also
had little say about it outside the famous dictum, "What . . . God
has joined together, let not man put asunder."[1] We could infer from
the story of the woman at the well that he passed up a marvelous
opportunity to comment on marriage when he told her that she
had had five husbands and that she was then living with a man
without benefit of clergy.[2] It could even be inferred that Jesus paid
surprisingly little attention to adultery. Moral defects seem to have
interested him much less than the spiritual conditions that breed
them. Remember his comment that it is out of the heart of a person
that evil things come.[3]

To go a bit further, it is worth noticing that scant mention is
made of the marital status of Jesus' disciples. Only Peter is explicitly

said to have been married. We do not know if he was married or widowed at the time of his discipleship, but we could safely surmise that he spent a good deal of time away from his wife if he had one at that time. Passages like Mark 10:29-30, in which Jesus says, "There is no one who has left house or brothers or sisters or mother or father or children or lands, for my sake and for the gospel" who will not be repaid a hundred times over, suggest that the renunciation of family was not only accepted but encouraged. How this might have affected marriages is a matter of conjecture.

I do not mean to suggest that marriage is treated flippantly in either the gospels in particular or the New Testament in general. We should, however, beware of two trends which characterize much recent thought about Christian marriage and family. One trend has been to make absolute pronouncements about the ordering of Christian families according to certain models of male domination, presumably derived from Ephesians 5:22-33. It is exceedingly dangerous to erect whole social theories on so slight a base as this, even if the model accurately reflected what the writer of Ephesians is driving at (a debatable issue). The other trend has been to romanticize and sentimentalize marriage as if somehow the married life is the universal Christian vocation. Such a view ignores the silence of page after page of the New Testament on the subject of marriage and family, while much is there about the spiritual priorities that call *all* relationships, including marriage, into question.

Marriage is placed first here because it is the beginning of family life. And it is upon a theology of marriage that a theology of family is built.

A THEOLOGY OF MARRIAGE

Covenant. One does not have to read further than the title page of the Bible to find the principal idea in the entire Book. The word which reveals it, of course, is "Testament," and testament means covenant. The whole history of salvation is a history of the covenant with humanity which God has voluntarily made, and by means of which he has pledged himself.

There are at least four covenants within the Old Testament. The first mentioned is that with Noah, of which the rainbow is the sign. The second is the one God makes with Abraham. In looking a bit more closely than we did in the last chapter, we can see some interesting implications for *family* in the Abraham story. God calls Abraham to leave his family of origin—his kinspeople. This radical break with the past becomes prototypical for the biblical understanding of faithfulness. Abraham literally does not know where he is going or whom he is obeying. Moreover, he is getting on in years. All of this emphasizes the amazing grace of God, who promises Abraham that he and Sarah will have a family of their own— notwithstanding their advanced age. God asks only that Abraham be faithful.

The outward sign of this covenant (every covenant must be "signed and sealed" in some way) is circumcision. Though circumcision may well have arisen much later in Israel's history, the important thing is that the family of Abraham are called out from among the rest of the people of the earth and are given a mark of distinction. God has created a new people, and has voluntarily entered into a covenantal relationship with them, in which both he and they can expect certain benefits. The covenant depends upon the "good faith" of both parties. Abraham must keep faith with Yahweh, and Yahweh will in turn keep his Word, his promises.

It is exactly this faithfulness on Yahweh's part which forms the background for the third covenant story, which begins with the call of Moses to be the instrument of delivering the children of Israel from slavery in Egypt. Moses is an unlikely candidate for religious vocation, since he has escaped to Midian after murdering an Egyptian. He, too, sets out on a journey in faith, returning to Egypt to argue with Pharaoh for the release of his people. It is clear in this whole episode that it is Yahweh who has the power, not Pharaoh or Pharaoh's gods. In the end Yahweh will bring about the deliverance he promised. Whatever layers of tradition might lie behind the story, in the form in which we have it, clearly God is "keeping his word" which he spoke to Abraham.

God does not make a covenant with the newly released Israelites, however, until they have departed Egypt and have arrived at Sinai. The giving of the Law to Moses, and thus to Israel, is the apex of covenant history in the Old Testament. God has lived up to his promises to the patriarchs by delivering their descendants from slavery. Now, through the Law, he is giving them the means by which to live as a holy people. Keeping the Law will thus become not the *means* by which they have a relationship with God (that is already assured), but will be the way they respond to his initiative and live within the covenant relationship.

The fourth covenant is that "everlasting covenant" Yahweh makes with the house of David. It stands in contrast to the Abrahamic and Mosaic covenants in that it is not made with the entire nation. The Davidic covenant becomes highly important in messianic thought, and in Christian theology is appropriated as having been ratified in the everlasting reign of Christ, the Son of David.

Crucial to a theology of marriage is what happens to the understanding of "covenant" in the hands of the prophets. An image floating in and out of the writings of the prophets is that of a marriage of Yahweh and his people having taken place on Mount Sinai. When he gave the Law, Yahweh chose Israel to be his bride. The Law became a kind of marriage agreement, and the Bridegroom expected fidelity to the Law, which was tantamount to fidelity to Him. In the prophets' view, Israel had clearly been unfaithful. She had forsaken the covenant with Yahweh, and had played the whore, running after the Baals, the Canaanite gods. This sexual imagery is important. Canaanite religion was characterized by fertility cults, which included temple prostitution. Sexual restraint came to characterize Yahwism, which needed to distance itself from baalism.

Nowhere is this imagery more significant than in the Book of Hosea. Hosea's story is that Yahweh came to him and told him to go marry a prostitute, and to have children with her. Yahweh wants the prophet to experience what it is like to be married to one who, like Israel, has abandoned the marriage covenant. Hosea does just that. He marries a woman by the name of Gomer, and has three children by her. Gomer leaves him, and Hosea goes and woos her back, buying her for fifteen silver shekels and nine and a half bushels of barley. He learns what it is like to be the God of Israel. Yahweh, despite his love for his people, has a bride who constantly forsakes him to play the adulteress. He feels the pain of spurned love, and yet goes after the faithless bride, winning her back and beginning again.[4]

Thus, covenant becomes understood as marriage—the wedding of Yahweh and his people. Derivatively, marriage of man and woman comes to be understood as reflecting the covenant between God and humanity.

In the New Testament, the imagery of Yahweh and Israel is transferred to Jesus and the Church. One of the first things we notice in the gospels is the abandon with which Jesus goes about life. His activity has a celebrative air, witness the amount of eating and drinking reported or alluded to in the gospels. At one point, the question is put to Jesus as to why he and his disciples go about eating and drinking, in stark contrast to John the Baptist and his company, who were known for their fasting. Jesus' reply is interesting. He refers to himself as the bridegroom, and notes that when the bridegroom comes, people naturally celebrate by eating and drinking. The day will come, he goes on to say, when they will fast because the bridegroom will no longer be around.[5] Schooled in the Old Testament, Jesus knew exactly what he was saying. He was applying to himself the imagery that Hosea and other writers had used to depict the relationship between Yahweh and his people.

A number of parables pick up this figure. The Kingdom of Heaven is like a banquet which a king gave at the wedding of his son.[6] Or ten bridesmaids await a bridegroom who has been delayed.[7] Or a man shows up at a wedding celebration without the proper attire, and is cast out, apparently because of his presumptuousness.[8] The community reading and hearing such parables cannot avoid their messianic implication. It is Jesus, the Messiah, who is the bridegroom. It is he who will return in the middle of the night when many least expect him. It is he who bestows the garment of grace by which alone one attends the messianic banquet.

In the context of such a communal understanding of Jesus as bridegroom, the writer of the Epistle to the Ephesians spells out the figure more fully. The relationship between husband and wife is like that between Christ and the Church, he claims. It is ironic that this passage has become the focus of so much talk about headship in the home. Perhaps the writer is emphasizing that. I think, rather, that the key to his thought is, "Give way to one another in obedience to Christ."[9] His is an understanding of marriage as *mutual* submission. Just as Christ gave himself up for the Church, though he is Lord, so husbands are called to give themselves to their wives. Wives are called to give themselves to their husbands. It is in this very context that the writer quotes the same passage in Genesis that Mark reports Jesus as having quoted in his comment on divorce: "For this reason, a man must leave his father and mother and be joined to his wife, and the two shall become one body."[10] Though he purports to work out his theory of Christian marriage on the basis of the relationship of Christ and the Church, the author actually does the reverse. Marriage becomes the way in which he understands the Body of Christ idea. "This mystery," he states, referring to the above quotation from Genesis, "has many implications; but I am saying it applies to Christ and the Church."[11]

Note the sexual implications of this passage. Christ sacrificed himself for the Church, so that he might make her holy. "He made her clean by washing her with water with a form of words."[12] In this obvious reference to baptism, we have a comment harking back to the concern for sexual chastity which distinguished Yahwism from baalism. Quite probably it was born out of the writer's perception of the similar contrast between Christian ethics and the sexual licentiousness rampant in much of the pagan world of his time. Christ did all this, he goes on to say, ". . . so that when he took her [the Church] to himself, she would be glorious, without spot or wrinkle or anything like that, but holy and faultless."[13] That is about as explicit as the New Testament ever gets with the sexual metaphor. The vision of Christ as the lover of a pure and holy bride, the Church, presents both the Ephesians and us with an amazingly high doctrine of marriage and specifically of sexual union. The implicit claim is that no relationship more closely approximates the love of Christ and his Church than does marriage, specifically the sexual union of wife and husband.

A final place in which we see the bride and bridegroom imagery is in the Book of Revelation. John, the visionary, looks beyond history to the culmination of all things and events. He sees the New Jerusalem coming down out of heaven adorned as a bride for her husband. Again, marriage is the experience which provides the picture describing the union of Christ and his faithful people. The bride is bedecked in the most radiant jewels, presented all beautiful to her husband. Accompanying this metaphor is the proclamation from the throne of heaven:

> Behold the dwelling of God is with men. He will dwell with them, and they shall be his people, and God himself will be with them; he will wipe away every tear from their eyes, and death shall be no more. . . .[14]

What is that but a final statement of the covenant? Out of Abraham, God has called a new people into being. Through the Blood of Christ the Lamb, they are now perfected. At last creation is restored. God and humanity are reconciled, united, at peace. "I will be their God and they shall be my people":[15] this refrain, played long before by the prophets, has been realized in Christ Jesus. The reality extends to embrace the entire human race, indeed the whole cosmos. For all the former things of the old world are gone. There is a completely new creation. And it is *marriage*—the relationship of lover and beloved—which is chosen to provide the picture in which all this is viewed.

Sign. Marriage is a joining together. That is the very first thing said in the Celebration and Blessing of a Marriage in the Book of Common Prayer.[16] The praying community gathers in the presence of God to witness and to bless that joining together of a man and a woman. The clergy do not do the joining; they facilitate it. The community does not do the joining; they witness and bless it. Were we to hold that the man and woman are not in some way changed through the rite of marriage, then it would be honest to say that they do the joining. But marriage is a sacrament: they are changed, transformed, given a new status, a new and qualitatively distinct kind of life. As in all sacramental action, God is the agent. God does the joining.

The next thing the marriage rite tells us is that "the bond and covenant of marriage was established by God in creation." The union of man and woman is part of the natural order. It is a union of "heart, body, and mind": emotional and spiritual, physical and intellectual. Our understanding is that God has in mind the mutual joy of the man and woman whom he brings together. They are, within this union, to help and comfort one another in all circumstances—prosperous and adverse. And, if God gives them the gift of children, they are to nurture them in the knowledge and love of the Lord. All this says clearly what the marital union is *in intention*. From this we can draw many inferences about how two people might live as married persons. This does not describe *the* (or even *a*) style of married life, but does say with great clarity what the *purposes* of marriage are.

In the middle of all this, the community is reminded of something else. Marriage "signifies to us the mystery of the union between Christ and his Church." It *signifies*. Marriage is itself a sign, pointing to the covenantal relationship uniting Christ and his people. Further on, in the Prayers of the People, the community prays that the life of the married couple might be "a sign of Christ's love to this sinful and broken world, that unity may overcome estrangement, forgiveness heal guilt, and joy conquer despair."[17] Just as baptism points to dying and rising with Christ, the immersion into divine life united with human nature, so marriage points to a reality, namely the victorious love of Christ which breaks down all dividing walls of hostility. Like baptism, which is intended not just for some but for all, marriage points to a universal truth: the union of all humanity with the life of God. Marital union thus operates as a sign on at least two levels: it signifies to the faithful the union between Christ and his community, and it signifies to everyone the love of Christ through which the whole world is redeemed.

When taken as a whole, a sacrament is a sign of God's redemption, of unity overcoming alienation, of Christ's death and resurrection. But each sacrament also contains a component which itself is a sign of the transforming Grace of God—the water of baptism, the bread and wine of the communion. etc.

I once asked Joe and Carol, in our premarital session on the Church's teachings about marriage, what they considered to be the outward, visible sign of marriage. Like three-fourths of their peers, they were stumped. Eventually Joe said, "The ring." When pressed, they admitted that the ring is not comparable in any way to the water of baptism or the bread and wine of communion. As Carol put it, "I guess our marriage wouldn't be over if one of us lost a wedding ring!"

I pointed out that the rubrics in the Prayer Book permit some other symbol to be used in lieu of a ring or rings. Joe tentatively suggested, "Then it's the service itself?" Indeed the service is the part of marriage available to the senses—like the laying-on-of-hands with prayer in confirmation or ordination. It would be correct to say that the vows of marriage are its outward, visible sign; vows accompanied by the joining of hands and the giving and receiving of rings. But what do vows, and the symbolic acts of joining, point to? Is it not to the literal joining of a man and a woman—two bodies, two personalities, two individual spirits—when they give themselves totally and completely to each other in love, specifically in full sexual union? The "outward, visible" part of marriage *is*, then, the man and the woman. Their joining is effected by the exchange of vows, the joining of hands, and the exchange of rings or other gifts. But the joining has not been "consummated," to use the old word, until they are united in body, mind, and spirit.

It is *this* joining that we are really talking about when we say that marriage signifies to us the mystery of the union between Christ and his Church, between Yahweh and his people. We are boldly claiming that in the whole realm and range of human experience, it is this joining together that most closely resembles the union of God and humanity. The Church does not say and never should say that marriage is the only good and proper human relationship. We do not even claim that there are no other kinds of love relationships. But marriage is the only one which we bless and call "*Holy* Matrimony."

This is an audacious idea! Sexual communion of man and woman is exalted to a far higher plane in Christian experience than in our culture. And, of course, there are dangers in that. It is possible, in claiming the specialness of marital union, to fence it off so completely from possibilities of abuse that we make difficult the very enjoyment God created it for. On the other hand, it is about time we dealt honestly with what Christian theology has to say about the sacrament of marriage and with why sexuality is deeply important to the Christian community. Our society has overreacted to the oppressiveness with which the Church has historically approached sexual issues, and we are left with few people, in the Church or out of it, who understand "what's so special" about sex. Christian tradition has placed sexual love within the context of marriage for good reason, which we have unfortunately lost sight of. It signifies what it is like to be in love with God.

Keeping promises. Because marriage is a sacrament, it conveys to us God's grace. One of the prayers in the Prayer Book marriage rite words it this way:

> Give them grace, when they hurt each other, to recognize and acknowledge their fault, and to seek each other's forgiveness and yours.[18]

Certainly married people will hurt and be hurt by each other. If they think they can avoid either, they are apt to be disappointed or at least deprived of the exquisite experience marriage can be. It is painful to be in a love relationship with God, just as (God knows) it is painful to be in a love relationship with humans. You trust. You are disappointed. You are angry. You want to turn and walk away. You do. And you are sorry. You feel the isolation, the estrangement. You know loneliness. You crave your lover. You return. And are ashamed. And accepted. And forgiven. You begin again. On and on it goes, day in and day out. Risk, trust, vulnerability are all words we use cheaply. We are surprised when we risk and lose, when we trust and are betrayed, are vulnerable and actually get wounded. But in a love relationship there are no guarantees, except the overarching faithfulness of the two, bound together within the covenant.

What enables people to stay married if that is what marriage is like (and it is)? Grace does. The Collect for marriage implores God to "look mercifully upon this man and this woman . . . and [to] assist them with [his] grace, that with true fidelity and steadfast love they may honor and keep the promises and vows they make. . . ." And it will be that grace alone which enables them to keep those promises.

Here is where the Christian concept of marriage differs radically from that current in American society. Almost everyone in our society (Christians included) thinks that the cement holding marriage together is *love.* From a sacramental viewpoint, it is not love but *grace.* And grace is not the same as love. Certainly it is not the same as *eros,* sexual love. Grace comes out of love and expresses love. If love is not the cement of the marital relationship, neither is love its foundation. In the Christian tradition, *covenant* is. One is faithful because one has given one's word, one's faith, to another. The terms of the covenant are that the relationship is not to be broken. If the relationship is instead founded upon feelings of love, then it is going to be in trouble when those feelings begin to change (not necessarily wane) as feelings inevitably will. If, on the other hand, the couple share an understanding that love is a foundational position in life, characterized by giving, caring, and finding a basic fulfillment in putting another before oneself—then perhaps, after all, it is reasonable to say that marriage is built on love. Needless to say, that is a very different idea from what most of us mean when we say, "We're in love."

A clamor of dissent will break out over this, especially over the suggestion that marital partners will be fulfilled by putting each other first. Many will quite rightly point out that men have exploited that idea by having women serve their interests at the expense of women's own self-fulfillment. Absolutely right. Not women only, or men only, but *both* are committed within the covenant of marriage to putting each other before themselves. The fact that we have so rarely done it does not render the idea meaningless or wrong.

Marriage is not the only place this is done nor the only means for accomplishing it. The great embarrassment of the American Church in the late twentieth century is that Jesus actually said, "If anyone would come after me, let him deny himself. . . ."[19] We are only slowly beginning to face the fact that self-denial, while it may fly in the face of the human potential movement, is not only healthy but necessary. What Jesus is claiming, and proclaiming, is that it is exactly in denying one's *self* that one reaches full potential! It is more than unfortunate—it is shameful—that throughout history so many have taken this idea to mean that they should have no sense of self worth, and thus have led themselves down the road to self-abasement and the most damaging kinds of self-abnegation.

It is only when we discover that we have a self that is lovable and beautiful that we can believe anything of value is being given should we give it away. The route to this discovery is to hear the gospel that God created us in his image and for his purposes. All that is defective is restored and redeemed in Christ Jesus. One does not discover God without discovering oneself. And one does not discover one's true self without discovering God. Marriage is one vocation, and only one, where the truth of this is lived and applied.

To be married means that a man and a woman have chosen to practice this self-giving life of Jesus Christ by giving themselves as wholly and completely as possible to each other. That is the dynamic underneath making and keeping promises: giving ourselves away—putting ourselves in another's hands—pledging our faith. Yet it takes awhile before the married discover this. Few people getting married, for the first time at any rate, come into marriage knowing it. We have to *practice* giving ourselves away. This is why experience keeps telling us that we cannot afford to be too restrictive and narrow in our affirmation that sexual love belongs within the context of marriage. Chastity is desirable. But young persons will indeed experiment, especially in an age when courtship is completely private, subject to no parental or peer supervision. They will practice giving themselves away. Sex education, particularly anything that goes by that name in the Church, should endeavor to help youth understand the theology of sexuality, and how sexual union is absolutely the most significant of all human experiences. We can hardly control sexual behavior; but we can go far to help people understand what it *means* in our tradition.

To keep promises—to be faithful—we have to learn not only how to love and be loved, but the limits of love. We have to practice the life of self-giving. We know that we kiss not only because we love, but in order to love. So it is with loving one another sexually. If it is true that marriage reflects the relationship of Christ and the Church, then marriage is a life-long journey of discovery. We pray not only because we know God, but in order to know God. We worship not only because we have found a reason to worship, but in order to find a reason. So we make love to our husbands or wives: not only because we love, but to learn how to love, how to give ourselves away.

Promises can be made. We are not necessarily able to keep them. We cannot, except by grace, love so unconditionally as we promise: "for better, for worse; for richer, for poorer; in sickness and in health. . . ." It is impossible to spell out where this grace is found and how God communicates himself to husband and wife. My belief is that however it is mediated, it is discovered within the context of real commitment, which is what covenant essentially means. If commitment is not present, there is not the freedom seriously to entertain the notion of what life would be like without each other. Anyone who is married knows that notion is sometimes irresistibly attractive to people not mutually committed. But more than that, wife and husband have to find ways to offer themselves and their marriage to God. Certainly prayer, both private and shared, is one way to do this. Reflecting on the relationship, working on it, celebrating it, and renewing it: all will be ways and moments when grace is discovered.

PREPARING FOR MARRIAGE

Separateness. A process of separation from family, friends and community is the first ritual connected with marriage. The problem is that the ritual is only present in abbreviated or secularized or vestigial form. What is called "Declaration of Consent" in the Prayer Book marriage rite is actually based upon the old Roman betrothal rite which took place a considerable time before marriage. In Lutheran and Anglican practice in the sixteenth century, the couple would come to the church, and probably on the church porch make public their intention to be married. They had to answer questions which probed the seriousness of their commitment.[20] The present rite incorporates these questions before the reading of Scripture and the marriage vows.

It is not difficult for the Church to seize the opportunity to begin the process of marriage preparation at the point of engagement through variations on this process of separation. In some sections of the country, couples are now beginning to plan a year or more in advance of the wedding. True, pressure to find a place suitable for a large and sometimes expensive reception is unfortunately one of the reasons behind this trend, but the Church has redeemed

secular trends before. Immediately when the couple contact the
priest about a date for the wedding, the priest ought to invite them
to come by for an extended conversation about marriage preparation as well as wedding planning. I find it best to extend this
invitation practically to everyone who asks anything about being
married in the church, including those with hardly any notion of
what Christian marriage is. It is a great opportunity for evangelism
—so long as they quickly learn that Christian marriage makes
absolutely no sense apart from participation in the Christian
community.

If the engagement has not been officially announced, and
possibly even if it has been, the priest or minister has an opportunity
to pray with the couple before they embark upon marriage
preparation, which might not commence for some months. It would
be helpful and interesting to do this with both sets of parents present,
either in a home or before the altar of the parish church. This brief
ritual, reminiscent of the old betrothal rite, could emphasize that
the couple are going to be psychologically, and in some sense
physically, separated from family and friends in order to get ready
for marriage.

When the marriage preparation starts, the couple should be
encouraged to spend ample time alone. That may sound silly, but
I am amazed at how little time some couples have together. If both
are working or in school, or if they are not living near each other,
it is not at all improbable that time will be precious. They will have
to make an effort to ensure that all the moments together are not
spent planning the details of the wedding.

One of the best pieces of homework to give a couple to enable
sharing is a questionnaire about their life history, including relevant
items about their mental, physical, and emotional health histories.
The most helpful questions for getting into life history are probably
those about family of origin. In anticipation of the first session of
marriage preparation, I ask them to answer some questions about
parents, grandparents, and the siblings of father, mother and
themselves. They also work individually on a simple family tree,
concentrating on a single phrase or two about the family members
who have affected them most. For many, this experience seems to
be their first serious reflection on their family. At this session,

after I have looked at their individual forms, I ask them to share with each other their family constellation, seen as best they can remember from their point of view as children. Going through the process of describing various family members, and the dynamics and bonds between and among them, is a very moving experience. Old wounds and unfinished business sometimes surface. Joys and happy memories come back. This is a holy moment: the couple are beginning consciously to weave their shared story out of their two separate stories.

This sharing of story will increasingly characterize marriage. The couple are not being asked to forsake their kinspeople, but they are being invited to bring their family stories with them into the new relationship. Clergy may suggest elaborations of this idea. It could be fun for some couples to work together during engagement making a family photograph album. I know a couple, for example, who purchased a "package" from a portrait studio to photograph all their parents and grandparents. They began by having good photographs made of their grandparents. Several years later, when one of the grandparents died, this picture took on added meaning, as it was the latest one she had had made. But simple and inexpensive photographs will do just as well as foundation pieces of shared family stories. Later, pictures of the wedding, photographs of the children's baptisms, and snapshots of the first home or apartment can be added to keep the story going. Variations such as taping the oral stories of some older family members, or writing character sketches or the rudiments of family episodes may interest those wishing to pursue more deeply their shared story.

Very early in the marital preparation, the couple are introduced to a husband and wife who will become guides, friends and mentors for them during the crucial months before marriage—couples who really understand something about the subtleties of marriage and especially who know what Christian marriage is about. Making this match will be a delicate matter in some cases, but will nearly always be a rich experience; faith is best shared through relationships with other people of faith. The priest, or a lay person whose special ministry is to assist those in marital preparation, must make clear to the couple who will function as guides exactly what they are being asked to do. I find it helpful to let them know something of the background and personality of the two people they will be meeting, and suggest that they invite them to a meal. This provides a good setting in which to converse about marriage, and especially about what makes Christian marriage distinctive. If the preparation is taking place over a number of months, perhaps the sponsoring couple can arrange two or three other occasions when the couples can get together.

Taking time to develop their stories, meeting with the sponsoring couple, and coming together regularly with the clergy are all ways in which a couple are ushered out of the company of peers and relatives to focus on the shared life they are beginning. Pastors will find other ways to enhance this process of separation, such as through bringing together two or more couples in marriage preparation. Seminars including such topics as financial management, communication, and role expectations are fruitful. Knowledgeable lay persons with expertise in various fields can offer their gifts and insights.

It is not so easy to persuade the prospective bride and groom to get some distance from each other. They will not enjoy being separated, literally or psychologically. Yet the possibilities make it worth trying. One priest I know has his premarital counselees go on a mini-retreat alone. During this time they write a simple essay or two on such topics as "What I Want out of this Marriage" and "My Personal Gifts and Liabilities as a Potential Spouse." They come back together with the priest and share what they have thought and written.

Creating a home. When people marry, they are forming not only a bond between themselves, but also a home, household. Marriage preparation must take this into account. Certainly if there are children from former marriages who will be included in a new, blended family, attention must be paid to their needs and concerns. One or more sessions with the whole blended family, and possibly additional time with the children alone are helpful. Often they have concerns, problems, and issues they are not comfortable raising with the parent and step-parent-to-be.

If there are no children, some issues about childbearing are still in order. I say this knowing full well that those who do not yet have children are ill-prepared to deal with them realistically. It is relatively useless to discuss who is going to change diapers and who is going to be responsible for what part of toilet training, but there is a point in looking at issues like value-formation. What will be the role of family rituals? Most couples will not have considered that they might do something with daily prayers at mealtime. What about their stewardship? Issues like the Christian standard of tithing should not necessarily be postponed until long after marriage. Establish a home with an understanding of giving. And what about their time management? The stewardship of time includes such issues as what to do on the Lord's Day, how they will spend time with each other, and how they will invest time in community and charitable causes. I have learned not to dodge these issues because couples might not be ready to address them. Though they may not do anything about much of this, at least they get the message that such issues take their place alongside communication and role expectations as valid concerns within a marriage.

Strike a balance between a purely clinical approach (dealing with the concerns and issues of the couple as they surface them) and a didactic approach. If there is no teaching component in marriage preparation, certainly many couples will be none the wiser about Holy Matrimony as a distinctive way of life.

One of the deepest tenets of the Christian tradition of Holy Matrimony is that it is undertaken for, if it be God's will, the "procreation of children and their nurture in the knowledge and love of the Lord."[21] It is upon the foundation of marriage that the home is built, as it is upon the foundation of Christ that Christian marriage is built.

From this beginning, growth is possible. It is to that we now turn.

FOUR

Holy Baptism: Growing

Clergy are supposed to know everything. One of the last things the parish priest is likely to know is when someone gets pregnant. Unless complications are present early in a pregnancy, a couple might not think to tell their pastor of the new member on the way. Since it occurs to many people slowly, if at all, to let the priest know of such things as ordinary illness and marital difficulties, it is not surprising that few people pick up the phone and announce a pregnancy. For baptism to become a point at which ministry to and in families is effective, we have to change this situation.

Preparation for baptism begins ideally with conception. Soon after a couple learns that the wife is pregnant, they should share that fact with the parish priest. A wonderful opportunity for pastoral ministry appears! The priest may wish to schedule some visits or counseling sessions with the couple, and possibly with the family if there are other children. Introducing a new member into a family is a delicate matter. Siblings need to be prepared, as appropriate, for all relationships and bonds to change. Parents are beginning to share with children much more directly than formerly about a new baby "on the way." It is an ideal time to address questions like "Where did I come from?" Many parents, however, seem to be unaware of or naive about the fears created in young children by the anticipation of a new brother or sister. Accurately, children may suppose that mother and dad will have less time, energy, and attention for them. Inaccurately, they may fantasize that a ready-made new playmate is about to come, whom they can enjoy (and control) from Day One. Effective pastoral ministry takes seriously the whole family into which the new baby will come.

FORMING COMMUNITY

Craig and I were finishing lunch when he said, "Oh, by the way, Nancy's pregnant." Craig and Nancy had three children, ranging in age from eleven to four. Things had been rough for them. Craig had job problems. Nancy had recently been through the illness and death of her father. And, in fact, Craig and I were having lunch because things had been troubled between him and Nancy for the last few months. This was *not* the time *I* would want to have another child. I doubt that I concealed my tempered enthusiasm.

"Gee, that's interesting." I sipped my coffee and went back to work on my Black Forest cake. "How are you and Nancy feeling about that?"

"Well, you can imagine. It's not the greatest time for another baby. But maybe it'll all be for the best. Nancy is depressed. She was looking forward to going to school this fall."

"And the kids?"

"We haven't told them."

I could imagine myself in his circumstances, and did not savor the idea. On the other hand, the baby was clearly coming. Maybe we'd better make the best of the situation.

Interestingly, it was Craig who brought up the subject of baptism. He wanted to know if they could plan a baptism. They had always felt that the baptisms of the other children had been somewhat perfunctory. They wanted this one to be special.

Something clicked. Here was the opportunity I had been waiting for. We could begin preparing for baptism right away. I mentioned a few vague ideas to Craig: I could get together with him and Nancy to talk about "parish sponsors." This, of course, meant zero to him then. Before we left each other, Craig and I had marked down a date when I would come to visit.

If I were going to see Craig and Nancy today, I would know much more about what to do than I did then. In addition to talking with them and their children about the oncoming change in their lives, I would offer to pray with them. Perhaps we would celebrate a home eucharist together, giving thanks for the gift of new life. I would offer to have the Blessing of a Pregnant Woman, a brief and moving liturgy in the Episcopal Book of Occasional Services.[1] At the very least, I would offer to lead some informal prayers and thanksgivings. At the time, however, I failed to suggest any of those things.

Nonetheless, Nancy, Craig, and I did talk about godparents and parish sponsors. I assumed that they, like most people, would want to choose relatives as godparents. It turned out that they had no relatives who were particularly involved in the church. So we began talking of parish sponsors. They had come to know another parish couple, older than themselves, who they suggested rather timidly might make good sponsors. "Good!" I cried. "The Padgetts are perfect!" And they were. Committed Christians, actively involved in the worship life of the congregation, Jake and Edy Padgett were marvelous parents with their own children. I knew immediately it was a wonderful idea.

Edy Padgett was ecstatic when I told her. She thought parish sponsors were a wonderful idea, since several of the godparents of her own children lived far away and had had minimal contact with them over the years. In this case, I told Edy, you and Jake will be the *only* sponsors. She assured me that she and Jake would think it over and pray about it and respond.

Needless to say, sometimes making a good match of parents and parish sponsors is not nearly so natural and easy. When an expectant couple are new to the parish, the priest can offer to introduce them to some parishioners. Over the years, I have learned to trust my intuition, and to make a match I think will work. Having gotten to know a bit about the prospective parents, I contact one or more persons (keep in mind that single persons make wonderful sponsors) asking them to consider being parish sponsors for the new baby. Until this ministry becomes well established within the congregation, sponsors need to be told what is expected of them. Edy and Jake Padgett joined my wife and me for dinner at Craig and Nancy's, and we talked about preparing for birth and baptism. In cases where the child to be baptized is already born, parish sponsors can have some contact with the parents and child before the baptism, and continue contacts afterward. Parish sponsors should know that they will be expected at several baptismal preparation sessions, and that they will, on behalf of the congregation, participate with other sponsors (godparents) in the liturgy of baptism.

Only if they feel positive about this ministry should people agree to be parish sponsors. Every opportunity to decline should be extended, with the assurance that in no way will their declining be viewed as a rejection of priest, baby or parents. When the one or more parish sponsors have consented to do this ministry, they and the parents of the child come together in an informal setting, such as the dinner that we and the Padgetts shared. First-time parents usually welcome such support as birth approaches. Sometimes parish sponsors can, in fact, be more supportive than relatives, especially when there are politics being played about which grandmother gets to come when. Even those who have had several other children will be astonished at the number of opportunities to prepare for birth and baptism which they never before considered. Parish sponsors and parents will naturally discuss how other members of the household might be included in birth and baptismal preparations. Sensitive sponsors will figure out ways to reach out to children, who can often feel especially left out during the final months of awaiting the new baby.

Ideally, there should be at least three of these pre-birth meetings, so that by the time the baby is born, a truly Christian community of support is in place to welcome a new life. If something happens to complicate the pregnancy or labor, or if the child is still-born or handicapped, there is a community of support already established to provide assistance and emotional strength to the parents. If, on the other hand, everything goes smoothly during labor and delivery, a variety of other supportive measures becomes possible: help with housework, child care, transportation for arriving grandparents, hospital visits, and perhaps above all, protecting the space and limited time of the new parents.

As soon after birth as feasible, the new parents bring the baby to church for the Thanksgiving for a Child. Other children in the family can participate in this brief rite, which should come directly before the "peace" at the eucharist. It seems desirable, however, to omit participation of parish sponsors at this point. Otherwise, the service might begin to resemble Holy Baptism in some confusing ways. And nothing should steal thunder from the day of baptism! The Thanksgiving should be kept simple, without elaboration of ritual, and certainly should not be followed by any celebration.

The day of baptism begins to draw near. One or more church school classes might be asked to make special presents for the newly baptized. When Craig and Nancy's daughter was born, the third-grade teacher (whose class included one of the older siblings) invited them to bring the new infant to meet the children the week prior to baptism, to give the class some connection with the child. They were designing a quilt to be given to the parents on the day of baptism (keeping that, of course, quite a secret!) In one parish, children often make banners to display when welcoming the newly baptized, to add color and festivity to baptismal days. In still another parish, various families make presents for the newly baptized, and these are presented immediately after the priest says, "Let us welcome the newly baptized." When there are many candidates for baptism, attention must be paid to coordinate these efforts so that all may feel equally included.

Prebaptismal instructions include, so far as possible, all parents, parish sponsors and other sponsors (godparents) of all candidates. Godparents often live some distance away, quite frequently too far to come for the baptism itself. All the more reason to make sure that parish sponsors are involved from the beginning. The first of three sessions should begin with a brief getting-acquainted period, followed by a presentation of basic baptismal theology. One of the many effective ways to do this is to discuss baptism in terms of the Holy Trinity: baptism as incorporation into the family of God the Father; baptism as union with the death and resurrection of God the Son; baptism as continual participation in the life of God the Holy Spirit. Another interesting approach is to unpack baptismal theology in light of the particular liturgical event (Epiphany, Easter, Pentecost, All Saints Day) on which the sacrament will be celebrated.

Selected passages of Scripture might form the focus for the second session. The flood, the giving of the Law, Ezekiel's vision of the valley of dry bones, the near-sacrifice of Isaac, Jesus' baptism, Romans 6:3-11 ("baptized into Christ's death"), Galatians 5 ("walk by the Spirit"), Matthew 28:19-20 (the "Great Commission") are all profitable passages to explore. Sometimes I have assigned one or more of these for parents and sponsors to study between sessions. One priest I know consistently uses the story of the near-sacrifice of Isaac as a paradigm of obedience as well as of parental willingness to give over a child to God. After talking about it at the first session, participants role-play the characters during the second session, and reflect on the elements of fear, courage, and deliverance —all of which are a part of the baptismal reality.

By the end of a third session, participants should be familiar with the liturgy of baptism—not only the logistics of the service, but also its meaning. Symbols like Paschal Candle and Oil of Chrism will have been thoroughly explained. Preparatory prayers are an essential part of this session, and perhaps fasting should be suggested (except to nursing mothers!): everything possible must dramatize that Holy Baptism is the single most important thing that can ever happen to us.

Several things should happen on the day of baptism. If the Book of Common Prayer is followed, it will normally be a major Holy Day: All Saints, the Baptism of Our Lord, Pentecost, the Great Vigil of Easter. By all means, the sermon should have some relation to baptism—not a hard task to accomplish, since any sermon to the baptized (and baptizing!) community should bear seeds of this already. It is especially easy to accomplish on the major festivals, chosen because they relate intrinsically to baptism. Periodically, as when, for example, a baptism is scheduled during that long period between Pentecost and All Saints, the sermon can in effect be an instruction about the liturgy itself, so that the congregation continues to grow in awareness of their role "to do all in [their] power to support [these] persons in their life in Christ."[2] This also is a day for taking many pictures (after the service, of course). Suggest that the family get at least one good picture of the font. They can use it later in telling the story of baptism to the growing child. Obviously, a picture that includes all the sponsors, and one of the priest and child, are desirable. If circumstances permit, consider taping the service. Recently, during our younger daughter's preparation for First Communion, she listened to herself wailing during her baptism at the Great Vigil of Easter—with interest and great delight.

Afterwards, the parish will surely want to have a party to celebrate! Some may protest that they need to rush home after the service to make ready for relatives and friends. Well in advance of baptism, however, the priest might explain the necessity of giving the *whole* parish some way to celebrate. A simple celebration during the coffee hour following the liturgy is all that is called for, perhaps dressed up with a bouquet of fresh flowers or greens and augmented by (why not?) a special cake, decorated by one or more parish sponsors.

One congregation I served had a parish weekend retreat that included both Halloween and All Saints' Day. Those planning the program decided to focus on Holy Baptism. Accordingly, they took an evergreen tree, and had each participant make a dove-shaped tag to hang on it, bearing the date (or approximate date) of that person's baptism. It would be possible to have a permanent "family tree," perhaps in picture or poster form, which could be displayed during these celebrations of baptism. New tags or pictures or names could be added to include newly made Christians. Incidentally, the connection of a "family tree" with the Christmas tree is an intriguing possibility. You might consider decorating a parish Christmas tree with symbols of baptism—our own "new life" in Christ—and keeping the tree up through the first Sunday after the Epiphany, the Feast of the Baptism of Our Lord.

After the baptism, family and sponsors may celebrate even more. Parents and sponsors, when they met to share a meal and plan for this great occasion, will have created ways to involve relatives and friends in delightful, memorable ways. In places where candles lit from the Paschal Candle are given to the newly baptized, symbolizing their share in the Resurrection through baptism, the candles can become focal points at home during the meal, or during prayers. Later, parish sponsors will need to keep up contacts with the family. Perhaps they can schedule a rendezvous with parents after six months.

Baptismal anniversaries are crucially important. It would be highly fitting for parishes to work on ways to include in the Prayers of the People those who are celebrating their baptismal anniversaries during the week. The parents, or perhaps sponsors, will wish to plan a party to celebrate the anniversary. Take care to consider the date and time. I recommend that the liturgical anniversary be celebrated, so that every Easter, for example, recalls our baptism into Christ's death and resurrection, or every Pentecost reminds us that we share the Holy Spirit through baptism. Individuals may weigh this against the easily remembered calendar date, and even the possibility of transferring the annual celebration to a time when it can be given even higher priority, not being eclipsed by seasonal festivities as an Easter anniversary might be. These anniversary celebrations are a perfect time to bring out pictures or tape recordings of the baptism and reminisce. Young children love to hear stories of their baptism, and these anecdotes become important pieces of the personal myths they are constructing.

Forming community in these ways is great fun, and much work. Pastoral ministry will shift emphases. Such changes often require enormous energy. Grooming lay leadership to lead parts of the process, such as sharing in the baptismal instructions and planning post-baptismal celebrations, will take patience. Continuing support of parish sponsors demands time.

The payoff is significant, however. Craig and Nancy did not find that making baptism central to their family life cured all their interpersonal ills, but they did find themselves and their other children able to prepare for and welcome the new baby with true joy and hope. Several years later, when the baby contracted a serious illness, Jake and Edy Padgett helped bear the family's strain. And later still, when Craig and Nancy experienced a severe crisis in their marriage, the Padgetts stood near them, offering friendship, encouragement and understanding. A true community of support had come into being around Katherine's baptism. I believe that Craig and Nancy's experiences around that baptism deepened their faith. Their family today is strong and healthy, in part because their faith has guided them through some very difficult seasons.

LIVING THE BAPTIZED LIFE

We are fond of speaking of baptism as the Sacrament of Belonging. It is more than merely belonging, however. Baptism is the process of becoming immersed in the missionary life of the Christian community. Setting up this model of sponsorship will almost certainly result in a heightened sense of belonging to the Christian community. But how do we go about bringing the newly baptized into touch with the heart of that community's task—reconciling the world to God in and through Christ?

The short answer to that question is that the individual will be formed in the context of the life of a church and that of a family shaped by the meaning of baptism. Church life and family life have to be interwoven. Both have to reflect clearly the Gospel message if the individual is to grow in the knowledge and love of God. Both have to share consonant values if our children are to have a consistent image of the "full stature of Christ."

In the Prayer Book baptismal liturgy, the celebrant asks five questions as a part of the baptismal covenant, after the traditional creedal questions calling for affirmation of belief in the Holy Trinity. They have to do with continuing participation in the life of the Christian community; repentance and resisting evil; proclamation of the Gospel in word and deed; service to humanity; and working for justice, peace, and human dignity.[3] All of these, especially the last four, demand a highly developed social awareness among the baptized. Development begins as family and church work together to build that social awareness from the very beginning of life.

Obviously, the only way this can happen is by having an educated adult population. The family's role in living out the implications of baptism assumes the presence of adults who are at least actively struggling with Gospel issues. Their Christian community must be doing the same thing. People do not struggle in a vacuum. Any systematic approach to family life education in the church will boldly raise questions (of clergy, necessarily) about what we do to help couples preparing for marriage carry on the struggle with the Gospel. Likewise, instruction for expectant parents requires attention. In short, the church has to carry on an endless effort to help adults at every life stage grapple with the implications of baptism. We have to be very clear with people about the *social* demands of Holy Baptism, else countless people will continue to rock along thinking that baptism has saved them from hell-fire. Period. We must stop foolishly assuming that the message gets conveyed every once in a while through a one-shot adult seminar or an annual Lenten study.

All true. But we still have to start somewhere. We cannot assume that the parents of our new-born child were married in the parish or even in the Church. For various reasons, preparation for birth and baptism may have been curtailed or short-circuited. So here, after baptism, is another opportunity to intervene with the gospel. If the parish has a director of Christian education, or a lay volunteer in charge of coordinating the parish nursery, he or she might call together a group of new parents with others in the parish, such as those who have agreed to staff the nursery or whose ministry is the care and teaching of young children. Many of these parents will either expect that bringing the child to church will be a convenience for them or that it will be a drag. Almost all will think that the presence of the child in pre-school at such an early date is optional. Change this thinking! *Perhaps the very most important experiences* we ever have in church are our first visits to the nursery! The way we are loved, touched, cuddled, cleaned and played with has much to do with what we come to perceive as "church." Parents are not going to bring their children into a dingy church basement with dangerous toys and poor heating and ventilation. If any of these circumstances prevail, enlist some parents in correcting them.

Beyond reflecting on the physical qualities of church nurseries, however, discuss the overarching aims of Christian education in the parish. Again, many young parents will not have pondered these. Indeed, some of the teachers of the very young might not have thought about them. Use this opportunity to raise a few basic issues about value-formation. Have some books available like John Westerhoff's books, *Will our Children have Faith?* and *Bringing up Children in the Christian Faith*. Find out in advance what kinds of support groups there are for young parents in the community. If none is available, perhaps those present may wish to start one.

Above all, come "through the front door" with the issues about living out baptism. Many a parent who will have responded to the baptismal question, "Will you strive for justice and peace among all people, and respect the dignity of every human being?" with great gusto saying, "I will with God's help," will dig heels into the dirt when confronted with what that might mean. It will do no good to clobber people with the social gospel; it might do much good to let them chew on its implications with each other. It has, after all, everything to do with the world in which their young children will grow and live.

Faith in families depends largely upon how well we equip parents as educators of and models for their children. No Christian education training is complete that does not constantly include parents in planning and reflection. Bringing together parents to focus on their children's religious development is every bit as important as the school PTA.

BAPTISM OF OLDER CHILDREN AND ADULTS

Shifting cultural patterns will likely produce an increasing number of children who will reach adolescence or adulthood without having been baptized. When children older than eight, or adults, come to be baptized, they bring unique challenges and opportunities. Frequently, they bring deep needs.

The Haleys had lived in half a dozen places in their ten years of marriage. Frances Haley had grown up in the Church and had always actively participated in it. She had been on the official board in two parishes. Joe Haley, in contrast, had never been baptized. Although he had attended church during his childhood and adolescence, Joe had never felt church to be important. He had become somewhat involved in one parish during the early part of his marriage, but only briefly. Aaron, their first child, was baptized in Frances' home parish. When, three years later, Jessica was born, they were between two moves. They chose to wait until they could settle into a parish before Jessica would be baptized. The wait lengthened. When Jessica was four, the Haleys moved into our town and into our parish. Joe was drawn into the church, slowly at first. After a year, he had embarked on an earnest religious search. Frances, meanwhile, felt pressure to have Jessica baptized.

When Joe decided to be baptized, we began to plan both his and Jessica's baptism. Jessica was a student in the daily pre-school of our parish. Her teacher, once aware of the upcoming baptism, worked very creatively to help Jessica overcome her shyness, reluctance and apparent feelings of embarrassment and fear about being baptized. Several weeks prior to the baptism, the entire class spent considerable time visiting the font, talking about baptism, learning about the importance of water, getting acquainted with central symbols like the Paschal Candle. Shy little Jessica became excited about her coming "Big Day." At the same time, Joe's pre-baptismal sessions were progressing. The Haleys planned for the baptisms in their family. Frances' regret over delaying Jessica's baptism melted in the enthusiasm she felt for the growth in their family. Joe's initial reluctance (he had felt self-conscious as an unbaptized adult in the parish) softened as he caught Jessica's excitement over their shared experience.

In a community with a traditional norm of infant baptism, unbaptized children and adults often feel awkward, uneasy, pressured either to conceal their unbaptized status or to conform quickly to the prevailing pattern. Clergy and lay leaders can work to assure folks like Joe and Jessica that they have a marvelous opportunity to prepare intentionally and carefully for the biggest moment in their lives: new birth in Christ. Never should we capitulate, in the guise of being "pastoral," to those feelings of embarrassment or awkwardness, sneaking people into the baptized community through the back door with private baptisms or rushed public ones. To do so denigrates baptism, and mitigates baptism as a public affirmation of the lordship of Christ and our obedience to him. Whether we are baptized as infants, as children, as youth, or as adults, baptism is a vocation to proclaim Christ in word and deed in the world. We can affirm that, and encourage candidates like Joe and Jessica to acknowledge and to celebrate the supreme importance of their identification with Christ through baptism.

I have never found a way successfully to include children under 12 in our regular pre-baptismal sessions. My own priority is to help adults to understand the meaning of baptism, and therefore I design the sessions as adult education. If children 3 to 5 years old are candidates for baptism, the officiating priest should plan one or more home visits, and endeavor to involve parents and children in a conversation about what happens in baptism. We approach the sacrament almost exclusively on the basis of what the children can expect to happen. We keep our theology appropriately basic: "this is the way we all become members of God's family." Children of school age and older are often invited to at least one session at the church, where we guide them on a tour of the church, perhaps visiting the sacristy (almost no young children have ever seen where vessels and vestments are kept and where the communion bread and wine are prepared). The tour climaxes at the font, where we act out what will happen on the day of baptism, trying to put the candidates at ease by showing them what to do. We take care to talk about the Paschal Candle, lit every Easter and at every baptism to remind us of the new Light of the Risen Christ. We let them smell the sacred chrism, pointing out how generations of people— such as kings and queens—have been specially anointed with oil for important purposes.

Sensitive parish sponsors will help immeasurably by extending a sense of welcome and belonging to older children, youth and adult candidates for baptism. The key for sponsors, clergy, lay leaders, and congregations is simple: remember that baptism, at whatever stage in life it comes, is the single most important, most wonderful thing that can happen to anyone, and *always* treat it accordingly.

DEVELOPING STRATEGIES WITH PARENTS OF YOUNG CHILDREN

Christian parents really do want to do everything in their power to nurture faith in their children. Rather than laying heavy expectations upon young parents who may feel bewildered by the routines of parenthood, lay educators and clergy can concentrate on demonstrating that Christian child-rearing is a real, workable, manageable possibility. Three simple strategies can become dimensions of an ongoing approach. If the group of new parents decided to come together for further discussion, these three themes might well provide the topics for reflection.

The first of these strategies is working together on the Apostles' teaching. That sounds like a monumental undertaking, but actually it need not be overwhelming. The Apostles' Creed sums up the tenets of the teaching of the apostolic community. Even simpler than that is the *kerygma,* or early Christian preaching, found in the Book of Acts. The apostles first preached sermons making the point that the Old Testament had prophesied a Messiah, that Jesus was he, and that Jesus, resurrected from the dead by God, had been exalted and had sent the Holy Spirit to the Church. To be sure, much more than this simple outline needs to be included in Christian proclamation. But that is not bad for beginners. It will indeed work quite well if it lures even the casual reader to take a fresh look at the Old Testament and to begin asking questions about the Holy Spirit.

Naturally, it will be years before a child can be taught all this explicitly. In the meantime, the teaching can form part of the backdrop against which the child will learn the story of salvation. Bible stories should be read, along with other stories, at bedtime and at other times. Though these need to be selected with sensitivity, the important thing is to tell and re-tell the story. We don't fear the goriness of fairy tales and folk stories and we need not be anxious that children are going to infer from the story of Noah that God is out to destroy the world. (Anyone who has paid much attention to children dealing with that story will know that it is the boat and the animals that captivate them.) Parents and church school teachers should be encouraged to read the stories as stories and not get hung up on whether they are literally true. They will tell the children about God: his creating power, his deep concern for what is just and right, his alignment with poor and oppressed people, and his willingness to go to any lengths (witness the Noah story!) to save people who make a mess of things.

Bible stories are just one way to get at the Apostles' teaching, however. Short, interesting, seasonal rituals can become a part of the family routine. (The next chapter deals with ways in which the family can create simple yet exciting rituals around seasons, activities, and crises.) As children grow older, these rudimentary rituals can be enriched and elaborated within the confines of overall simplicity.

A second strategy to help children and their families grow in understanding what baptism means is learning and practicing intercessory prayer. My experience is that praying for other people comes naturally to children—moreso by far than prayers of confession, for example, which require a highly developed conscience. While children will inevitably relate to those in their own sphere of experience—family, friends, neighbors in need—they can be helped to understand the broader needs of others in the world. There is now no dearth of pictures showing the devastating effects of hunger and war on children throughout the world. I believe it is appropriate to focus on these with our growing children from time to time. We do our children no service by trying to shield them from unpleasantness and pain. The point is not to get them to feel bad, but to teach them how to care and how to be concerned—for *all* God's children, not just for those closest to us and most like us.

"Repenting and returning to the Lord" is the name of the third strategy. The education of conscience begins very early, as a child is taught good from bad, right from wrong. Learning to say "I'm sorry" is an important step in moral development. Learning how to accept forgiveness and to be affirmed, even after being scolded or punished, is equally important. These basic patterns have much to do with the way we grow to deal with the themes of sin, judgment and forgiveness. Children must learn that we are accountable to God for our decisions—good and bad—and that he loves us and accepts us and continues to provide for and love us, no matter what.

One way to practice repentance within the family is to go through a simple exercise at bedtime in which parent and child together share "one thing that happened today that I feel bad about," which can be altered to "one thing *I did* today I feel sorry for. . . ." Far better than augmenting guilt feelings is to take the feelings and raise questions about what we can do with them. Is there something I can do as a parent to make amends for what I did that I am sorry for? Is there anything the child can do to correct a situation? If so, we can decide to do something. If not, we need to confront our helplessness to do anything constructive, and to give up (confess) our helplessness to God. Doing this regularly, taking care to celebrate and offer thanks for forgiveness, is a way of living out the sin/forgiveness dimension of baptism.

Other approaches to repentance will be found in the chapter on reconciliation. Suffice it to say here that inculcating a healthy understanding of sin and forgiveness in young children is a delicate matter. Our society has become neurotically afraid of shame, guilt and anything that smacks of the judgmental. Christians need to recognize that we have to deal with those themes because they are realities. Healthy shame, in some form, is necessary for any sense of social responsibility. Guilt is healthy when it is real instead of needless, false or imagined. Guilt is healthy because, like pain, it signals the entire organism that something is wrong. It is necessary because it spurs us to accept responsibility for changing what is harmful in behavior or attitude. Judgment, if we can believe the Bible, is something we really have no choice about. God is a moral God, who cares deeply about our decisions. Judgment is God's response to our decisions and actions. Most often we experience it as that "moment of truth," that word, crisis or event which exposes us to the real truth about ourselves and our lives. There is no way we can bring up children to know God and to love him without dealing with sin and our responsibility for it.

On the other hand, people are rightly scared of unhealthy guilt. Too many Christians have been brow-beaten with the Church's great club—the threat of no forgiveness and ultimate damnation. While speaking what purports to be the mind of God, the Church has often used guilt and shame as means of social control. The ends have not justified those means. Sensing the lie behind all this, many sincere people have left the faith community, preferring any doctrine more promising and affirming, or none at all. And that is the real shame. What is required of us now is not to dodge the difficulty of the issue, but to look for creative ways to deal with sin and forgiveness with growing children—ways consonant with the Gospel of God's love in Christ.

Yet another strategy to implement the reality of baptism in the life of the growing child is a basic approach to stewardship. In our culture, most families will find soon enough the need to teach young children how to manage money. While this is only a fraction of what stewardship encompasses, it is a good place to begin. Even

more basic is the natural process of teaching children how to take
care of their toys, books, clothes, rooms, bodies. Make a point from
time to time, as children begin to approach the age of four or five,
that God very much wants us to take care of his world. Practically,
few children are going to buy the argument that their possessions
are not really theirs but given them by God to keep. That does not
mean they should not be told so, however. And, in fact, children
are far less possessive than we suppose. A friend recently told
me that the children in his parish were invited at Christmas
to bring a toy as a gift for the Christ Child, and told that these
would be taken and given to some children who had few, if
any, toys. The priest encouraged them to select something from
among their own toys, rather than go out and buy a new one.
Interestingly, the children brought some of their best and most
expensive toys to share, and in some cases parted with much
loved toys. Who got upset? The parents, who complained, "Do
you know what these toys cost?"

Committing to give a dime, quarter or more each week to the
church is a good way for children to be taught the rudiments (note
well the choice of words!) of Christian giving. If the amount is tied
directly to "work" they do as a gift to the family, it takes on even
more meaning. Parents need help in understanding that, contrary
to the great American fear of being ripped off, the Gospel asks us
to place emphasis on giving, not on where the money goes. That
is indeed an issue of stewardship, but on the corporate (congregational) level. The parish, like the individual, must decide what
to do with what it has. That is stewardship.

Of course, the ramifications of stewardship are endless—because
absolutely nothing in life is not "given." We thus have to care for
everything. Certainly the issue of what we eat is one the faithful
family will need to work on. Can we in good conscience stuff junk
food into our bodies while many of God's children are hungry? This
critical question of values demands to be addressed. Parents cannot
skirt responsibility for it by arguing that their children must eat
this or that. Rather than be heavy-handed, parents can invite
reflection from all family members on what it means to take care
of our bodies in a way that expresses love for our Creator and for
the other children in his world.

There are no surprises in all this. We simply need to make connections between the ordinary, routine stuff of life, and the Life of Christ into which we have been baptized. We need our consciousness raised about how we can live out our baptism. It will not happen automatically. Nor will it be particularly easy, because baptism calls us to new life, a radically new kind of life. It is not only resurrection in Christ, it is also death to life in the world without him. It is transforming. What families are called to do in this age is to facilitate this transformation. Parents are called to provide a framework in the home where they and their children can live daily the life into which they have been baptized, which is no less than the life of the Risen Lord.

FIVE

Holy Eucharist: Ritualizing

If baptism is birth into God's family, eucharist is family mealtime. Of all the sacraments, the eucharist is the one whose images most vividly suggest home. No activity bespeaks "family" so much as being gathered around a table to share a meal. Nothing provides an image of fellowship and caring better than having dinner.

It would seem that Jesus thought so. Notice how many times he compares the kingdom of heaven to a feast of some sort, usually a wedding banquet.[1] Luke, in particular, pictures Jesus doing a great amount of teaching at mealtime. In the house of Simon the Pharisee, Jesus uses dinnertime as the occasion to speak about loving much and being forgiven much—prompted, to be sure, by the actions of a woman who was anything but welcome at Simon's table.[2] On another occasion, he notices how guests scramble for the places of honor, and again comments with a teaching about humility and service.[3] In different ways, both Luke and John relate how the Last Supper was an occasion for teaching about discipleship —Luke telling how the disciples were again squabbling about who was the greatest, a question that seems to have endlessly intrigued them, and John relating how Jesus delivered the supreme parable by washing his disciples' feet. One can easily imagine how both accounts stem from the same experience, especially if one has been present at almost any family quarrel at mealtime.

Perhaps the single greatest discovery of the Church in the twentieth century has been the *re*discovery of the eucharist as meal. It is the holy meal of the holy people of God. It is the passover meal of the New Covenant. It is the sacrificial meal which serves to seal the New Covenant of Grace through Christ's death and resurrection, much as the Old Covenant was sealed with a sacrificial meal involving Moses and the elders of Israel on Mount Sinai.[4] It is that symbolic meal which foreshadows the messianic banquet when the kingdom of God shall have fully come. It is itself the affirmation that the marriage supper of Christ the Lamb is a present reality for those who live in him, as well as a future reality for all of redeemed humanity.[5] It is a celebrative, joyous meal at which we respond to God's grace with thankful hearts. It is a meal through which God pledges to welcome sinners, and through which sinners pledge loyalty and fidelity to God. It is a mystical meal, in which believers participate ritually and symbolically in the life of Jesus, who is identified with the elements of bread and wine.

Incredible as it may seem, for much of the Church's history, this aspect of the eucharist as meal has been obscured. Until recently, eucharistic theology has focused upon issues about the presence of Christ in the bread and wine, upon the benefits received through the experience of communion, and upon the issue of whether it is primarily a sacrifice or a memorial. Nowadays, with the reintroduction of something more closely resembling honest-to-goodness bread than little slick white discs, and with more frequent celebrations of the eucharist around free-standing altars where people experience a sense of sharing, the mealtime aspect of the eucharist has become rather obvious.

I go into this much detail because we need to get straight what we are doing when we prepare young children for, and "admit" them to, the eucharist. If the eucharist is a meal, and if it is for *all* the holy people of God, then *all* the baptized should be welcome, invited and indeed expected to participate in it. We waste no time in giving infants food. There is no need to delay welcoming the newly baptized to the Lord's table.

Yet we worry. Should a child not be able to communicate in both kinds (bread and wine) before being expected to participate in communion? And what about eating and drinking "unworthily," to use St. Paul's word?[6] Some feel strongly that being able to discern what is happening and understand its importance is essential to appropriate reception of communion. These issues will be with us for a while. Clearly the Church is moving towards a younger age for beginning regular participation in the eucharist. That is likely to continue. We need to be clear that there is no way that we can "understand" the eucharist, at age six, sixteen, or sixty, if by "understanding" we mean rationally comprehending it. It is, and will always be, a mystery. Nor, if we believe what we say about grace, will we ever be able to qualify for communion, through moral rectitude, age, intelligence, spiritual state, or anything else. Thus, if we argue for postponing reception of communion, let us honestly admit that, at least theologically, there is no reason to deny a young child participation in the ritual meal any more than we would deny a very young child a place at the family table at home.

This does not mean, of course, that there are not other considerations besides theology. If a congregation does not grasp what is happening and what it means when young children participate in the meal, then it is wise not to press the point too far. Perhaps the most important consideration for pastoral practice is abandoning any idea of an "automatic" age. Though I strongly support communicating all the newly baptized and continuing to communicate them, so that there is never a time when one does not remember being fed at the Lord's table, I would argue more strongly still that we be flexible. Community pressures are such that norms will naturally arise over time. Multiformity will not result in absolute chaos in the congregation. There should be no one automatic time to begin receiving communion any more than there is any one correct time to be baptized, married or confirmed.

Whether or not a child begins receiving communion when baptized, there is a clear need to involve both child and parents in reflecting on that participation within a few years. Periodic catechesis for eucharist should ideally take place regularly. At the very least, set aside a time around the age of five or six when those who have been receiving can reflect on what they are doing, and when those who have not begun may prepare to receive. The following section describes an initial catechesis for participation in the eucharist. It is designed for children around school age (five, six or seven years old).

COMING TO THE TABLE

Nothing has been more rewarding in my ministry than seeing young children make connections between the eucharist and their lives. I am repeatedly astonished at what children grasp, and what they see.

Gail, age five, was preparing for her first communion. To her mother she commented, "Mom, Jesus will come again some day, won't he?"

"Well, yes, I suppose so, Gail. What makes you think of that?" Her mother was practiced at being caught off guard by some of Gail's deeper questions.

"When we go to communion I think of that," responded Gail matter-of-factly.

"And what at communion makes you think about Jesus coming again?" her mother pressed.

"Well, when Jesus comes and is here, all that flesh and blood will get back together and we won't have to eat bread and drink wine any more, because Jesus will be here, right?"

On some level, Gail had heard that in the eucharist we continue "a perpetual memory of . . . [Christ's] precious death and sacrifice, *until his coming again.*"[7]

The *preparation* needed most is for parents: to learn unexpected insights from their children about eucharist. I share this and similar stories regularly when parents come together to launch a ten-week period during which they will catechise their children in understanding the eucharist. The frank goal and expectation is for parents themselves to grow in their understanding. Material, books, audiovisuals, and all the rest will help; but their children are by far the best teachers. Interestingly, over nearly ten years I have had almost no resistance from parents in taking responsibility for preparing their children for first communion.[8] They sometimes evince quite a little anxiety, which is quickly allayed with promises and offers of support from clergy and others.

Of course, if parents have been coming together since their children's baptism, there is a core of real community in such gatherings. As pastoral ministry continues to address the needs of growing children and their families, this will become more and more the case. At the initial meeting of parents, clear expectations spell out what is asked:

Set aside regular times (once each week) to work with children on their lesson for that week;

Involve, as appropriate and possible, both parents and other siblings in the preparation and discussions;

Plan for at least one parent to accompany the child to a "mid-point check-in" during the preparation;

Make an effort to plan one or more sessions with another family involved in the preparation;

Have the entire family join the other families at a simple supper during the final week;

Be present with the child on the occasion of first communion.

The "mid-point check-in" emerged when some parents began to ask for more assistance and support from each other and from clergy. It has proved to be useful as a means of fostering accountability among families and as an occasion for offering support. Everyone typically receives assurance that they are "on track" and progressing well. Children have a chance to share some of their work, especially artwork they produce in their books.[9] After a brief filmstrip focusing on the theme of community, we gather in the church around the altar, and one of the priests talks about the way the altar is vested, pointing out the symbolic meaning of various vessels and cloths used during the celebration of communion. Often questions of children (and parents) consume much of the half-hour. The aim is to connect (a) the parish eucharist, (b) their preparation, and (c) the Last Supper of Jesus. We emphasize that this holy meal is one in which we share with Jesus not only as his disciples shared the last supper with him but because, as the Risen Lord, he is present with us in the Holy Communion.

During the course of the ten weeks, children receive letters from clergy and other staff. Every attempt is made to have one of the clergy visit the home of each child during the preparation, to offer encouragement and to build relationships with the children.

The supper during the final week of preparation has become an institution. Each family brings some element of the supper (it is possible, of course, to connect the gifts for the supper with the gifts of bread and wine which make the eucharist possible). While supper is being prepared, children work together on a project, sometimes a mural on a theme they have encountered in their sessions at home. Older and younger siblings are given tasks to do, sometimes a project all their own. After some singing, supper is served, after which children share what they have liked and disliked in their preparation. They are trained how to receive communion according to the customs of the parish, and given a taste of unconsecrated bread and wine. Parents, meanwhile, reflect with another adult leader on what they have learned, sharing stories about what their children have done and said during their sessions at home.

The evening concludes with actual rehearsal of receiving the bread and negotiating the chalice. We stress simple devotional practices—how to pray during communion, upon what to focus when coming to the altar, how to exercise proper "manners" at the Lord's table. Obviously, in a parish situation where a majority of the children have been receiving since baptism, some of this teaching would either be eliminated or take on a different cast.

First Communion Day is important, but in no way should it be viewed as a rite of passage. Ceremony should be kept simple. Nothing should give the idea to children or others that they are any more a part of the community as a consequence of receiving communion. (Of course, it is impossible *not* to imply this: a major reason for consistently communicating *all* persons from their baptism on, thus avoiding this double message!)

THE NEED FOR RITUALS

A key way to build faith in families is to nurture a process of ritualizing in the home. Making and doing rites and rituals, if grounded in the eucharistic experience, will both reinforce what happens around the parish altar and extend that experience into many crevices and corners of family life.

What we need to see first is that the eucharist is not only a *sacred* meal, it is a *ritual* meal. All eating, of course, is ritual—in the sense that we biologically ingest food regularly to maintain normal body temperature and to obtain the energy necessary for work and play. Eating thus lends itself to ritualization because it must be regularly done, and regular repetition is one characteristic of ritual. The eucharist from its inception, however, was more than a meal, inasmuch as Jesus identified what was eaten with his body and blood. *Words* of a particular sort—"This is my body, . . . my blood" —have always accompanied the sharing of the eucharistic bread and wine. Eating is thereby lifted from the level of the commonplace to the realm of the symbolic, the transcendent. Not only that, but the particular verbal formulations, which according to the gospels Jesus himself gave, point to his death upon the cross—so much so that one can scarcely engage in the meal without recalling what became of his body and blood in his death and in the resurrection which followed.

This kind of ritualization, out of which supper becomes Holy Eucharist, is precisely the kind of ritual-making that families already engage in. We can, and should, become more conscious of it. In short, we have to learn in our families how to take just such simple, ordinary things as bread and wine and water and mealtime and bathtime and bedtime and to look beyond them to greater meanings. In some cases, we shall have to develop rituals from scratch. In other cases, we shall have to assign meaning to activities already a part of family experience. At still other times, rituals like grace before meals and the celebration of birthdays and baptismal anniversaries, will be present, and we shall have to make the time to reflect upon their meaning.

It can by no means be assumed that every family, even every intentionally Christian family, wants to have a ritual life as such. Despite the number of Sunday school curricula that have been developed with an "at-home" component, very few families have ever done much with household religious rituals. We consistently leave the job of ritualizing to the church, which in turn protests that education in Gospel and liturgy must take place in the home on a regular basis. The result is that very little meaningful ritualizing goes on in the upbringing of children. Outside grace before meals, some family Bible reading (rather rare in my experience), and bedtime story-telling, there is not much of a day-to-day ritual life in most homes. Holidays provide the occasion for many important rituals, but most of these in contemporary American society have to do with intensifying family ties and loyalties (certainly a worthy goal) without much if any sense of transcendence. Thanksgiving, for example, is one of the chief American holidays—and one which has perhaps suffered the least corruption by the commercial establishment. What seems to be most important about that day to a great many people is not the giving of thanks to God for all his benefits, but being with family. My guess is that the only expressly religious component in the Thanksgiving Day experience for most Americans is the grace before the great meal of the occasion, if indeed one is said at all. Church attendance patterns on Thanksgiving tend to document the accuracy of my guess.

In the absence of a sound ritual life, parents are left with few means to inculcate values in children. Some years ago, Erik Erikson averred that it was precisely the absence of meaningful ritualization that accounts for the fact that children now grow up in our society with shaky values. Erikson suggested that the *judicious* is an element in ritual which implies a function of discriminating between what is sanctioned and what is out-of-bounds. He noted,

> . . . the decay or perversion of ritual does not create an in-different emptiness, but a void with explosive possibilities. . . . It explains why "nice" people who have lost the gift of imparting values by meaningful ritualization can have children who become (or behave like) juvenile delinquents; and why nice "church-going" nations can so act as to arouse the impression of harboring pervasive murderous intent.[10]

We need rituals to reinforce values. We need occasions and times to call attention to those things which we want to hold up as exemplary to our children. We need to find ways to celebrate the presence of people—friends, relatives, family heroes—who are worth emulating. Parents also need to find times and ways to mark for their children what is negative, unhealthy and wrong.

In the sections that follow, various kinds of ritual-making are outlined. A high priority for any parish interested in building faith in families is to gather together groups of families—adults and children—to examine, experiment with and evaluate such ideas as these.

TABLE RITUALS

There is little doubt that mealtime is the central activity in most families, just as the eucharistic meal is the central act of worship in the Christian community. It is the time, perhaps the only time, in the course of a day that the entire family is likely to gather. To maximize mealtime as an occasion for family ritual is altogether natural.

Before trying to get super-religious, with Bibles, Prayer Books, and other paraphernalia, families might well work on making mealtime a pleasant time. Start with whatever table is used for the evening meal. For some families it would make good sense to make breakfast the family meal of the day—that being the time when all the household members are usually together. Do it right! Whether at breakfast or dinner, have some flowers or some other suitable centerpiece on the table. If dinner, add candles. Our children may never become acolytes, but they love candle-lighting (and extinguishing!) at home. I am prejudiced against that kind of informality that sees fit to sling dishes on the table. No matter how humble, a table can be set to suggest that something important—indeed holy—takes place when we eat, whether the food be cereal, hamburgers, soup, bread or leg of lamb. Needless to say, teaching children by giving them responsibilities for setting and clearing the table is itself practical and important to family ritual life.

Then take the next step. After designating one meal per day as the main occasion for family gathering, select one particular day or evening as family time. For many years, our family chose Thursday, partly because of its association with the institution of the eucharist, and hence a natural day to celebrate a "holy mealtime." The sacredness of Sunday dinner seems to have given way to soccer games and other events; but in places where Sunday is less fragmented, a midday or evening meal will be quite workable. On family day or night, things can be added to enhance the specialness of the time: tablecloth, cloth napkins, special dishes, candles, flowers. This is the time to put extra energy into preparing the meal.

Take care to see that everyone at the table is included in the conversation. This is crucial. Even very small children can be

included. Story-telling and other more complex activities will work
better in families that know how to converse with each other and
how to listen to each other. Something our family has had to learn
is that we cannot always be preoccupied with table manners, or
else mealtime can become one constant harangue for the children.
We have had to stake out particular nights to be especially mindful
of instructions in manners, letting the other nights get lighter
treatment. In any event, do all you can to avoid arguing at table.
Families perhaps need to plan, to set policies which affect everyone,
and to hash out concerns at mealtime, but the table is not the place
to do all this unpleasantly.

Once family night (or day) is in place, a basic ritual component
is established. Add prayer. I assume all families can easily commit
to saying a grace before every meal. If this simple tradition has fallen
into neglect, reinstitute it. Even perfunctory thanks are better than
none at all, and thanksgiving is at the heart of living eucharistically.
On family night, look for ways to make family prayer a bit more
special than on any other day. Play music, for example. Perhaps
read a short passage of scripture, following a lectionary or some
manual of devotion like *The Upper Room* or *Forward Day by Day*.
If a special event is being celebrated, such as a birthday or wedding
anniversary, prayers and a passage of scripture can emphasize that.

From this point, the family can elaborate on the table ritual and
really begin to have fun. The natural thing to do will be to select
important dates in the family's life and mark these with either a
special menu or a more detailed kind of celebration. The start of
school is an excellent time for families to renew their ritual life.
Why not celebrate it with special prayers for students, teachers and
parents? Cap off an evening in late August or early September with
a "last fling" at summer swimming or ice cream. Leaving for camp,
the night before vacation (or the first night home afterward), first
communion for a child, the completion of a special project, a
promotion at work, retirement—all can become occasions for family
celebration. All it takes is a little extra time and effort to make an
attractive table, and remembering to pray.

Somewhat less natural, but potentially as enjoyable, is for the
family to be creative at celebrating saints days and holy days. The
first thing to do is to get a good church calendar, and a good

resource such as a book on the lives of the saints. One family in a parish workshop decided to design a unique celebration for the Feast of the Conversion of St. Paul. They were particularly fond of dramatics, so they read the narrative of St. Paul's conversion and acted it out, each one taking the part of one of the characters. This opened up a good discussion on Paul's life, the relations between Christians and Jews, and the matter of religious conversion. Quite a full evening's worth! They ended their experience with free prayer and the Collect of the Day.

Our family adopted from friends a tradition of celebrating Twelfth Night—the Eve of Epiphany. Other families come for a potluck supper, which is concluded with a special cake in which are hidden symbols of the Christmas-Epiphany stories and charms of good luck for the new year. After supper, we dispatch children to the attic to round up suitable costumes for all the characters in the story of the Wise Men. As hosts, we assign parts to guests of all ages. Nearly everyone has a part, including one person who is the star of Bethlehem. The story in Matthew 3 is read, after which the drama is enacted by everyone, *ad lib*. Lines can be hilarious— and the children never forget the Epiphany story and the interesting corruptions thereof! Epiphany hymns and Christmas carols conclude the party.

Another elaboration of the simple table ritual can be based on the ancient *lucernarium*, or lamp-lighting ceremony. In the early church, the faithful would gather at the close of day. While lighting the lamps, they would meditate on the Light of Christ, which dispels the darkness of sin and death. The 1979 Prayer Book reintroduces this service to modern worshippers in the form of An Order of Worship for the Evening.[11] One of the most beautiful parts of this simple rite is the *Phos hilaron*, the oldest extant Christian hymn. It has been translated into some lovely verse, and can be found in *The Hymnal 1982* at numbers 25, 26, 36, and 37. Since, as I mentioned above, children are so fond of lighting candles, this idea is patently cut out for them. Set, or make, some candelabra that will hold three or more candles, and put them on the table. The service can be used with or without adaptation. The family might learn a simple tune for the *Phos hilaron*; or learn a refrain to go with each of the verses read by a parent; or chant it. *The*

Book of Occasional Services[12] contains some seasonal anthems that can easily be recited, read or sung during the candle-lighting.

When we deliberately make mealtime, at least occasionally, a holy time, that dimension of the Holy Eucharist which gives thanks to God the Father for all creation will spill over into home life, as we thank God for food and other blessings, and as we acknowledge God's presence in the fellowship of the family.

SEASONAL RITUALS

Most families have a natural seasonal rhythm. Encourage your families to discover theirs! For many Americans with school-age children, the year really runs from September through May or June. Summer is a distinct season, and spans whatever time there is between academic terms. Some churches tend to run on this schedule, with different hours of worship in the summer, and frequently a break in on-going Christian education classes. Neither the civil nor the ecclesiastical calendars are much attuned to the rhythm of family life; yet both obviously impact it and have clues to offer for family ritual patterns.

Surely the beginning of the school year should be marked in some way. As I mentioned above, it can become the focus of family mealtime, even over several evenings or days. To go beyond this, families could well make an annual event of spending an evening together talking over hopes, expectations, fears and goals for the new school year. Such a conversation will become a religious ritual when all of these things are committed to God in prayer. One diocese, through its education and training committee, offered families a manual containing day-by-day Scriptures, prayers, and meditations for the first week of school. Parishes can easily do the same thing. For that matter, the family, or a group of interested families, can do their own. This will take seriously the stress connected with all beginnings, especially the anxieties children often bring to a new academic year. If there are those in the family leaving home for school or college, the time may be even more important, and thus an even greater opportunity for ritualizing.

Probably the next seasonal event for American families is Halloween. As a child, I positively hated Halloween. I couldn't stand orange and black, and found little excitement in jack-o-lanterns and candy corn. As an adult, however, I have come to appreciate it. Halloween, it will be argued, has been taken over by the commercial establishment, and thus is lost for religious purposes. Nonsense. I am far less worried about that than about the attempt in recent years by neo-evangelicals to strip Halloween of its darker side. In some sections of the country, churches have sponsored gatherings for children, who they urge to come dressed up as angels and other "good" beings. They rob Halloween of its importance as a rite of reversal. A rite of reversal offers people the possibility of getting into exactly the opposite role or position to the one they usually fill. When I was in high school in the early 60s, before the age of gender liberation, powderpuff football games did something of the sort by allowing boys and girls to swap their conventional (and traditional) roles for an evening. At least two things happened. First, girls who really relished playing the "masculine" role on the football field, and boys who really enjoyed leading cheers (and/or dressing up like women!) could do those things at least for one evening with permission and impunity. Secondly, because it was a one-evening event, the "normal" roles for boys and girls were therefore intensified. A rite of reversal intensifies the norm by allowing a circumscribed departure from it for a brief period.

Halloween, seen theologically, may be more necessary today than ever. It is essentially for poking fun at evil, and at the same time is a reminder that we deny our monstrous, mischievous and sinister sides to our own peril. All Hallows Eve can thus be understood only in relation to All Hallows Day (All Saints Day), November 1. *This* is the festival when it would be appropriate to dress up as saints and angels! What power it might have for us were we to see those who were costumed as demons and monsters on Halloween gather as saints the next day! At a time when many are scared to death of Satan and the hosts of evil and when others are scared to admit they are susceptible to anything evil, we need both a potent reminder that evil is real—whether personal, cosmic, or systemic—and an equally potent reminder that evil is ultimately conquered in Christ Jesus.

With such an understanding, the family can celebrate Halloween and All Saints with meaning and delight. Though I have lost, some years, to fairy-tale characters and fads for dressing like Wonder Woman, I do my best to get the children to dress in as macabre a fashion as possible. At least *I* have fun doing so. In places where Halloween has itself become the victim of evil, in the form of razor blades in apples and drugged candy, families can offer some redemption to the experience by hosting a get-together of neighborhood families and either supervising the trick-or-treating or turning one residence into a haunted house. (Public libraries are resources for records with eerie sounds.) Or perhaps a group of families can take over the parish house of the church and provide a safe place to celebrate Halloween. Reflecting on its meaning, particularly in the context of a simple service preceding or ending the party, would probably be easier at church. A well-planned evening could end with a service, during which everyone might take off their Halloween costumes and light candles or put on crosses to emphasize the transition to a celebration of All Saints.

I suspect that my next suggestion will strike some as inane. That is to reclaim St. Martin's Day, November 11. Many school systems and businesses in fact keep the Veterans' Day holiday, which falls on or close to November 11, so at least there is some secular support for a minor holiday at that time. Martin is worth remembering for several reasons. Though of course his being a soldier has nothing to do with Veterans' Day, Martin was indeed in the Roman army. He had a conversion experience while on duty. He cut his cloak in two and gave a beggar half of it, and dreamed later that the beggar was Christ. Sharing with the poor, and remembering people who are subject to all kinds of pressures in the armed forces, are appropriate themes for family discussion and prayers on St. Martin's Day. Moreover, Martinmas was, in some places in medieval Europe, the beginning of what we now know as Advent. My own finding is that, year after year, Advent sneaks up on us, because it always coincides with whatever is going on around Thanksgiving. Martinmas could appropriately become associated in the family schedule with beginning to make the Advent wreath, Advent calendars, and those other things that need to be ready sometime before midnight on the Saturday before the First Sunday of Advent.

Thanksgiving hardly needs comment. Fortunately, there is a set of cultural rituals belonging to Thanksgiving, widely shared throughout American society. The Christian family should find it natural and easy to develop its own customs around Thanksgiving, which can very well include making a significant gift to alleviate hunger. Attend the Thanksgiving eucharist as a family, and share a gift with house guests by inviting them to worship with the family and join in other family rituals.

Such rituals at Thanksgiving will probably be focused on the traditional meal. I remember John Westerhoff telling the story of how in his family at Thanksgiving Day dinner five grains of corn are placed on each plate. It is the job of the youngest person present to ask, in the fashion of the Passover Seder, the question "Why on this day do we have grains of corn on our plate?" A parent replies something like, "Because when our fathers and mothers had made it bravely through their first year in this country, they gave thanks to God that they had grain to eat."

Advent is most suited for family rituals. Various family members can participate in making the Advent wreath, now in many Christian families as important a symbol as the Christmas tree. Many books are available on how to make one and what its various parts mean. Let me add a plea that we depart from the one-pink-candle notion. That was a Roman Catholic custom which made sense when there was a "Gaudete (Rejoice) Sunday" on Advent III, when the emphasis on penitence lightened. Now that the accent falls on expectation, hope and preparation, its sense has been obscured or lost. Certainly a more relevant symbol—one that would re-enforce what the family is hearing in the Advent lessons at the eucharist—would be something to recall the figure of John the Baptist. The middle two Sundays in Advent highlight his ministry as Christ's forerunner. Some rich possibilities are a shell (ancient symbol for baptism); a honeycomb, beehive, or locust (recalling John's preference for health foods); or a piece of leather (symbolic of his clothing). Any or all of these could interestingly be added to the Advent wreath to underscore the message of preparation for the return of God's Messiah which we infer from John's preaching.

My favorite kind of Advent calendar is the simple paper chain my wife makes. She writes on the inside of each link either some activity that the family can do together, or the name of one person in the household whose special day has arrived. Even the dog is given a special day. As a result of this device, Christmas preparations happen at a manageable pace, and the family is able to have some fun amid what everyone knows can become an insanely frantic time.

Advent's biggest blessing is also its major curse. That, of course, is the spirit and mood of Christmas—clearly our society's major holiday. Until fairly recent times, people really waited until December 24 to begin celebrating Christmas. In this generation, however, putting up door wreaths and trees on Christmas Eve is everywhere the exception. People seem to think that celebrating Christmas is a month-long bash that starts in late November and culminates on December 25. Even the Episcopal Church, which has been a hold-out for keeping Advent Advent and not pre-Christmas, is now seeing abominations like Christmas pageants on the Fourth Sunday of Advent and choral concerts of Christmas music scattered throughout December. The integrity of the Church year is lost this way, and thus one other foundation for a coherent, meaningful ritual life is undermined. We desperately need to keep Advent the time for getting ready, not for letting all the stops out. Then, possibly, we can reflect on the *real* preparation in which we are called to be engaged, which is getting ready not so much for the Christmas blast as for the coming of God's kingdom in all its fullness.

Hence, the family should use in its rituals whatever opportunities there are to keep Advent unique, and should postpone celebrating Christmas until December 25. Sing Advent hymns at least until late Advent. Instead of putting up the Christmas tree so soon, hold off until December 23 or 24, and do a Jesse Tree, an evergreen or other tree (perhaps even a big house plant) on which symbols of Old Testament characters are hung. It is an effective way to teach something about that first Advent before God's Messiah came, and a delightful way to get into the treasures of the Old Testament. Look for ways to get ready for Christmas without celebrating it, such as putting up a crèche without the Baby Jesus until December 25. Far from detracting from the Christmas spirit, the added note of anticipation will build excitement, and Advent will take on memorable and enjoyable features all its own.

One way to ease some pre-Christmas tension and have a mini-Christmas in Advent is to celebrate St. Nicholas' Day, December 6.

Like many parents, we had some problems with the distortions and secular accretions in the Santa Claus myth. St. Nicholas' Day became a way for us to deal with Santa Claus in a new key. St. Nicholas (Santa Claus in northern Europe) was a real bishop, as a little girl in a children's service once said when someone asked if there really was a Santa Claus. While he is mostly wrapped in legend, his importance to children has been a venerable tradition. In our family, December 6 is a highlight of Advent, when we pull out and decorate with all the Santa Claus paraphernalia: Santa Claus mugs, placemats, figurines, doorknob decorations, stockings, music box. An icon of St. Nicholas that normally hangs in our front hall might be placed on or near the dining table. After supper, family members exchange gifts. Naturally, all gifts are from St. Nicholas, who sometimes has left them in our shoes, which (following Dutch custom) we have taken off and left at the door. The issue of gifts from "Santa" has never really come up in our family—I am sure because of the connection now made in all our minds between Santa Claus, gift-giving, and St. Nicholas' Day.

Some Advent planning needs to focus on the Twelve Days of Christmas. In our family we have learned that unless we have the Twelve Days planned well before December 25, we never seem to celebrate them well. Fortunately, the children will be out of school most of that time, so Christmastide can be a family time somewhat easily, especially if working parents can save up an extra vacation day or two. If not, the Christmas season always includes one, sometimes two, weekends. During this brief period, Christian families can do exactly the opposite of the culture. Radio stations are back to "Moon River" or Michael Jackson or Madonna or Neil Diamond on December 26. Let the house ring a little longer with "O Come, all ye Faithful" and "Deck the Halls with Boughs of Holly." Burn Christmas candles nightly. Follow the Christmas lectionary of the Church. Read a Christmas passage of scripture each evening at mealtime. If the family has used a chain-type Advent calendar, have a Christmas one of a different color. Families can sit down together and decide what they really would like to do to keep alive the festival spirit. They might wish to set aside several days during the twelve for special activities, like delivering presents, mailing late cards (why are they "late" if it's still

Christmas?), visiting shut-ins, writing or calling relatives. We have sometimes made the saints days (St. Stephen, St. John) following Christmas special by asking a friend named Stephen or John to have dinner with us on those days (December 26 and 27 respectively), or by doing something for a young or newborn child on Holy Innocents Day (December 28).

New Year's Eve is a disaster of a holiday in our culture. No other occasion is so intimately tied to abusing alcohol and acting silly. There has been for some time a Protestant tradition, doubtless an attempt to redeem something of the New Year, of having a Watch Night service on New Year's Eve. One family I know does something of the sort by inviting other families (adults and older youth) to a midnight party, which begins with a eucharist by torchlight out in the woods. When snow is on the ground, it is a beautiful (if cold!) moment. Afterwards, everyone enjoys a covered dish supper. A similar event could be shared by families with younger children earlier in the evening or on New Year's Day itself. Since January 1 is the Feast of the Holy Name of Our Lord Jesus Christ, it would be timely to reflect on the gift of our own names, or to make a decorative banner or centerpiece celebrating the various traditions of the family carried on in the members' names.

Epiphany is a major Christian feast which has been nearly eclipsed by Christmas in the Church and lost completely in the world outside the Church. The three great Epiphanies of our Lord's life and early ministry are the coming of the Wise Men, his baptism in the Jordan, and the manifestation of his power in the changing of water into wine in Cana of Galilee. In the old days, churchgoers on Epiphany heard all three stories: the story of the baptism at morning prayer; the story of the wedding at Cana at evening prayer; and the story of the Wise Men at the Holy Eucharist. It was the latter that stuck. This story, which obviously belongs with the nativity group, has thus become what Epiphany means to most children in Sunday schools. Actually, it is the baptism of Jesus that is the most deeply rooted tradition of this feast. The 1979 Prayer Book restores this idea by designating the first Sunday after the Epiphany always as the Feast of Our Lord's Baptism. Thus the Sunday congregation gets to hear and celebrate this event in salvation history every year. Either on the Epiphany itself, or on

the Sunday after, or sometime between, the family can celebrate
the great gift of baptism. The celebration can be as direct as having
some prayers at mealtime or bedtime or a bowl of water placed
in the center of the dining table. This could quite naturally be a
time for pulling out pictures of various family baptisms, and perhaps
finding in an art book from the parish or public library a picture
of our Lord's baptism. If one of the children was baptized on the
first Sunday after the Epiphany, the celebration of the anniversary
of that baptism and our Lord's would naturally lift this occasion
to a really major family observance.

For the next several weeks, and sometimes as much as two
months, we are in the ritual doldrums. But it does not have to be
that way! The Lincoln-Washington birthday holiday can be
celebrated with cherry cobbler at home as well as at school, and
Valentine's Day might as well be redeemed from Hallmark and
Whitman's captivity with red carnations or a special dessert.

Particularly in years when Easter comes early, Ash Wednesday
will slip up on our blind side. The first day of Lent came to be called
"Ash Wednesday" when the original custom of doing penance
("repenting in dust and ashes") for serious sins became gradually
extended to the whole community of the faithful, with all taking
ashes upon them as a mark of repentance. The first thing the family
will want to do to mark Lent's beginning is to worship together
at the parish church, and receive ashes. Some will wish to limit
ashes to those old enough to understand, and this sentiment
doubtless has merit. It must be remembered always, however, that
all ritual actions are only in part cognitive and conscious. Participating in them without understanding everything they convey does
not lessen their power. On the contrary, young participants will
have their faith and understanding formed partly by the rite itself.
Little children sense that there is something naturally abhorrent
about being smeared with something dirty. One little girl at an Ash
Wednesday service remarked to her grandfather, "Boy! That Father
Dunn had better not make *my* face dirty!" At dinner or at bedtime,
parents can very effectively help young children to understand the
"ashes to ashes and dust to dust" idea. Don't worry if children
cannot grasp the notion of our mortality. (Adults aren't too
proficient at getting it either.) This is an opportunity to deal

forthrightly with the fact that we come from God, and through the gate of death we go back to God forever. It is also a chance to underscore that, like the rest of creation, we are dust, and therefore close kin with the rest of God's dust. I also find the idea appealing that the ashes on Ash Wednesday veil, as it were, the cross with which we were signed in baptism, reminding us that we share not only in Christ's resurrection, but also in his sufferings too. We ourselves suffer, and we also, like him, identify with the sufferings of others.

Lent, by its very nature, militates against celebrations. Good! All rituals are not joyous, celebrative and helium-filled. We need to balance the themes of mercy, joy, love, and gladness which are so much a part of Easter, Christmas, and even Advent, with the themes of responsibility, self-giving, obedience and sacrifice. This is not to say that Lent should be a dour, somber, gloomy time. While we need to be sorrowful for our sins, we need to find an authentic element of joy in our penitence. Lent can help us do both. Since it fixes our attention on our Lord's temptation, passion and death, it carries a motif of repentance and responsibility. This, however, is coupled with the fact that Lent comes in the springtime and is also historically the time when the Church prepares candidates for Easter baptisms (and by extension prepares itself to renew the baptismal covenant)—all of which suggest life, growth, hope and renewal.

In recent years, the fashion seems to have become to take on some new effort or responsibility, instead of giving up something. To my mind, neither proposition is bad and neither is very satisfying. Rather, Lent can be a time to do a family, as well as a personal, inventory. A week or so before Lent, the family can sit down and discuss together a topic like, "What do we have too much of in our life together?" This recently turned up some interesting data for our family. A piece of posterboard visually told us where our family life was overlived. Very rapidly some things emerged that the family wished to give up not just for Lent, but permanently. Other things we wished to shelve just for Lent. The next step is facile enough: reflect on what the family has too little of. Time? Mutual endeavor? Privacy? Parents have a responsibility to guide the younger ones to see whether certain social concerns are getting short shrift.

Enumerating these things, the family may see clearly enough the benefits for restructuring some dimensions of its life.

Silence is worth trying in Lent. One minute, or even a half-minute, of silence before or after prayers at mealtime may add refreshing sensitivity. Most of us Americans abhor silence. A minute will seem like an eternity to children, so effective is even a drop of silence. Some prior reflection on the importance of silence will be helpful, as will introducing it with this or some similar prayer:

> O God of peace, you have taught us that in returning and rest we shall be saved, in quietness and in confidence shall be our strength: By the might of your Spirit lift us, we pray, to your presence, where we may be still and know that you are God; through Jesus Christ our Lord. *Amen.*[13]

I find myself supposing that everyone, especially children, will resist keeping silence. I should point out that children are not the only noisemakers in the family. They, like all of us, can gain from others' silence, not to mention their own. And, if resistance seems too great, before giving up the idea, experiment with eating in silence. Sometimes it helps simply to be doing something like that while being silent. Or play a record or tape of good, quiet music. Children will make a game out of who can keep silence the longest, and while that might detract from the pristine purity of the experiment, so be it; at least you will come away with some deeper appreciation for the gift of human speech!

Some parishes take the trunk of a Christmas tree and turn it into a cross the following Lent. A family can easily do the same thing. A small cross on or near the dining room table, especially if it recalls the merriment of Christmas, can be a powerfully effective symbol upon which to reflect while pondering Christ's temptation, passion and death.

Holy Week is a very different preparatory time from Advent. It does not carry a sense of gradual build-up, a heightened sense of joy. Everything which anticipates Easter should be kept suppressed during these all-important days. Keep family ritual simple and streamlined, with all energies exerted on the rites of Holy Week being celebrated at the parish church. Meals ought to be the simplest fare, in stark contrast to the Easter feast to come. On the other hand, some preparation for Easter must take place. Special foods will have to be prepared, and this will help provide some balance to Holy Week. Eggs can be dyed, especially on Holy Saturday. In our family, for years we have gotten a dead or leafless tree branch upon which are hung gaily decorated egg-shells and other symbols of new life and resurrection, such as butterflies.

If Easter foods are to be blessed at the parish church, it certainly adds to a sense of corporate celebration to take lamb, eggs, milk and honey, and other traditional Easter foods to have them blessed, usually at the parish love feast or agape meal, which traditionally follows the Great Vigil of Easter. Bringing these home, together with possibly a taper lit from the Paschal Candle is a visible, tangible link between the eucharistic community and the family's own life. If this is not possible, using special thanksgiving for Easter foods, and the Easter prayer for light[14] may be helpful.

The Great Fifty Days of Easter, stretching from Easter Day through the Day of Pentecost, commemorate all the mighty acts of the Risen Lord. Until the fourth century, there was no particular program to historicize them by placing, for example, the date of the ascension forty days beyond the Sunday of the resurrection. The point is not so much for us in our day to reverse the process of historicizing, but for us to set aside the Great Fifty Days as a unique block of time. The family can borrow from the liturgy the Easter acclamation,

V. Alleluia. Christ is Risen.

R. The Lord is risen indeed. Alleluia.

as a preface to the grace before all meals in the Easter season. Or some reference to Luke 24, such as the prayer that Christ may be made known to us, as he was made known to his disciples, in the breaking of the bread,[15] would serve to amplify the importance of *eating* in the Easter stories.

Celebrations with wind and water seem to be particularly apt during the Great Fifty Days. Wind recalls the coming of the Spirit, and water emphasizes the association of Easter with our death and resurrection through baptism. Kite-flying, windmills, banners, flags, sails and other wind-activities can be done with a simple sentence of connection: "We are doing this because it's Easter (Pentecost) and the wind of the Lord's Spirit is blowing!" Washings, bathings, swimming, drenching and other water activities might serve to fill a night of waterworks in celebration of the crossing of the Red Sea, the crossing of the Jordan into the promised land (God's everlasting kingdom) and our union with the Crucified and Risen Lord in baptism.

Summer provides ample possibilities for ritualizing. Certainly (according to Genesis) gardening is one of God's oldest activities! Blessing crops, tilling soil, practicing the stewardship of the earth: all are potentially rich opportunities for learning, growing, and giving shape to faith in the family. Of course, the real summertime festival—this will surprise you—is the Nativity of St. John the Baptist, June 24. In medieval times, and for considerable time thereafter, it was known as "Midsummer Night," and in many places it was the occasion for the St. John's Day bonfires. All young boys and girls used to come together at the community bonfire and pair off during the course of the evening.

Bonfires are out of fashion, and outside the law in most places; but there are other kinds of fires: campfires, charcoal fires. A contemporary version of Midsummer Night would be for a group of adults to throw a cookout for teenagers, replete with "their" music and "their" food. Adults are doing this kind of thing in our town in Connecticut on the night of the high school prom. They seek an alternative to the risks of drinking, drugs and driving all mixed in deathly proportions. A similar, yet simpler, thing can be done on St. John's Day in the parish, or by and for a group of families.

Summertime is punctuated by three civic or secular holidays: Memorial Day, the Fourth of July, and Labor Day. All three are times when prayers, hymns, scriptures and decorations can add an expressly religious dimension to the occasion. Of the three, the Fourth of July especially suggests a variety of possibilities for ritualizing: hanging the flag; special red, white, and blue table decorations; and the reading of a historic document (I suggest the Gettysburg Address, not only for its brevity but for its power and pertinence). Both the Fourth of July and Labor Day are provided with proper readings, psalms, and collects in the Book of Common Prayer.

STORIES

"Read me a story" is itself the beginning of a ritual in many families. There must be something deep within the unconscious of *homo sapiens* that yearns for a story either to forestall going to sleep or to hasten it. By the choice of bedtime stories, parents have an unusual amount of power to inculcate values. Many stories do not need commentary. Many will invite comment and discussion from children. Still others will need or demand a clarifying *midrash* (commentary). Especially some from the Bible will fall into the latter category (Cain and Abel come to mind). Most stories should stand on their own. Nor should the darker side of human experience be neglected. Bruno Bettelheim, for one, has taught us that we need not fear the gruesome and the macabre—not even with children (within the bounds of reason, of course). Our psyches need to find expression for the negative, dark and evil in us.

Families need help to see that story-telling is not something just for the children. Nor, for that matter, only for bedtime. Storytelling is a vastly important human activity, and intrinsic to biblical religion. Story gives way to holy story, and holy story provides the reason—the only reason—for celebration. Who we are, what we have done, where we have come from, where we are going, and what has happened to us thus far are all the themes of the holy story of the people of God. Without being conscious of some of that every time we celebrate, our festivities fall flat. That is why at least some reading of the Gospel is required at every celebration of the eucharist, no matter how simple or informal. The story not only reminds us of who we are and who God is and what He has done in Christ, it "gets us to the table," asks of us a response which is nothing less than *eucharistia*—thanksgiving.

Nothing forms and holds family identity better than the family's own story. Photograph albums, baby books, home movies, video-tapes and tape recordings are means to construct and to preserve family story. "Remember the time when . . ." is usually the way into recalling events and people that have made us who we are. Tell family stories. Pass on the tales and traditions from one generation to another. Those who appreciate and revel in family story will likely honor, enjoy and celebrate the holy story of the family of God.

STARTING

I cannot imagine a family doing *all* the things I have suggested. I *can* imagine, very easily, families intentionally choosing a few of these ideas, or similar ones, and getting going with one or more—such as the weekly family night and a few of the seasonal rituals. Add things gradually. The family, led by parents, can select occasions they wish to celebrate. Christian educators, clergy in particular, can aid the cause by making a priority of educating families in ritual-making. Workshops, short courses for adults, whole family events, family cluster training, and parishwide weekend retreats are all settings in which these and similar ideas can be shared, shaped and tested.

Ultimately, the family itself will fashion the character of its own ritual life. An effective process of ritualization depends upon the family's determination to choose its unique occasions for celebration and prayer. If at least some of those occasions relate family table, season and story to eucharistic table, season, and story, then family rituals and church rituals will reinforce each other. What we need to avoid at all costs is a clutter of unrelated rituals adding to pointless busyness in the home.

When, as a schoolboy, I took piano lessons, my teacher would sit patiently by my side while I sometimes massacred a piece— sometimes from ignorance, often from sheer lack of practice. (I never play Bach's *Two-Part Invention No. 4* that I don't recall his saying that was the absolute worst he'd ever heard me play!) The way he taught me best was to move me off the bench occasionally to play a piece as it was meant to be played. I learned by imitating. That is much the way clergy and lay educators have to train families in the art of ritualizing. We have to *be alongside* families as they experiment with rituals, sorting out what does and does not work, what is authentic and what is not. Occasionally, we shall have to take charge of the keyboard and model how a thing might be done. Eventually, others will catch on. Keep in mind that, when we help families make rituals, we are helping them develop a powerful tool by which to build their common faith—a faith that offers their whole life as eucharist to God.

SIX

Reconciliation: Shaping the Soul

About three months into the final lap of my preparation for the priesthood, it occurred to me that among my duties would be hearing confessions. For a thoroughbred Methodist, that was a sobering thought. I was not at all sure how I felt about confession. I was sure that I knew nothing about what to do, say, or expect.

I began reading, trying to find out, first, how one goes about making confession in the Anglican tradition. Before long, I was testing myself to see if this might be something *I* should do. At twenty-five, I had a fairly long list of regrets. My adolescence, still in progress though I was married and nearly out of school, had left its share of scars on my character. Like everyone else, I had invested considerable energy in developing dependable shells behind which to hide at least most of the weaknesses. Yet, fortunately, I had chosen to be in therapy for a brief while during my last two years of college. I knew there could be much worse things than unburdening one's soul to a listener. Though I had never thought of it as "confession," I had peeled off layer after layer of my mask before my dear friend and confidant, the college chaplain. Thus, a little fear hung over the prospect of making confession, tempered by a trust that "it wouldn't be so bad," and a belief that I'd feel better once I had done it. Still I delayed.

It happened that Father Mark Gibbard, an English priest and monk of the Society of St. John the Evangelist (the Cowley Fathers) was spending a year at General Seminary. Father Mark was gentle, quiet and approachable. I think I sought him out not only because he was a monk, and therefore somebody who ought to know about confession, but because he seemed genuinely interested in students. Rather than being put off by somebody in garb I was unused to, I was drawn to him. I intuited that he was truly a man of prayer. But I needed someone who was friendly and down-to-earth as well. "The only way you can learn to hear confessions," he said without hesitation, "is to make confession."

"One thing still troubles me," I told him. "How do I know if something was a sin? I mean, maybe it was, maybe it wasn't." He saw through me. I had been scared by some of those long, depressing lists in priest's manuals. There are sins on those lists that I would never have considered feeling guilty about until I read them there.

"Looking at the lists is not the important thing," Father Mark assured me. "Measure yourself by what you know of Jesus' life. He was a man of prayer. Are you? He was keenly attuned to the needs of others. Are you? He was faithfully obedient to what he perceived to be his Father's will. Are you? Where have you been less faithful than you know you ought to have been?" Father Mark continued and I began to get the point. Confession was a stock-taking, an inventory. It was a chance to look into the mirror and confront those things in myself—those habits, behaviors, actions, thoughts—that distorted the image of Christ in me. I needed to make a periodic check of where I was going awry, and what was missing from my life. We made an appointment for my first confession, and I got on with my preparation.

One of Father Mark's counsels to me when he heard my confession was that once I had confessed something I was not to go back over it. Drop it. I have never forgotten that wisdom. I often fail to abide by it, but I do remember it. I remember even more clearly what he said to me just before pronouncing the absolution. "You must hear these words not as my words, but as if Christ himself were at this very moment speaking them to you personally. He is speaking to you his word of acceptance, freedom and release. I am his instrument, but the forgiveness is his." Never before or since has anyone made such an evangelical proclamation to me. That was a statement my Protestant upbringing would permit me to understand without strain. The Word of God was declaring his love for me through one of God's other children.

I have made and heard many confessions since that time. I don't think I've ever heard or spoken the words of absolution that I haven't remembered that those were the words of Christ, speaking to me or through me, granting freedom and release to the penitent sinner. Later I was to flesh out my understanding of this sacrament. I would come to understand that it reconciles the penitent to the Church just as much as to God. I have grown to appreciate the need to name before another human being those things that are the hardest for me to face. And I have learned, as all priests do, that no one can tell me anything that they have thought, fantasized, spoken or done that I haven't thought, fantasized, spoken or done myself. The core of the good news in the Sacrament of Reconciliation remains: the Word is present, loving us, forgiving us, healing us.

That night I went to the eucharist after receiving absolution from Father Mark. I only remember sitting in the pew reading again and again the 139th psalm:

O Lord, thou hast searched me out and known me.
Thou knowest my down-sitting and mine up-rising;
Thou understandest my thoughts long before.
Thou art about my path, and about my bed, and art
  acquainted with all my ways.
For lo, there is not a word on my tongue, but thou, O Lord,
  knowest it altogether.
Thou hast beset me behind and before, and laid thine hand
  upon me.
Such knowledge is too wonderful and excellent for me;
I cannot attain unto it.

I remembered from childhood listening to a tape of Charles Allen, the well-known Methodist minister, preaching on that text. Now I knew what he meant. Jesus was the lover of *my* soul, and had come and swept it clean. He had laid his hand upon *me*. Such knowledge was too high for me. Too much.

> Try me, O God, and seek the ground of my heart; prove me
> and examine my thoughts.
> Look well if there be any wickedness in me; and lead me in
> the way everlasting.[1]

TELLING OUR STORIES

At least as late as the Letters of John, there were those in the Church who seriously contended that there could be no such thing as sin after baptism. Theoretically, that is a defensible position. If the believer is united with Christ in baptism, how can he, as St. Paul argued, "who has died to sin, still live in it?" We do not think in those categories, in our guilt-ridden Western Church. To us, it is all too obvious that we can and do sin. But the Early Church took baptism with high seriousness. Washed away were the sins, drowned was the old life of wickedness. Christ's newly born were clothed with purity and holiness. It was unthinkable that anyone could fall away. But they came to see that the newly baptized could indeed fall away, especially in times of persecution. Smelling lion's breath a few inches from you can induce you to say you believe you'd better rethink this commitment to Jesus. Many apparently did. The first big sin for the Early Christian was not murder or adultery or theft, but apostasy. Falling away from the true faith of Christ: this was the sin that could undo the whole Christian enterprise very rapidly. Ignatius, Polycarp, the Johannine literature, the letters of Peter—all exhort Christians time and again to hold steady to the faith.

Yet some continued to argue that it was at least possible to live sin-free lives, though not everyone does so. So the writer of 1 John puts the matter squarely to those who would deny specific sins or general guilt or just general cussedness:

> If we say we have no sin, we deceive ourselves, and the truth
> is not in us. If we confess our sins, he is faithful and just, and
> will forgive our sins and cleanse us from all unrighteousness.
> If we say we have not sinned, we make him a liar, and his
> word is not in us.[2]

One way or another, sin had to be dealt with, and the community had to develop ways to address it. *Exomologesis* is the term denoting a confession made before the Christian community. Those who were guilty of sins were expected to do this, engaging in self-humiliation, acts of penitence such as wearing sackcloth or rags, and possibly in some situations publicly disclosing those sins which had been done whereby Christ's Body was offended. Sin, of course, could never be merely personal; the concept of the Body was entirely too strong to allow that. Later, the bishop had the job of assigning penance to those who had undergone *exomologesis*, and particularly heavy penance to those who were guilty of rather notorious sins. Penance came to involve excommunication from the eucharist, though not necessarily expulsion from the community. The Great Vigil of Easter became a time to reconcile those who had done such penance. When the newly baptized were brought into the gathered community, those who had been excommunicated would join them and the Peace would be given to those who had been separated, as well as to those new brothers and sisters who had never shared the eucharist.[3]

Problems naturally arose from these practices and it is not hard to imagine why. *Exomologesis*, if it included public accounting for specific sins, was more than many communities could bear. We see something of the stew into which a community can get over serious sin in Paul's First Letter to the Corinthians.[4] In some situations, bishops began prescribing heavy disciplines which became permanently binding after reconciliation. Sometimes they required abstention from sex. They often barred penitents from ordination, public office and military service.[5]

Despite everything, however, the public dimension of confession seems to have lasted for the first several centuries. As best we can tell, the monastic communities in Ireland were the first to begin practicing a different kind of confession. Monks began going to each other to confess their sins privately. Within a relatively short time, this practice caught on on the continent and quickly replaced the practice of public penance. The Eastern pattern, however, has retained something of the flavor of early public confession. In the Russian Orthodox Church, for example, the penitent stands facing the priest, with an icon between them. The priest, on behalf of the entire community, will hear the confession. Often this takes place prior to the liturgy, and the congregation will, in fact, be gathering, watching the process. Anglicanism has, in general, retained confession in the church, instead of in a private confessional or separate room, although no congregation is present.

Protestantism swept away auricular confession,[6] though not nearly as entirely or as radically as many would suppose. When Luther developed the doctrine of the priesthood of all believers (not original with Luther, of course) he meant not, as many came to infer, that every person should be his own priest, but that each Christian had the responsibility for being a priest to others. Thus, Christians were to confess to fellow Christians, who acted as priests within the fellowship of all the baptized. A different kind of development actually made this idea viable for a while in the Methodist movement. The Wesleys organized class meetings, small groups expected to be intimate communities of faith. Class members talked over their faith, their trials, their sins and shortcomings with each other. They took seriously their shared responsibilities for each other's growth. This was definitely a mode of confession, not unlike the one practiced in the Early Church. The model of "giving testimonies" to other Christians in prayer meetings and other small groups is widely practiced within evangelical Protestantism. What has happened is that the need for "honest confession" has been met in a way different from the Roman Catholic tradition, but met nonetheless. It is interesting that Alcoholics Anonymous, and all its off-shoots, have relied essentially on the same method. There is something sacred about one's story. And nothing is more essential to health than to be able to make a clean breast of everything, telling one's story honestly *to others.*

Sharing one's story with others is cathartic. It is freeing to get out what has been bottled up. That is the root meaning of *exomologesis.* Metaphors of regurgitation and defecation are often used to describe the process of confessing one's story. Psychologically, it feels like that.

Telling one's story is also clarifying. We do not know, let alone understand, our stories nearly so well before we have told them to another individual. We become more conscious of their content and meaning. Recent developments in spiritual direction, workshops in intensive journal writing, and dream-reflection used in depth analysis attest to the importance of taking one's story seriously. It is easy to see that the functions of spiritual director, analyst and confessor are quite similar. The process of telling our stories *works*, because the community, whether the Methodist small group or the personal analyst or the priest, *accepts* us in spite of our stories. This acceptance is the single most important thing in the healing process. It is even more powerful than committing all our secrets to a journal. Clear and conscious though that may make us, we still need the acceptance—and the assurance of love—from someone outside ourselves.

Finally, the process of sharing our stories, when done within a context of taking care of our own faith development, is a discipline of referring all things to God. Someone has called that the task of theology. It certainly is the task of anyone who would seriously reflect theologically on one's own life. We learn through telling our stories how God has been present in our lives. Oscar Wilde, in *De Profundis*, says that when we look back at our experiences, we see that even in the midst of the most sordid affairs, the Holy One was present. To see him is why we keep telling our stories.

Few things claim higher rank on the Church's agenda than helping people learn to take their life stories very, very seriously. Underlying all our contemporary crises of faith and belief is a pervasive suspicion, if not outright conviction, held by a host of people that God is not real; that he has nothing to do with their ordinary lives; and that religious experience is either so rare as to be of negligible interest or so psychologically questionable as to be avoided at all costs. The Church must change this kind of widespread thinking by training people to treat their ordinary experiences as holy. We need to equip people to reflect on those experiences theologically. We have to aid people in seeing the presence of the Divine within the ordinary flotsam and jetsam we all are anxious to trash. Journals, dream analysis, active imagination, prayer— all are tools by which we can grow towards a deeper awareness of the life of God within us.

The Church has no better context in which to begin helping people tell their stories than families. Most families are surprisingly cut off from any sense of story. Studies show that not only in this country, but also in western Europe, the average child cannot say who his or her grandparents' siblings were.[7] An exercise that Herbert Otto frequently uses in family enrichment events is the doing of a family history or a family tree. Over and over, we have to engage families in honoring both the positive and the negative elements in their individual and collective stories.

FACING THE COMMUNITY

Like the penitent in the Orthodox congregation facing the priest to make confession, the individual Christian in our western congregation has to be helped to face the community. This is a crucial issue in the whole phenomenon of confession. In our radically atomistic, highly private form of Christianity in the West, not many people, lay or ordained, believe that. Such emphasis has been put on "a personal relationship with Jesus as Savior and Lord" within Protestantism that the corporate dimension of that faith has sagged. Of course, the individual is important, as we shall see in the section below on individuation. The Gospel is that we are connected intimately and personally to Jesus. We have to learn, however, that when we sin, we injure not only ourselves but his whole Church of which we are a part. Theologically, confession of that sin is corporate for just as we are a part of the Church we are accountable to it.

Psychology bears this out. The integrity of the individual does not have to be sacrificed for us to see the fundamental relatedness of every person to the whole human community. Certainly Carl Jung's insights into a shared "objective psyche" or "collective unconscious," to which we are all related, points up our unity as human beings. Our failure to take the social fabric seriously has led to debilitative behavior, social negligence and mass projections onto others of traits that do not fit with ours in our highly precious notions of ourselves. This failure leads to aggression and war. We cannot stand much more on this planet. Churches, whatever their traditions, have to find ways of getting out of exaggerated personalism and into a heightened sense of social connectedness. The matter is urgent.

Nathaniel Hawthorne, for all his ambivalence about the past in *The Scarlet Letter*, grasped the truth that even when one is driven out of the community, some sort of bond has to remain to tie the individual to the social order, which is the source of healing. Hester Prynne, branded with the scarlet "A" for the adultery she has committed, lodges on the edge of Salem and beats a path to those in the village who need her help. She becomes known for her good works, and gradually people either ignore her scarlet letter or observe it like a piece of jewelry. Of course, because Hester is unable to come to terms with what we would call her own internal psychic material, she is unable to experience the depth of healing that leads to true wholeness. Yet, under the circumstances, she does the best she can. She works out the consequences of her adultery within the very community whose laws she has transgressed. Over the years, she becomes reconciled to that community,

Not so Arthur Dimmesdale. He can hide his complicity in the adultery behind the *persona* of minister. His guilt eats him alive. With a whip he tears his flesh, and flails his soul more fiercely still. The presence of old Chillingworth cruelly haunts him, hovering over him like an unrequited conscience, knowing his sin yet never offering any compassion or absolution. Dimmesdale's guilt burns, and inevitably the fire must break out. Though he will be destroyed, he has to mount the scaffold before the community and bare his own scarlet letter, seared onto his flesh. The community has no knowledge of his sin, and therefore neither compassion nor condemnation for Dimmesdale. He carries all the guilt himself. And, like every other mortal, he lacks the capacity to heal himself. Of the two, Arthur is immeasurably more tragic than Hester.

Puritan society hardly represents a loving and forgiving Christian community. Yet, Hawthorne's message is that, for all its sins of self-righteousness, the community is primary. We must face it eventually and the sooner the better, else the privatization of guilt will consume us totally.

The Christian always has a two-edged relationship. As penitent, the Christian comes to the community to face responsibility for having fractured that community's life through involvement in sin. But then the tables are turned, and the penitent becomes one among all the other penitents in the restored and forgiven community extending that acceptance and forgiveness to the others who come for it. Whatever our traditions—catholic, evangelical—we need to recover this dimension of Christian community. All our talk about being the Body of Christ is empty if we are unable to face the Body with our sins and weakness, asking to be restored and forgiven. Likewise, we are hampered in exemplifying true forgiveness and charity to the world as long as we find no way to extend that grace and forgiveness to each other. A priest, a lay confessor, a small group—we can use any means at our disposal and consonant with our self-understanding. We cannot back off from the integrity of the community if, as we teach, the community is the source of healing grace.

Paralyzing us from affirming corporate accountability more than any other single thing is the deathly fear of being judgmental. Most Christians, thank goodness, have progressed in their awareness to the point of seeing that one self-righteous prig can drive away a host of people from the church. We want desperately to shun anything that smacks of a holier-than-thou attitude. That is, of course, all to the good. If we err, let it be on the side of compassion and generosity. Yet, one of the gravest problems in the Church today is that, amid the confusions of a pluralistic society gone wild with options, we are left not having very much to believe in. We find ourselves apologizing for traditional Christian values. Part of this is the creative tension that should always exist between the Christian Church and the culture in which it finds itself. But another part of it is our fear of taking *any* stand lest we be perceived as spiritually smug. Church leadership has to help people strike a balance between having no values and believing that "our way" is the only way.

The Church can help families discover ways in which they can deal with the corporate dimension of sin. Two such ways are (1) to become communities exercising responsibility within a climate of compassion; and (2) to teach children that when one sins, one harms not only oneself, but also those to whom one is related—not only other family members, but the other members of Christ's Body. Senior highs on an Emmaus weekend, an intensive experience for teens built on a strong sense of community, said that they were quite surprised to learn that there were others who would not only *not* shun them when they opened themselves in community, but in fact drew closer to them. Perhaps it is inevitable that that come as a surprise to young people; but it need not be quite so rare. Were we to experience sharing ourselves in Christian community, and an accompanying acceptance on the part of that community, we would doubtless find the courage to build a stronger sense of corporate responsibility. Through the Sacrament of Reconciliation, we encounter both our responsibility to, and the gracious acceptance of, the Christian community.

DEVELOPING A SENSE OF RESPONSIBILITY

John Updike's *Rabbit, Run* is a classic story of the twentieth century's evasion of responsibility. Harry ("Rabbit") Angstrom is immensely likable. A high-school basketball hero, Rabbit meets Janice in the department store in which they both work. They marry, Janice being already pregnant. We are introduced to Rabbit as he comes home to Janice, a boring young wife who watches much television and is drifting down the road toward alcoholism. She is far along in her second pregnancy, though all the signs are immediately apparent betraying a deteriorating marriage: nit-picking, projections, arguing, fault-finding. Rabbit leaves to pick up young Nelson from his mother's, and instead of getting his child and coming home, is almost hypnotized by what he sees through the window: Nelson being cared for by his own mother and father. Rabbit, if he is conscious of anything, realizes that he and Janice cannot *care* adequately. He runs away, with a half-baked idea of continuing to drive all night until he comes to his Promised Land, the South. There he can—do what? Rabbit has not thought that far. He just has the urge to run. We see in this young husband and father an undeveloped teenager.

Into Rabbit's world soon steps the Reverend Jack Eccles, the Episcopal priest of Janice's parents' parish. Eccles reacts like all the other adults and authorities in Rabbit's world: he sees and treats Rabbit as a naughty child—one whose company he enjoys a great deal as a means of escaping much less pleasant involvements.

Rabbit comes to the hospital where Janice is in labor. There his mother-in-law, whom he intensely dislikes, and who has never liked him, gives Rabbit what no one else has offered: a confrontation.

"If you're sitting there like a buzzard young man hoping she's going to die, you might as well go back to where you've been living because she's doing fine without you and has been all along." . . . Mrs. Springer's attack, though it ached to hurt him, is the first thing anybody has said to Harry since this began that seems to fit the enormity of the event going on somewhere behind the screen of hospital soap-smell. Until her words he felt alone on a dead planet encircling the great gaseous sun of Janice's labor; her cry, though a cry of hate, pierced his solitude.[8]

Though it is her comment about the possibility of Janice's death that hooks him, Rabbit is really caught by Mrs. Springer's open confrontation. Everybody else seems to go out of the way to be gentle and understanding; or, like his father, to avoid confrontation; or, like his mother, to side somewhat angrily with Harry, projecting blame and disgust onto Janice, whose fault, of course, the whole mess is anyway.

The story rings true. For whatever reason—and it is not easy to say—Harry Angstrom has never grown beyond being "Rabbit." His family, his culture, his in-laws, his wife, have insulated him from developing an adult sense of responsibility. No one confronts Rabbit, and he confronts no one. Even his own Lutheran pastor, straight-laced and somber, believes, as he tells Eccles, that it is not the business of the clergy to meddle in people's lives. Let the clergy pray. In all Rabbit's life, there is no one who truly calls him to be accountable for his behavior and his decisions.

Through this story, we gaze at an almost photographed picture of contemporary men and women. It is clear that Rabbit is able to feel. He can even feel guilt. He can even feel responsibility. Guilt and responsibility "slide together like two substantial shadows in his chest."[9] He doesn't know "what to do, where to go, what will happen, the thought that he doesn't know seems to make him infinitely small and impossible to capture. Its smallness fills him like a vastness."[10] The tragedy for so many people like Rabbit is that there is no one, no group, no institution which can help them to *know*, either themselves or the truth—two things which are deeply related. Families are sometimes, though not always, conscious of having the job of rearing children to become "responsible adults." Rabbit's parents might even have said that that was their job, had they been asked. But how is this task to be done? Few seem to have any idea.

And yet, our society seems to be coming ever so slowly to realize that we have a widespread problem. Colleen McCullough's novel *An Indecent Obsession*, attempts to deal with a sense of duty. Its title suggests how many people perceive duty. "Responsibility" in some minds is equated with drudgery, uninteresting work, "heavy-duty" obligations, a stultifying life. Duty is for them much like the printing establishment where Rabbit's father works: the force that sucks life out of you. From that, who doesn't want to run?

Dan Kiley, in *The Peter Pan Syndrome*, writes of men who never grow up. Kiley, I am certain, would diagnose Rabbit as a Peter Pan. But there are women, too, who have the problem of wanting to run away from the drudgery of "responsibility." If there is anything in the concept of accepting responsibility worth saving, and for society's sake let us hope so, then the family must become more conscious of the issue, and more skilled at dealing with it.

The Church's role, here as elsewhere, is to work together with families in order to do the job. Eccles' role in Updike's story is instructive. He models the kind of pastoral care that the Church has come to accept as standard since Eccles' day—the mid-fifties. No doubt he had been through clinical pastoral education. He knew better than to push religion down Harry's throat. He knew enough to establish a relationship with the one he wanted to help. And, no doubt, he had a view towards building faith in families, and wanted to begin his job with the young Angstroms by getting them back together. For all of this, Eccles is commendable. On the other hand, he is passive. He may or may not be in touch with his own inner life (I guess not), but for whatever reasons—his own immaturity, a shyness, a fear of rejection—he does not confront Harry Angstrom. He does not insist that Harry and Janice sit down and talk things through. He shows no plan to refer them to anyone. And, to Harry's clear-cut testimony that he does not *want* a reconciliation, Eccles offers no response. He vaguely suggests that it might be God's intention that Harry grow up; but when Harry retorts that he does not cry over being immature—"mature" being very close to dead—Eccles replies that þe is immature himself.[11]

Clergy can sympathize with poor Eccles, navigating with a runaway husband in-between dealing with deaths and services and sermons. But what we cannot do is to opt for Eccles' idea of supporting faith in families. If indeed Eccles *has* an idea, it seems to be to keep people married because marriage is a sacrament and it is not God's will for husbands to make their wives suffer by leaving them.[12] That does not get the Angstroms very far. Among the host of things needed by the Angstroms and the world they symbolize is for the Church to say, "You have a responsibility. It is not primarily a responsibility to your family, though that is not negligible. Nor is it a duty towards God, though you have that too. But you have a responsibility to your self. If you do not know where you are going, let us face that together. You can learn to discern a path to follow, one that will be true to your nature. You can learn to live in a way that, while not pain-free for yourself or those you love, will steer away from needless hurt to others around you. You can become more conscious of those forces that are swamping you and urging you to run. You can confront them, and you can begin, with the grace of God, by getting to know yourself."

That is a tall order, but that is what the Sacrament of Reconciliation is fundamentally about. It is about "coming clean" to ourselves, in the presence of another human being and to the community of faith that person represents, and to God. It is about looking in the mirror, and seeing in that moment of judgment also the presence of grace accepting us and freeing us, not to run away from truth, but to "mount up with wings as eagles," and run towards it.

TRANSMITTING VALUES

It is by no means certain in the minds of many just who is responsible for responsibility(!) A sense of responsibility, like other values, should be delegated to extrafamilial institutions, say some students of the contemporary family. Philip M. Hauser says,

> . . . The family today is not the main source of transmission of moral and ethical values to the next generation. Probably the family does still play a very important role in shaping

the child's character in his early years. But when it comes to value systems, to consciousness of social order and its requirements, and to other basic patterns of human behavior, the family no longer performs the functions [of value formation] . . .[13]

Until recently, and perhaps still in less urbanized parts of our culture, families assumed control of the process of forming and transmitting values. As Edward Shorter notes,

In the heyday of the modern nuclear family, the prime burden of transmitting values and attitudes to teenage children fell upon the parents, and the rules of the game were learned in the cloistered intimacy of countless evenings about the hearth. But as the post-modern family rushes down upon us, parents are losing their roles as educators. The task passes instead to the peers, and with its transfer passes as well a sense of the family as an institution continuing over time, a chain of links across the generations. The parents become friends (an affective relationship), not representatives of the lineage (a functional relationship). If this is so, we are dealing with an unprecedented pattern.[14]

There are voices that say, with Richard Farson, that this is indeed the case, and that it is all to the good. Why should the home be the place where values are acquired? What qualifies the family to inculcate values in the young?[15]

My own point of view is that Shorter is correct; that the family is fast ceasing to be the setting where values are formed, except for the basic values in young children. I am not so sure that we ought to view the demise of the value-making function of the family with enthusiasm. Furthermore, I am convinced that the Church is an institution to which families can turn for help in forming values, reinforcing values and judging values. I am not talking about the values underlying nice, middle-class respectability such as cleanliness, achievement, success, politeness. No question that the Church supports those values. I am talking about the values of the Kingdom of God: peace, justice, righteousness, honesty, holiness, compassion, love, freedom, sexual integrity, wholeness. The church needs to be the setting where serious issues get discussed, where people can confront each other's opinions with respect, tact and honesty. The church must be the place—if indeed the only place—where parents can come to talk about the stresses and challenges of child-rearing, and expect to get helpful criticism and positive reinforcement.

Our parishes have to become the places where parents and young people work out the difficult existential issues of human sexuality, political involvement, spending money. We cannot perform that function if we keep dodging hard issues and burying our heads when anything controversial is raised. Where will the world change its course now set towards nuclear confrontation? In parish houses and fellowship halls, as people begin to see that peace is not a nice suggestion for Christians but inherent in our very identity. How will we build faith in marriages that are free and not constricted, mutually satisfying and not oppressive for one or both spouses? By bringing people together in groups to learn from each other, to share their own pilgrimages of ascents into ecstacy and descents into hell. How will families become stronger? When parents and children, become much more aware of the direction for their lives and of how it is that God is working in everyday events to bring us to himself.

What has all this to do with the Sacrament of Reconciliation? First, one cannot face one's accountability in a vacuum. We must offer a practical understanding of the moral and ethical demands of the Christian life before we can expect people to confront their sinfulness appropriately and their responsibility to self, neighbor and God. Second, reconciliation in its widest sense is something that *flows from* the sacrament, not something that is bottled up within it. One of the things incumbent upon us once we have confessed our sins (whether to God in private or to a priest or to a group of Christians) is to amend our lives however we possibly can. Carrying on the process of reconciliation, then, involves working and reworking the value systems that we are constantly shaping and applying.

The essential purpose of the Sacrament of Reconciliation is to rid the soul of all that keeps it from growing and developing fully. To be reconciled in this sense means to be reconciled to one's truest and deepest self, from which we become continually split off.

Values—what we cherish and cling to, what we are willing to affirm publicly—shape our souls. Values can interfere with our growth into the image of Christ, or they can enhance that growth. Thus, the church, in helping individuals and families to become more conscious of value-forming processes, not only has to ask what values are, but whether the ones we have are good ones. Values are not static. An opinion we treasure highly one day is cast aside in favor of another the next. Utilizing the Sacrament of Reconciliation, and helping people to prepare for that sacrament by means of healthy introspection, the Church can aid them to see what they truly value—what they really live by and believe honestly to be important. Values clarification, for all its worth, is inadequate for this process. Once we are clear about what is important to us, we still have to see whether it is in line with our basic identity.

In my estimation, the Church, as it goes about helping families to become more conscious of value-formation (and thereby enlisting the help of parents in the Church's larger task of value transmission), needs to emphasize the creation of a certain quality of "climate" in the family. Essential to the very young child's absorption of positive values is an atmosphere of security, love and order, provided by parents who free the child to judge his own actions and set his own course of conduct, within appropriate limits.[16] This atmosphere does not have to be saccharine. Rather, in such a climate, the family will treat anger and hostility realistically. One writer puts it this way:

> Anger is evident in new-born infants who scream and kick and demand what they want when they want it, in unmistakable ways. Persons of every age normally undergo some frustrations, the result of which is often feelings of aggression. Frustrations are inevitable in a child's early experience in his family, and it is toward his parents and his siblings that his anger is first expressed. Somehow, over the first few months and years, families have to accept a child's angry feelings and at the same time curb his harmful expression of them against himself and others. This takes some doing. To deny the presence of anger is to be emotionally dishonest, but to allow rage to go uncurbed is to allow the child to do disservice to himself and to others—now and later.[17]

Within such a climate, parents can practice some spiritual direction of their children. (We are always doing this; to call it "spiritual direction" is simply to become more keenly aware of it as such.) John Wesley's mother, Susannah, who had twelve children, used to spend an hour every week with each of them, talking about the state of their souls. For Wesley, this was the most important hour in his whole week.[18] That idea, given twentieth-century content, makes good sense. Parents today, who normally have fewer children than Mrs. Wesley, can look for a significant block of time each week to engage their children individually in conversation about what is on their minds, what is troubling them, what is helping them to grow, what is keeping them from being the person they want to become. This is where theological reflection can begin.

My own observation over the years is that most of our children's training comes when their mother or I tuck them in at night. That is the time of conversations about what they love, fear, worry about. It is as if the psyche comes to the surface as the body is readying itself for sleep. The dark waters underneath the placid surface are there to be plumbed. Opportunity to shape the soul is present.

In a healthy family atmosphere, parents will encourage their children to exercise self-discipline. Children in many homes are not expected to do *any* work—not even pick up their clothes or make their beds. They are readily and easily "forgiven" if they fail to keep commitments to attend a function or to be on time for an event. "Children will be children"; yet this attitude undermines the growth of needed self-discipline, which is, in a basic sense, the inescapable goal of all moral training.[19]

The texture of family life should allow children, as they grow into adolescents, to carry on the struggle for adult status. Parents will find it increasingly necessary, as their children grow older, to recognize their need for independence and autonomy. Here the situation becomes delicate, as far as the place of religion is concerned. *If* religion has been consistently presented as a way toward wholeness and meaning, related to everything we are and do, then young people are likely to see it not as a deterrent to their emerging selves, but as a friend. If, on the other hand, religion has always been presented as restrictive, inhibiting and oriented towards keeping people children, then naturally adolescents will want no part of it. How we wish the situation were this simple! I have known people to rebel against the religion of parents who gave them what seems to me to be a very healthy religious upbringing. The point is not that we can push the right buttons and guarantee that our children will grow up to be people of faith, but that we can intentionally recognize the needs for personal autonomy, connecting religion and faith with the emergence of the true self.[20]

Church educators and pastors can help families develop values by guiding them to discover their *strengths*. Herbert Otto's contribution in this regard is immense. He has brought to awareness the need to replace exclusive problem-solving with strength identification. I have used his ideas repeatedly in family counselling and in family enrichment settings. Family strengths include these capacities:

To provide for the physical, emotional and spiritual needs of family members;

To give and take in child-rearing practices and discipline;

To communicate effectively;

To provide support, security and encouragement;

To initiate and maintain growth-producing relationships and experiences within and without the family;

To maintain and create constructive and responsible community relationships in neighborhood, school, town, etc.;

To grow with and through children;

For self-help and ability to accept help when appropriate;

To perform family functions and roles flexibly;

For mutual respect for individuality of family members;

To use crisis or seemingly injurious experience as a means of growth;

To have concern for family unity, loyalty and intra-family cooperation.[21]

Helping families to claim what in their life they can feel positive about, celebrate, and build upon, is one of the first goals of family ministry. This, too, is an implication of the Sacrament of Reconciliation. It is never sufficient to confess one's sins and to leave it at that. Often the very form of absolution in the liturgy reminds us that the grace of God strengthens us in all goodness, confirms what is healthy and life-giving within us. So there is no reason to limit helping people to identify their strengths—always a much harder task than to name weaknesses. In family workshops, parent education, adult seminars and family clusters, we do well to ask what the various individual family members bring to the family constellation of strengths. We should enable families to see their most effective functions, and how they can prize individual members for their contributions to those functions. Family inventories, which we spoke of in Chapter Five, are helpful ways to determine not only the weaknesses which need to be worked on, but the strengths that need to be affirmed and stimulated.

PREPARING FOR CONFESSION

In this positive kind of climate, parents, working together with clergy and Christian educators, can have a decidedly good experience helping children to prepare for confession. Children can, with guidance, enumerate those things which they need to confess, and to make their confessions in whatever way seems appropriate. We can intervene in this process to dispel many of the counter-productive and downright neurotic ideas of sin that become so fixed in many people that they never develop a mature understanding of sin. Rather than give children lists of no-no's, and lead them towards scrupulous examination of their lives for all the naughty things they have done, we can help the child of nine or ten, for example, to see that sin is the way we put what we want ahead of what God wants. We do not always do so; but when we do, it is sin. Wayne Oates has reminded us in his *Psychology of Religion* that the basic form of sin in the Bible is idolatry.[22] Children at nine or ten do not possess the cognitive and moral development to deal effectively with idolatry as an existential category, but they can certainly talk about what they love the most, what they prize most, what they would *give anything* to see or do. It is not inappropriate to help them ask, "Do I let that take away from my love for God?"

Several years ago a friend gave us tickets to a Jackson Brothers concert. Barbara and I kept them secret until we could surprise our children the evening before. They craved nothing so much as to hear Michael Jackson in concert, and, of course, they never expected to. When we revealed the news, Anne burst into joyful tears. She and Sarah Marsh immediately began planning what they would wear. I had never seen them so excited. I was moved by their joy. Some minor fracas started about who was going to wear what, and I intervened. "Let's keep this in perspective," I pleaded in my most reasoned parental tones. "After all, what is the most important thing you're going to do tomorrow (which was a Sunday)?"

Both of them caught my meaning, but answered (naturally), "Go to the Jackson Concert." We laughed. They could in no way have grasped how the Sunday eucharist is more wonderful than a rock concert. Yet, for a moment, they at least heard someone else suggest otherwise. I think I avoided waxing moralistic when I pointed out that their mother and I knew how excited they were, and that one day I hoped they would feel just such overwhelming joy at coming to the table of the Lord.

We do not have to teach children to look upon God as the enemy of everything fun and happy. God wants us to honor our bodies, to celebrate our physical natures. One does not have to apologize for one's love of soccer or music or ballet in order to be right with God. Christians in our culture have to learn, however, that we cannot ignore what it means to be faithful to the Lord. We have to help our children work out their understanding of faithfulness. Learning to affirm ourselves and to offer our gifts, our love, our talents to God has never been optional, and it is not optional now.

There are other ways of looking at sin that children can relate to. Sin encompasses our destructive habits. Leading a life that is careless and unsafe is destructive and therefore sinful, as is being cruel to animals and other people. Sin can also be just plain "acting stupid," doing things we know better than to do. Sin always causes separation between us and other people, between us and God. Children can understand all this on their own levels. Naturally, it is not going to work to expect them to deal with the reality of sin on an adult level; but neither will it do simply to glide over the presence of sin in our lives and in their lives.

Some will object that I sow the seed of all kinds of neurotic guilt. I do not believe so. Neurotic guilt (false or misplaced guilt) springs from wrong ideas about what we can and should be responsible for, and germinates *when there is no way of receiving forgiveness.*

Western society is guilt-ridden, not because we have altogether inappropriate or unrealistic ideas of what we are guilty of, but because we have ceased to have any faith in the rituals, like the Sacrament of Reconciliation or its counterparts, which are designed to remove our guilt and to assure us of pardon and absolution. I once knew a boy who told me that the "best thing" he got out of church was the priest standing up and forgiving him his sins. He always felt relieved and free when that happened. Then, of late, he "confessed," he had ceased to believe that the priest had any power at all. He no longer got anything out of church. Behold: a tragic little cameo of Western civilization. The boy did not discover the truth; he reached the point where he could no longer *rationally* accept the symbolic ritual, and dismissed it. Perhaps in the Western world, we shall learn one day not to judge everything by how well it shakes out rationally. The power of symbols and rituals, including those which could assure us of absolution, is rarely comprehensible on a rational level. We have to be honest about that with children. Better to be a little off the mark in what one thinks is sinful, and to confess it, than to try to talk oneself out of feeling guilty, and be eaten up by unconfessed and unabsolved guilt within.

INDIVIDUATION

Both Church and family have the task of soul-shaping. I say soul-shaping, not soul-making. The latter is God's job. And the soul is made through the presence of the Holy Spirit, operating in each one of God's children. The foregoing sections of facing community, developing a sense of responsibility, and transmitting values point up three of the major issues in the task of shaping the soul. Community, the inner sense of responsibility and values that are fit for life in the kingdom of God all aid in shaping the human soul. By far the most helpful concept elucidating this process in our own times comes from Carl Jung in his term *individuation*. For two ample discussions of Jung's treatment of the structure of the psyche, the reader can turn to Ann Belford Ulanov's *The Feminine in Jungian Psychology and in Christian Theology* and to Wayne G. Rollins' *Jung and the Bible*. The process of individuation, centrally important to the workings of the psyche for Jung, is the integration of the various elements in the personality which extends throughout the whole of life. Jung's initial definition of individuation was "becoming an 'individual,' and insofar as 'individuality' embraces our innermost, last and incomparable uniqueness, it also implies becoming one's own self."[23] The process of growth is towards wholeness. In the process of the ego's emergence from the unconscious, and in the ego's interaction with the surrounding society, we deny the value of certain aspects of ourselves, and banish them to live within the unconscious. The process of individuation integrates these parts of ourselves into our conscious life.[24] From infancy to midlife, the individual is occupied in the development of the ego—the sense of *I-ness* and with adapting the ego to social expectations through the development of the *persona*—the social or public presentation of the ego. During the rest of life, from midlife on, the person concentrates on the discovery of the "other side" which has been repressed. Ann Ulanov writes:

> Becoming whole includes realization of our innermost uniqueness, and hence the process also means becoming one's own self, as differentiated from having only a collective identity, as a member of a certain family, or group of people, or nation.[25]

Individuation is not the same as the emergence of the ego and its differentiation from the unconscious. It is the process which involves the ego in relating to and coming to terms with the "objective psyche," the central representation of which is the self.[26] It is also important to distinguish individuation from individualism. The latter often means the willful assertion of the ego itself. Individuation, in contrast, opens the ego to discover its limitations, and the person's fundamental relatedness to all other selves in the world.[27]

As the self more and more replaces the ego as the center of personality, we develop an awareness of a world beyond the small ego-centered struggles and conflicts that often fill the first part of life. The self "knows" that it is related to all others. An enlarging sense that we are related to the whole of history of humanity accompanies our growing awareness. We see that our lives fit into that broad picture. To us, the self indeed represents all that we are as individuals: our past, our connectedness with the rest of humanity, our potential. And, as Rollins sees in Jung's thought, the self and its emergence is what the future of humanity depends upon. So long as we are unconscious of the elemental forces of the psyche which keep propelling us into war and other violent upheavals, we threaten the whole life of the planet. Individuals radically regenerated in Spirit will renew society.[28]

The process of individuation is tied to what the Sacrament of Reconciliation seeks to accomplish: the purging of the soul (the whole human life) of its destructive and alienating elements, and the healing of the soul so that eternal life can be fully lived now, and enjoyed forever. Only the grace of God can accomplish such a thing. The sacrament is a direct means to that grace, and therefore a powerful gift in the process of becoming conscious of this self which begs to be the center of our personality. The self for Jung, incidentally, is symbolized by Christ. It is possible to see that the self, at our very core, is the point of contact between the Great Self of the Universe—God—and our own individuality.

There is a difference, of course, between the Sacrament of Reconciliation and depth psychology. We need to be clear that the process of individuation cannot take place exclusively within the context of confession and absolution. We need three things. First, we need to see the Sacrament of Reconciliation within the large framework of the life-long goal of the emergence of the self. Second, we need to prepare for this sacrament being attentive to its place in a comprehensive growth in wholeness. Third, we need to see the sacrament as offering a gift of grace which we need very intentionally to use and to explore, as our ego becomes more secure and as our self begins to take its place as the center of our personality. Let us look at these things one by one to see how, in the course of parish ministry, the church can focus on them, and thus give families indispensable tools by which to carry on the continuing soul-shaping of its members.

The Sacrament of Reconciliation is not an isolated part of the ongoing process of individuation. We must understand confessing our sins and receiving absolution not simply as a ritual process connected to life beyond the grave, nor simply as a way of getting temporary grace for this life. We need to experience this sacrament as a way that, to use an image of Yeats, our souls abandon the graveclothes of repression and take on the resurrection power of new life. My best guess as to why Protestants are offended by sacramental confession and why Anglicans and Roman Catholics are defensive of it is that almost none of us deals directly with the process of individuation. We do not emphasize taking our personal experience as the place where we meet grace. This situation is beginning to change. We are beginning to talk more openly about spiritual growth. We are beginning to take seriously efforts like keeping a journal. And in some quarters we are speaking frankly about the necessity of giving and taking spiritual direction. All of these are signs of hope and help. Yet, the vast majority of Christians in most churches know nothing of these things. We have much work to do in helping people to pay attention to their lives and to take them seriously *in a new way.*

This way is different from the egocentric preoccupation with ourselves that, if anything, much pop psychology and self-help techniques have fostered. The Church needs very earnestly to help people reflect on their experiences with a view towards what is enhancing, and what is blocking, development of our selves in the image of Christ. I hasten to add that to do this adequately, we need to say over and over that the Church's business, as the Body of Christ, is precisely the bringing about of this wholeness. We need to help people see ever more clearly that the life of the parish is not fundamentally a cozy little club into which they can fit and "get support" for life's problems, but is, on a deeper level, a community which must challenge each of its members to live under the merciful judgment of God so we can live truly under his abounding grace. We need as well to be very clear with our people that "making our confessions" and "telling our stories" are not just rituals that belong to a highly privatized religion which sees the salvation of the individual soul as distinct from what happens to the rest of the world, to all other souls, and indeed to the entire created order. We are in the business of reconciliation: to bring together, in the name of Christ and by the power of the Holy Spirit, all the parts of the created order that are estranged, including human beings and including the different fragments of ourselves, into the whole of God's peace. We need to preach and teach that with a full sense of urgency.

Our second need is for a kind of preparation for the Sacrament of Reconciliation which will place it in the context of the growth into wholeness. Here is where we have much work cut out for us with adults as well as with young people. The traditional means of preparation for the Sacrament of Reconciliation involved those lists of forbidden behaviors that I had come across before going to Father Gibbard. There is a better approach. The most basic element in preparation for the sacrament is to affirm those things which the ego needs for a healthy life. Remember that the process of individuation includes, but is not limited to, the development of the ego. Thus, we need to be extremely careful that we do not put down legitimate ego needs in the name of fostering spiritual growth. The ego, as a part of the whole person, is redeemed by Christ. Our willing, choosing, striving, and self-assertion are some of the ego's basic functions. They beg to be affirmed *before* we test them against the teaching of the Church—such as the Ten Commandments. My willing is good; sometimes my willing gets distorted, however. Where does my will interfere with my love of God and my response to his Lordship in my life?

That is the way the process of introspection works; it is considerably differently from starting off with the commandments and checking to see all the places that we are guilty of infractions against them. Likewise, we may see that our ability to choose, or to assert ourselves, is good. These are basic functions the ego must perform. Like all things about us, however, they get out of line. The process of measuring our ego functions against the standard of God's commandments and the Church's other moral and ethical formulations must happen *after* we have basically affirmed them. In parenting classes, in preaching, in training church school teachers and catechists, we must affirm this process. It provides not only the outline of healthy self-assessment for purposes of confession, but also an anchor for that elusive term our culture exalts, "self-esteem." God wills our appropriate self (ego) esteem. This does not mean that everything our ego wants our ego should have.

Preparation for the sacrament can be more than periodic inventory. Ideally, it takes place within the larger context of ongoing spiritual direction. The process of giving and taking spiritual direction has been greatly clarified in recent years by writers like Tilden Edwards in *Spiritual Friend* and Kenneth Leach in *Soul Friend*. My personal finding is that spiritual direction is not necessarily related to the process of confession. Nor need one find a spiritual director who will necessarily hear one's confession in the narrowest sense. When I made a separation several years ago between spiritual direction and confession, and sought two different individuals to be director and confessor, my most astonishing learning dawned when I realized how difficult it was for me to go to my spiritual director and to talk about something other than my flaws! Until I made the break between the two processes, I was not conscious of always seeing my spiritual growth as too closely tied with those things I needed to get rid of. I am learning the great value in putting spiritual direction on a larger and more positive plane. Now confession becomes just one among many things I do for my soul's health—not the main thing or the only thing.

Spiritual direction is a relationship in the context of which one can share and reflect upon one's life. All the various styles of spiritual direction—passive, directive, etc.—presuppose that the listener will be able to help the talker become more conscious of those things that are aiding or hampering the soul's growth in the image of God. Or, to use the language of individuation consistently, the emergence of the true self which bears the image of God. The church can help parents become more skilled and sensitive "spiritual friends," directors, models for their children by helping them to understand and to avail themselves of spiritual direction. The necessity of doing this is grounded in the truth that Father Mark told me. "The only way you can learn to hear confession is to make confession." The way for parents to become "qualified" to be their children's spiritual directors, helpers, friends, is to be under direction themselves. That may be, in the final analysis, the greatest single goal for any church which hopes to build faith in families.

Our third concern is to see, and to help the Christian community see, the grace of the sacrament as something we need to use consciously and employ intentionally. That is not quite so obvious as it appears. The Sacrament of Reconciliation presupposes that the penitent purposes to amend life wherever possible and appropriate.

This is the beginning. And, of course, it includes making restitution for wrongs we have done except, as AA tradition puts it, where to do so would cause additional and unnecessary harm. Beyond this, however, is a whole other dimension. Whereas for very young persons, confession and forgiveness may be understood as an intensely personal process, as we get older and our ego becomes more stable and secure, we can be more serious about our role in the wider world. A function of the confessor (or the spiritual director) is to point out to us our prejudices, our bigotry, our pig-headedness when we might not be conscious of them, and especially when we want to hang on to those things. Having availed ourselves of the Sacrament of Reconciliation, we become empowered with the grace to seek ways in which to make good our baptismal promises to "seek and serve Christ in all persons" and "to work for justice and peace among all people and to respect the dignity of every human being."[29] The power of the Holy Spirit frees us to do those things when we let go of our sins, failures and harmful attitudes. Confession leads us to a fuller life, which expresses the love and wholeness of Christ.

Specifically, priests hearing confession might well keep in mind helping the adult penitent to examine what might be done to foster such values in their family lives. One of the most helpful things a confessor, having heard my manifold laments about my failures with my wife and children, ever gave me to do was to go home and carve out an extra day or night, and spend it simply being with my family. The same priest, on hearing another lament about how I had not been faithful to the demands of my social conscience, told me to go back to my parish and to stake out with them one piece of social ministry which we could corporately undertake. When I did so, that parish launched a remarkable effort to relieve hunger locally and beyond. Those are ways by which one can "pick up" the gift of grace from the Sacrament of Reconciliation and translate it into the terms of the larger love and peace of Christ for the world.

Finally, we need to remain aware that the process of reconciliation is not the elimination of conflicts, but the reconciliation of opposites. Here, as in all sacraments, the human is reconciled with the divine, the body with the soul, the masculine with the feminine parts of ourselves, the darkness with the light. Tensions between these opposites are neither repressed nor obliterated. They will continue to provide the dynamism needed for a full life. The "reconciliation of opposites" always means that one side of us is not pulling against or trying to deny another side. In the process of reconciliation, nothing is more critical than letting go of the false and inflated instances of power which one part of us has used to keep another part suppressed. In its most basic sense, that is sin on its most profound personal level. All of that sin, that brokenness caused by the lopsided, imbalanced, distorted parts of ourselves, we have to let go. We have to hear the words of absolution as the very words of Christ, speaking release and peace and wholeness to us, reconciling us to the self within, to the Great Self of God, and to all the other selves of the universe.

For individuals and for families, that kind of reconciliation is not only the shaping, but the saving, of souls.

SEVEN

Working

In this chapter, we make a sharp departure from the pattern we have been following. Marriage, baptism and eucharist have obvious applications within the life of a family as well as being public rites of the Christian community. After forming a home, having children, and establishing a viable ritual life, the single most important part of life to deal with is work. Who in the family works? How is work handled? Is it perceived to be faith's enemy or faith's expression? Central as these concerns are, the Church has no sacrament that explicitly sanctifies work. Ordination is as close as we come.

But ordination is different from other sacraments. It is the only one that is reserved for a particular subspecies of Christian. While it is true that most of what clergy do is derived from their baptism rather than their ordination, still ordination has evolved into a rite that sets apart certain individuals for special work. Originally, of course, this work was seen as very different from what modern people associate with professions within Western society. Once, we spoke of those who were "called" to ministry. Then we thought in terms of vocation—slightly different, inasmuch as vocation came to be thought of as "full time work." Then we began speaking of full-time church workers as "professionals." Nowadays, church leaders of nearly all stripes think of themselves along lines that parallel other professions—doctors, lawyers, teachers, etc. Thus, ordination is tantamount to the conferring of professional status in our society—a long hike from the Early Church's understanding that "to ordain" meant simply to set apart or to designate certain individuals for certain work *within the Christian community* on behalf of the whole body. From all we can tell, the Church of the first few centuries was not the least concerned with the status of its leaders within the surrounding culture.

At any rate, the Church now has a way of sacramentalizing the work of its "professionals." All the bishops, priests and deacons are a tiny sliver of the total Christian population, however. Is there no way to sacramentalize the work of the other 98 percent of the Church?

What we shall see in the following pages is one approach to broadening the meaning of the Sacrament of Ordination to include the total Church. Specifically, I take the point of view that everyone, "ordained" to Christian ministry in baptism, can view work—not just life's work, but all work—as an expression of that ministry. This argument will in turn lead us to see that families and church can work together to put work into a new, positive light.

WORK AND MINISTRY

Our baptism into Christ's death and resurrection is also baptism into Christ's ministry. Our "job" as the Church—Christ's Body—becomes to do the very things he spent his life doing. There is only one *ministry*, and that is Christ's, though that ministry takes many and varied forms within the Church. And all ministry is directed to the same end as was his ministry: the reconciliation of the whole world to God.

Though nothing less than astonishing, the recovery of the concept of total ministry throughout the Church during the last decade has unfortunately edged away from this central truth. We have talked much about "lay ministry." Often "lay ministry" has been a slogan to suggest that lay persons can do certain things, customarily reserved for the ordained, as well or better than the ordained. True enough. But that suggestion does two things that we need to get beyond. First, it fails to ask whether the Church really needs to do what it does, whether through the efforts of laity or clergy. Second, it tends to perpetuate the notion that lay ministry is something that lay persons do *within the Church*. Thus, teaching Sunday school, ushering, singing in the choir, reading lessons in the liturgy and serving on church boards come to be seen as "lay ministries," and there we stop. The guts of ministry, lay as well as ordained, is *the reconciliation of the world to God in Christ*. Lay persons, like clergy, will find ways of concretizing that reconciliation through "internal" ministries directed to building up the Body of Christ, and through "external" ministries more clearly addressed to the needs of the world.

Ministries come in three kinds.[1] First, there are ministries of ordering. Primarily the function of the ordained, these "internal" ministries of administration and oversight are shared by laity—to the degree depending on a particular denomination's tradition. Second, there are ministries of proclamation. At first glance, these seem to be the special work of the ordained; but proclamation is far more than formal preaching and teaching. Every word and deed of a Christian is an act of proclamation, and it either counts positively or negatively in the total effort of reconciling the world to God. Proclamation takes place in worship and prayer, and also through daily living by word and example the message of Christ. A third kind of ministry is that of service. We are beginning to get over the centuries-old malady of seeing service as what the professional Christians do for the non-professionals. Service is for all Christians. *Diakonia* is something the entire Body shares. We engage in service whenever we do acts directed towards "seeking and serving Christ in all persons, loving our neighbors as ourselves" and when we work to bring about the reign of God expressed in justice, peace and dignity among all humanity.[2]

Ministries of proclamation and service are directed towards the world as well as to the Christian community itself. This dual direction needs to be obvious in, for example, worship. Prayers need to be offered for the world as well as for the Christian community. Likewise, the church, ever strong on doing good deeds among its own members, must see that the ministry of service encompasses working for a more just and equitable social order.

All ministry is a matter of representing Christ and the Church. This is true for the priest who represents Christ while ministering among the flock, and for the lay person who goes about his or her work in the factory, store or office. As parents, children, friends, neighbors or strangers, everything we do is an act of ministry. As I write this, I am returning from an hour-long episode of trying to extract something from the eye of my younger daughter. I shall have to wait until morning to find if we were successful. As I put her to bed, I said our usual nighttime prayer:

Michael be at your right hand,
Gabriel be at your left;
Before you, Uriel,
Behind you, Raphael,
And the Presence of the Lord God Almighty
Above you, bringing you to perfect Peace.

We have been praying that with her every night since she was born. Tonight, before we prayed, I asked her if she knew that Raphael is the one of God's messengers who brings health, and protects us from all danger to our bodies. We got into a conversation about prayer, healing, the Sacrament of Unction, whether priests are the only ones who can bless, and "if that blessing *works*, or if it just *tries* to make us better." As I explained to Anne, what I do in giving her a special blessing (which I did at the conclusion of our usual prayer), I am doing not so much as a priest, but as her father, and even moreso as a fellow Christian. I told her that she could do the same for me. This was an act of ministry—not of my priesthood, but out of my baptism. I prayed with my child. But it was not the prayer which made it an act of ministry, as if for *ministry* to occur, something overtly religious has to take place. It was ministry because I engaged in an exchange with another person. Because I prayed, and became rather catechetical with Anne, it might have been *better* ministry (I am not certain). But it would have been ministry had I only hugged her, kissed her, and done my best to get the object out of her eye.

Life abounds with such instances of ministry. Literally every moment, especially when we are interacting with others, is ripe with possibilities for proclamation and service. The difference between the Christian and others who made do the same thing is that we are motivated to proclaim the Gospel and to serve others by the example of Jesus: we do what we do in his name. And the difference between the Christian who ministers knowledgably from one who does not is the degree to which we are aware of our actions as ministry, done because of Christ who is our motive and our model.

Church leaders can bring their congregations to see that when we look at our whole lives, and everything in them, as ministry in the name of Jesus, our daily work becomes an important setting for both proclamation and service. Most adults spend the greatest portion of their time in "work." Whether senator or housewife or secretary or janitor or assembly-line worker or priest, we can view our work as a way that we live out the meaning of our baptism.

VOCATION AND WORK

What we are talking about is, of course, seeing our work as itself sacramental, though there is not, for the laity at least, a capital "S" Sacrament dispatching them to specific jobs. Their work can be every bit as instrumental in the proclamation of the Gospel and service to humanity as that of the bishop, priest or deacon. Quite possibly, even moreso. (I pause to add, for the sake of the ordained, that no ministry is more inherent in the vocation of bishop, priest or deacon, than the raising of Christians' awareness of their centrality in the Church's mission of reconciling the world to God.)

With this view of work as a backdrop, I believe the language of "vocation" becomes viable for the laity. We need to shuck the notion that vocation is synonymous with job, however. And we certainly need to disabuse ourselves of the foolish idea that "vocation" is something that has to do with a "trade" or with a (white-collar) profession or with a life as a full-time religious insider. I have a vocation because I have a sense of call. And I believe that my call materializes not only in a particular job that may occupy me for a period of time, but in the instances which demand my response as a person baptized into the ministry of Christ. Thus, to get a speck out of my daughter's eye was an instance of vocation. So also was my "call" (which I truly sensed and still believe) to get married, or to have children, or to become a priest. "Vocation" is not a term to be used only for the big, life-shaping choices. It is what a baptized person is continually attempting to find, to exercise and to act out. One of the purposes of spiritual direction, stated in these terms, is to help the individual identify what God is calling him or her to become. That is to seek one's Christian vocation.

Of course, to talk the language of vocation can border on the ridiculous (like nearly anything else). We can overdo by talking about how we are called by God to go to the grocery store or to walk the dog. But, I am urging us to bring the concept of vocation out of the clouds and into the realm of the ordinary lay person's experience. I remember an exchange of notes with a leading lay member of one of my parishes. He was debating about whether he ought to accept a certain position within the parish structure. My counsel was that he address the issue in terms of what he felt himself called to do. This does not seem to me to be a rarified, bizarre thing to say to experienced Christian leaders. My friend retorted, however, that he was not sure what I meant by having a sense of call. He could remember only once or twice in his life having a sense of call to follow a particular course. Granted, he and I might simply have been on different wave lengths; yet, I suspect that he was one of a legion of honest, intelligent, practiced Christians for whom it makes little sense to talk about being called by God.

What do we think has to happen in order to be called? To be struck from a high horse on the Damascus highway? To be asleep in the precincts of a shrine in the middle of the night and hear Yahweh calling your name? To be tending sheep on a mountain and see a bush burning? Surely, the extraordinary experiences of Paul, Samuel and Moses are not the standards for the garden-variety *call* to Christians.

Go with me one step further and explore just what *is* a call. I have used the word "sense." I sense that God is calling me to marry, or to take a certain job, or to have a conversation with a certain person. What this means for me, as close as I can describe it, is having a "gut feeling" that to do something is very right. (I may have doubts about it, and quite often, I have a sense of uneasiness;

but these are overruled, or at least overshadowed, by a prevailing feeling of "rightness.") I suspect that for other people, who operate more on the basis of logic than personal value, the sense of rightness is less a "gut feeling" and more a matter of being persuaded of the logical correctness of a particular action. To obey this sense of call is at the heart of having a vocation.

A word of caution: I am not anxious to say that when I have this "gut feeling" that something is "right" for me, I am ready to say categorically that it *is* the leading of the Holy Spirit. Though I often do assume that my feeling coincides with the Spirit's leading, before I can responsibly claim such things, I have to take a couple of extra steps. First, I have to submit my "sense" to the Scriptures. I do not mean flipping through the New Testament to find where I can proof-text my decisions. I mean submitting my opinion to God as I understand his revelation of himself in the Scriptures. Second, I often have to check my "sense" with the mind of the Christian community. The person to whom I usually turn for this checking is my spiritual director, who knows me intimately and who is also grounded in Scripture and tradition. Third, I need to test my "sense" against what I believe to be true in my personal story and the larger composite story of all Christians.

Let us clearly understand why it is necessary to define vocation in a way that unhooks it from identification with one's occupation or job. First, to be called by God to particular choices, tasks and actions is the very stuff of ministry that is constantly happening in our lives, on or off the "job." Second, how can the bored, underpaid piece-worker on an assembly line possibly view his or her drudgery as a vocation? It is all very well for middle-class writers to argue to middle-class audiences that we ought to see our work as our vocation and as a calling that comes from on high; but that will not wash with the textile worker in Roanoke Rapids, North Carolina. And yet, I maintain that the Christian who is a textile worker has every bit as much the privilege and responsibility to have a sense of vocation. God might not have called her to stand over the loom for half of what she ought to be paid; but God may be calling her in that situation to treat her fellow-workers with concern and respect, and indeed may be calling her to support a campaign

for the improvement of working conditions. Vocation may mean
that we are called on the job, not to the job.

It is, incidentally, instructive to note how often in Scripture God
calls individuals on the job. Gideon is at the wine press, Moses is
tending sheep, Matthew is collecting taxes, Amos is dressing
sycamore trees and keeping a herd, David is out in the fields with
his sheep, Saul is busy looking for lost asses, James and John are
fishing, Elisha is plowing. We do not remember any of these
individuals primarily because of the work they were doing. Nor
do we remember them because they were promoted to some loftier
job—Saul and David being arguably the exceptions. We remember
them because they sensed, or believed, or accepted, a call from God
to proclaim or to serve. That proclamation or service may be worked
out between nine and five, but proclaiming or serving, not the
setting or the hours, is always the heart of *vocation*.

FAITH AND WORK

If it is true that all Christians, regardless of employment, have a
vocation to bear witness to Christ wherever they may be, then a
major part of the Church's job is to equip its people to take their
faith to work. Some great movements in this century have happened
because Christian business people were committed to this ideal.
Wainwright House in Rye, New York, is one institution that directly
descends from a group of businessmen who were convinced that
they had a witness to make in the world. They established a place
where now, a generation later, people come to search out their role
in deepening personal and public consciousness, exploring practical
possibilities for peace, wholeness and justice. Executive and laborer,
craftsman and apprentice, teacher and student, all have to recover
the vision of work as a setting in which they are called to proclaim
and to serve in the name of Christ. To facilitate this, Church leaders
can emphasize some basic points, such as the following.

Care about Christian values on the job. Fundamental among
these are to respect the dignity of those alongside whom we work.
Going to prayer breakfasts and reading scripture during coffee
breaks are commendable; but the Christian is called upon to take
a stand for honesty, for fairness, for equal treatment of persons

in the marketplace. People of faith have to look for ways to voice concerns about shoddy workmanship, about price-gouging, about discriminatory hiring practices. Often the raising of questions, not to mention objections, will be costly. Battles must be picked carefully and issues chosen shrewdly. The greater the scope of a person's job responsibilities, the greater the potention for effecting positive values in business.

For starters, every parish might have at least one major event each year to emphasize the importance of taking your faith to work. A seminar, a Labor Day celebration, Rogation Day workshops, a Bible study group, or at the very least a Sunday devoted to special sermon and reflection are ways we can elevate the importance of this. Over the years, my observation has been that the most successful among such attempts are the ones when local lay people are willing to share openly with others about their work: the temptations they face on the job, the difficulties of taking stands motivated by their faith among uninterested or hostile fellow-workers, their navigation between on-the-job success and faithful Christian witness. People crave hearing others talk about these issues because we all face them (including those of us who work full time for the Church.)

Be attentive to human relationships as the most important part of any job. There are, of course, jobs that rarely involve any human interaction. But nearly everyone comes into contact with customers, fellow workers, subordinates, bosses, or the general public. Most effective proclamation happens through the interaction of Christians with these others. Here we run up against one of the most serious defects in American Christianity: the dearth of positive models for evangelism. Some of us err on the side of saying nothing, lest we offend those who might perceive us to be clobbering them with our Christianity. Others of us err in the opposite direction: committing what has been called the crime of spiritual mugging. We need to learn how to equip lay people to become comfortable, articulate witnesses of the gospel of Christ. Our repertoire for "witnessing" for too long has consisted solely of passing out tracts on the street corners, buttonholing people on the phone or at the door, or standing up in an assembly of Christians with a unique story to tell. In one parish, a lay person who works in a particularly difficult environment shared with other lay persons on a series of Sundays about how she shares her faith without being offensive. She offered an alternative approach. Without pushing her religion on anyone, she openly talks with co-workers about her church (not very unique). She is engaged in social work within a large, state institution, and her sense of ministry is strongly marked with a need to range herself on the side of the forgotten, neglected, ignored patient. Her stands outside the normally expected positions for a social worker to take often lead others in her department to ask her why she advocates these people who count little. Why is she the sole voice in the institutional wilderness crying on behalf of the powerless and neglected, often on her own time and to no avail? Most of all, why does she keep doing what she does? Then she tells them. She lets them know that her strength comes from the One who made heaven and earth. She tells them that her understanding of being a Christian leads her to believe that what she is doing is right and appropriate.

People like this are rare, perhaps, but not unique. All our parishes are populated with people who apply their faith to their work. They raise moral, ethical questions about business practices. They jeopardize their jobs occasionally by the questions they raise or the statements they make. And on occasion, they are fired. Church leaders need to make a priority of surfacing such Christians as examples of how one takes seriously the persons around them in the office, classroom or marketplace.

Do your work, whatever it is, with care. Recently I indulged myself in the pasttime which Eric Berne called "Ain't it Awful!" with a neighbor. This particular morning we talked for an hour about how awful the automobile industry is—how one cannot depend on cars, how disappointing the service one gets, etc., etc. We wore out that subject, and perforce turned to talking about the personnel in another organization with which we are both familiar. They are superb at what they do. Their clients are viewed with interest, courtesy, compassion. They seem to go to any lengths to please their public, far exceeding minimal expectations. As a result, their business thrives. I had a feeling of deep sadness as we concluded our conversation. Why should that kind of attitude be so rare? Where did we lose the sense of care with which people did even menial jobs? Whether through an overemphasis on the panacea of education, or through a devouring greed for more money at the expense of solid workmanship, we in the United States are paying a terrible price in more than just dollars. We are breeding generation after generation who apparently see no reason why work should be done with care, pride and dignity.

Church leaders have a responsibility to cultivate a very different attitude among our people. Beginning with our preaching and teaching, we need a systematic emphasis on the importance of caring about what we do. The basic theological underpinning for this effort is the concept that our work is a way we participate in the Creator's work. This basis is buttressed by the incarnational reality, worded by John Oxenham in his hymn:

All labor gained new dignity
Since he who all creation made
Toiled with his hands for daily bread
Right manfully.

No work is commonplace, if all
Be done as unto him alone;
Life's simplest toil to him is known
Who knoweth all.[3]

Our employment need not be romanticized for us to believe that everything we do can be done as unto the Lord. I do not pretend to know whether such a view would redeem the drudgery of the factory worker; but I do know that it could not hurt. And maybe we would build, at least among the faithful, a population of people who saw more than profit as their motivation to do their work as caringly and lovingly as possible.

A NEW POSTURE FOR THE CHURCH

The church has to do more, however, than get its people to apply their faith on the job. We have a considerable agenda within the life of the parish itself, overhauling our attitudes about work and our approach to work.

Trouble Number One which calls for attention is what Wayne Oates has called "workaholism" in the church. Considerable evidence points to clergy as a group with a heavy incidence of hard-core workaholics. Judging from the way clergy frequently brag or complain (which?) to each other about the amount of work they do, it would seem that the first thing we ought to do to foster a new outlook on work is to ditch our own calendars and start afresh. One of the most helpful chapters in all the mountain of literature on this subject is in Jim Glasse's book *Putting it Together in the Parish*, which he named "Driving the Demons from the Datebook."[4] Carving out time for what we want and need deserves a high priority. Without doing so, even the most disciplined are hounded by the demons that ingest hours and hours. Borrowing from Chapter Five the idea of a family night, I can think of few more positive steps for parish clergy than to make one night (at least) sacrosanct, free of all church activities. Announce it to the congregation, and stick to it. That would be a piece of helpful, healthy modeling.

Clergy are not the only ones with a problem of compulsive work in the church. Consider the lay people engaged in all manner of activities. Jackie McMakin, in an article published by the Alban Institute, has researched cases of burn-out among parish leadership, and has written a list of antidotes.[5] This is an issue that church leadership, clergy and lay, need to take with utmost seriousness. I have a rule that I never ask lay people to do more than one major task in the parish at a time. If it happens that some do more, it is rarely because I have asked them; perhaps they have said yes to somebody else. Once I shared this policy with another priest who surprised me with his comment, "At that rate, I'd never get anything done!" Why in blazes are we *doing* so much if we do not have the people to accomplish it? Is the Kingdom built on the burned-out shells of overworked laity? Official boards and committees ought to be encouraged to take a serious look at what we are doing in the parish: to laity, to families, to marriages, to the mission of the Church.

Wayne Oates, in his book *Confessions of a Workaholic*, prescribes what must be done to refashion the life of the work-addict. Some organizations, he notes, are actually built on a work-addiction ethic. He cites one person who said, "I can remember when there was such a good morale in our company that you could come here any night and find men burning the midnight oil in their work. But this is no longer the case. I hope we can get back to that spirit."[6] That comment could easily and honestly be made by scores of clergy and lay leaders, substituting the word "church" for "company." Oates goes on to say that grace is the antidote to workaholism, which takes us back to the point made in Chapter Two: when the church puts a premium on achievement and reward, we are missing the heart of the Gospel of grace. We need to begin a massive reorientation in our parishes by placing some limits on the work clergy *and laity* are expected to do within the church. The logical place to begin is to devote a weekend in discussing the issue frankly. Clergy and lay leaders can resolve to examine, with the help of a trained consultant, what they personally expect of themselves and each other. From there, they can proceed to set some parameters for the rest of the parish. I hasten to add that clergy must be willing to confront their own issues before this can get off the ground. As long as we hold on to our own workaholism, all we can expect is to infect the whole parish system with our illness—the way all "aholisms" function. Though it is not about either time management or compulsiveness, a good starting point for rethinking this web of issues is John C. Harris' *Stress, Power, and Ministry.* The real issue is power, and that is what we must confront.

After the necessity of dealing with our own overworking in the church, we can turn our attention to the way we address *leisure* in our liturgies and in our programming. The last decade saw the discovery of the celebration of leisure and play, with Harvey Cox's *Feast of Fools,* Sam Keen's *Apology for Wonder* and Robert Neale's *In Praise of Play.* The celebration of leisure is far from normative, however. Work (!) remains to be done. Theatre, the arts, clowning, storytelling have all acquired an enlarged role in many parishes. They should be encouraged. Something troubles me, however, about relying on these tools to foster a greater sense of play. What we really need is to cultivate an atmosphere of joy. Though I know many parishes where such a climate is a reality, I know many others that engage in everything from liturgy to potluck suppers with a dour seriousness. Lighten up; have some fun. Bring old people and young people together for parish suppers, talent shows. Little children and youth can teach adults to loosen up in intergenerational educational ventures and at parish picnics. Sacraments can be administered with a sense of joy without sacrificing one bit of reverence and awe.

We do not need a helium-filled spectacle every week to celebrate leisure and fun. Bulletin boards can say it. The tone of the parish newsletter can echo it. Small groups, big groups, Bible study groups, can eat, play, relax. One of the most memorable Bible study groups I have been a part of decided to fix a fancy lunch before we broke for the summer. Such rejoicing in what we had learned together and how far we had come!

Needless to say, the recovery of a celebrative cycle of holy days can greatly aid us in rejoicing in leisure. Whatever our tradition, we need occasions for song, dance, shared meals, stories and laughter. As a beginning, we can pick one of the major holy days (Ascension Day comes to mind as a logical choice, or perhaps Saint Michael and All Angels) and let it become an occasion for frivolity and fun. Traditions which know secular days better can select one or more holidays (Memorial Day, Mothers' Day, Valentine's Day) and do the same thing.

In a very different vein, most of our churches need drastically to rethink the way we deal with—or ignore—unemployment. When the major breadwinner of a family is out of work, the possibilities for building faith in families multiply. Unfortunately, if job loss occurs in a social context where unemployment is perceived to be rare, such shame and embarrassment accompany it that people are loathe to tell even their clergy. While we are teaching and preaching about work, and celebrating leisure, it would be profitable to throw in a sermon or two, or possibly write some articles in the bulletin or newsletter, about the fact of unemployment. Openly encourage people to tell the pastor. Support groups can draw together several people who are out of work. Similar groups or pairings can refresh spouses and other family members. The jackpot is to have a family in the parish who is willing to be open about their experience with unemployment and to invite others to join them in reflecting on it. This is unlikely to happen unless church leadership brings unemployment (a very much dreaded status in an achievement/ production society) out of the darkness and gives permission to cope with it openly.

In a similar fashion, the parish is the place to deal with

retirement. All of us have known those who represent the extremes of sad, depressed retirement and happy, productive, truly joyous retirement. No parish program of stewardship is complete unless we talk about what we do with our *energies*. (Energies are usually referred to as talents, but that is too narrow for my taste: it suggests things we're good at.) We pump much of our energy into our work. Many people, especially the work-addicted, have not learned the spiritual lesson of living in the present. Rather than "saving for retirement," we need to invest in some fun and leisure in the present. Beyond this, we can begin in the parish to make a person's retirement a very significant occasion. In *Liturgy and Learning Through the Life Cycle,* John Westerhoff and William Willimon have a chapter on retirement, in which they suggest ways to prepare people for this important transition in life, and ways to celebrate it liturgically.[7] Availing ourselves of their suggestions would make a sound beginning towards placing retirement in the honorable position it deserves.

THE CHURCH, FAMILIES AND WORK

The church and its families can join forces to revise the place of work in our lives. We can start by helping adults to put work into the perspective outlined above. Work need not be the enemy of spirituality, the demon that attacks family togetherness, the resented intruder. On the other hand, work does not have to be our whole life, nor even the same as our vocation. Conferences, study groups and other settings for reflection can help introduce the significance of work-related issues to a parish's adult members. Rest assured, all the workaholics (who aren't working) will show up to discuss work. Tilden Edwards' *Sabbath Time* is an accessible, easy, provocative book on which to focus an adult study group. Edwards presents practical ways in which families can recover a sense of the Holy Sabbath, so endangered in our culture. We cannot deal well with work unless we also deal with rest.

Having in place a core group of people who understand the significance of work and leisure, we can take a group of families and begin to develop some simple rites to sacramentalize work and leisure. First, there is a need for a service celebrating the beginning

of a new job. Such a rite can be used either within a public
celebration of the Eucharist or within a small circle of family and
friends. As such, rites should accord prominence to reading and
reflecting on Scripture. Prayers might be offered, and a special
blessing, preceded by the renewal of baptismal vows, can be given
to the person embarking on the new work.

The Book of Common Prayer provides A Form of Commitment
to Christian Service. Similar to the celebration of a new job, the
commitment service is intended to signal the taking on of some work
on behalf of, and with the blessing of, the Christian community.
This is a dimension of work which should not be overlooked, and
in fact might be more related to vocation in the real sense than some
kind of regular job (of course it might be that too). Definitely, this
kind of commissioning ought to take place at a major service of
worship.[8]

In some localities Labor Day is a perfect time to focus attention
on the place of work in the Christian life. The Rogation Days,[9] can
be appropriate occasions for celebrating the role of commerce and
industry in our common life. Saints Days can be times for focusing
on those in particular professions or occupations. In many parishes,
physicians and others in the medical professions are invited to gather
for eucharist and special prayers on St. Luke's Day. The custom
can be extended for people in government on the Commemoration
of William Wilberforce, for military personnel on St. Martin's Day
(November 11, fortuitously), for persons who work in crafts on St.
Joseph's Day, and so forth. A few such celebrations scattered
throughout the year (and not necessarily the same ones every year),
will serve to enhance a new vision of vocation.

Within a parish setting where work is valued but not overvalued,
and leisure given its proper place, church and family can work
together to nurture in young people positive attitudes towards work.
Fitting recognition can happen within the family of a young person's
job—a paper route, waitressing, clerking in an office. The parish
church should not miss the opportunity to signal the importance
of the job. During the time of stewardship emphasis, encourage
young people to evaluate the place of their work, and to tithe their
income in thanksgiving for their jobs. Work, including all the issues
we have examined, must be a high priority on any list of youth

programs. In my recent experience, one of the most popular courses for senior highs was led by a woman and a man who raised issues like those posed in this chapter. The youths responded enthusiastically. They need, in an age of cynicism, to know the possibility of viewing work as a setting in which they can live out their baptismal covenant.

And families can play together! Of course, that is much of what a healthy ritual life produces. Camping, parish family weekends, hiking, boating and similar occasions can pull together groups of families. We have to practice leisure in order to become good at it. A good setting for young people to practice creative leisure is one that includes the presence of relaxed, accessible adults.

Vocational guidance is something that the church should offer young people—but a very different variety from that available in the schools. Not that the scholastic version is unimportant; but the Church views "vocation" very differently from the culture. While it might be helpful and advantageous for the church to introduce young people to the possibilities of careers in ministry or life as monastics, the heart of our task is to help our people identify and use their gifts to the fullest. Gift identification is any process that helps individuals to discover and to claim their strengths. To my mind, the most effective process involves people asking themselves questions such as:

What do you do well?

What do you enjoy doing?

Who are the people you most admire, your models?

Gifts Differing, by Isabel Briggs Myers, is one of the best resources for helping people discern their particular gifts. Another resource, developed around the insights of the increasingly popular Briggs Myers type inventory is Lawrence Gordon's *People Types and Tiger Stripes*, which is particularly helpful with senior high youth. All "vocational guidance" offered by the church must underscore that to respond to God's call means to use our gifts as fully as we possibly can in Christ's Name.

Nearly all young people *work* as students. Family and church need to remember that young people are not merely in training for jobs they some day will have, but are indeed working now—in school or out of it. We can do our best to erase the distinction between adult jobs and kids' jobs, as if somehow the latter were not quite real. I was impressed that in his monumental book *Working,* Studs Terkel wrote as seriously about paper boys as he did about executives, miners and models. As communities of faith, we can set a goal of sanctifying learning, whether it is academic, training for a craft, or education in one of the trades.

As surely as on the Sabbath we find that rest that prefigures a greater leisure in the presence of the Creator, so in our working we spend our energies responding to his unceasing call to bring the world to know him and to glorify him. The time we spend trying to work more thoroughly towards that end is time that will bless the life both of family and of church.

EIGHT

Holy Unction: Facing Our Mortality

The Body of Christ has a vocation to heal. Where has all the power gone?

In Ursula LeGuin's *The Farthest Shore*, we have a parable that gives us a big part of the answer. Arren, a young prince from a distant island, visits Roke, center of wizardry and the arts of magic. He reports that something strange is happening in his homeland. All the magic seems to have vanished. Wizards seem unable to cast the old spells and to work with their accustomed power. The tested, venerable formulas from the old days are being forgotten, or are no longer working. What is more, people have heard reports from a traveler that the inhabitants of one neighboring land, far from being alarmed, go about not caring, but lethargic, "like sick men, like a man who has been told he must die within the year, and tells himself that it is not true, and he will live forever." People go about without looking at the world.

Ged, the Archmage of Roke, listens to this report with interest. It is not singular, for similar news has been arriving for a time from other lands as well. Something seems to be draining the powers of magic from all the lands of Earth-Sea. After preliminary discussions and consultations with the wise powers of the Great House of Roke, the Archmage sets out with Arren as his companion to hunt down

171

the source of the trouble. They understand from the outset that it will be a treacherous voyage. They might have to go to the end of the creation in order to find what is sapping the power from the world. Finally, they reach the farthest shore, an island called Selidor. There they discover Cob, an old dead man, once himself a wizard on Roke, who found "what you cowards [he tells Ged] could never find—the way back from death." Cob had opened the door that had been shut since the beginning of time: the door separating life from death. Ever since, he has been lord of the two worlds, of the dead and of the living. Both dead and living come to Cob, seeking from him the power to live forever.

Ged's task is to find the door and shut it, to make the world whole once more. For, if that door remains open, it will "suck all the light out of the world in the end." To shut it requires all the skills of Ged's life's training and all the strength of his heart. By the time he has closed the gaping fissure, he has all but spent his entire energy healing the world.[1]

For those who think that the Christian Gospel is primarily a denial of death, this must be a confusing story indeed. It would seem superficially that the Christ-saga is about finding a way back from death. Did Jesus not open the door separating life from death? No, Jesus is the one who faced death, who headed into the finality of death, and accepted his own death even when a part of him argued fiercely for death to be avoided. Furthermore, many of his teachings caution against the seductive illusion that death can be skirted successfully. "For whoever would save his life will lose it; and whoever loses his life for my sake, he will save it."[2] Most of the things that Jesus abhorred—greed, covetousness, self-righteousness, pride, stinginess—are ways in which we try to stave off death, to insulate ourselves from the horror of facing our mortality.

Far from shielding us against death, Jesus bids us face it in the knowledge that when we do, we shall indeed die *and be raised to new life*. The trouble is, we keep selling out. We keep believing that there is a way we can avoid dying and live forever. And because we are not willing to die, we never come to new life. No death, no resurrection: Christianity's fundamental axiom.

The "Cob" who squeezes this world in his grip may or may not be called Satan; but whatever the name, he comes in a thousand forms. He promises in all sorts of ways that if we play our cards right, we will not have to die. The right investments, the precise choices of mate and work, the correct surgeon, the proper place in society: all these are the sweets that he uses to lure us. Always we are so enchanted that we lose all interest except in what we fancy can give us "life," happiness, fame, meaning, pain-free days, secure nights. One of the results of this is that we lose true power. Ironically, the very rationalism that enables our culture to control so much of nature is the thing that sometimes leads us to covenant with the forces of death that can destroy us (armaments, over-indulgence, violence, overworking), and can even block us from believing in the supernatural power available to us when we are weak, sick or threatened. We believe in our reason so much that we cannot let go of it. Logic, our power, becomes our impotence. Cob dies laughing.

The Gospel calls us to face our mortality. Christ's cross and resurrection do not obliterate death; they transform it. Death is a part of God's created order. It is good. It is only when we deny it and try to fight it off that we fall under its sway. The affirmation of the body comes with the affirmation of the natural order. And the natural order includes the truth that we must die.

If Christianity has done anything about that, it has redefined death, not trashed it. In effect, the New Testament tells us that what looks like death might not be death at all. Sacrifice, martyrdom, giving ourselves away in charity, becoming "enslaved" to God: all look like sure and certain death. But they are not. These are truly life-giving things. On the other hand, worldly success, the accumulation of goods, riches, status, all taste like life's icing. They might well be the reverse: the grist of death. Things are not always what they seem. Real death, final and complete death, is to be cut off from God. Those who are united to God through faith, by baptism, and through sharing in the Paschal mystery of Christ by which he has overcome death, are the ones truly *alive*, no matter that they may lie breathless in their coffins.

It is a paradox. But letting go our need to control everything, having a sense of our own limitations, and an attendant posture of dependence, are marks of grace. "Whoever would save his life will lose it" always stands as a reminder to Christ's followers that holding on to life (and the hope of life) too strongly is a sure way to choke it.

There is an intimate connection between facing our mortality and claiming our power to heal. The two do not seem to mix; yet a quick glance at the Early Church reveals that they do. No generation of Christians has ever been more aware of its inherent contingency than the apostolic age. Peter, Paul, the other apostles, and their successors like Polycarp and Ignatius of Antioch were ready to face death without argument or delay. It was clear to them that there was nothing about "life" that could be more precious, more desirable than giving themselves totally to the cause of Christ Jesus. It is in this same generation of Christians, however, that we see abundant manifestations of the power of the Church to heal. Though we see Paul accepting his "thorn in the flesh," we hear him imploring God to heal him of it. We see Peter and John going through the streets of Jerusalem with a power so palpable that the sick tried to get in the way of their shadow. But we see none of the apostles suggesting that sickness may be good for people, that illness ought to be tolerated as one's lot in life. We do not notice them throwing in the towel with a resignation ready to succumb to illness, infirmity, or demons. The obvious inference from all this seems to be that the apostles were ready to face death at any moment, but were convinced that as long as we live, God wills that our bodies, souls, and spirits be unfettered from sickness of any kind.

POWER

The apostles, it is no secret, got that idea from Jesus. He was ready to face death when "his hour had come," but he never preached the message that humanity was to make a truce with illness and sickness. He clearly assumed that it was the will of God that people be whole and well. It is less than clear, but arguable, from the three stories in which he raises persons from the dead that he saw nothing necessarily desirable in death itself.

How do we hold all this together? First, we grasp the fundamental datum that God is life, and that his will and his righteousness are all that matter. Second, we come to understand that God's rule is under attack from the forces of evil and wickedness. This evil infests our world, corrupts and destroys the creatures of God, and displays itself in physical, emotional and spiritual disorders. The Son of God directed his power to the undoing of this dreadful evil. Putting God's righteousness where it belongs entailed driving away all sickness and weakness from human bodies. Freed from sin (all that opposes God), people could be "right" with God, through spirits and bodies functioning the way God created them. Finally, we can come to see that the "Resurrection of the Body" is our faith's central symbol for affirming our link with the rest of the created order. Like everything else organic, we die. But when those who are already united to God (through faith, through sacrament, in Christ) die, death becomes the "gate of larger life," and is to be welcomed, not feared. In the words of Norman O. Brown, we can come to see in "the old adversary" [death] "a friend."[3]

I state all this at length because we have to be sure we know what we are doing when we go about the ministry of healing. If we are not careful, we will slide into a denial of death, and a warped religion will result. On the other hand, if we are too quick to "accept death," we will deny Christ's power in us to heal, to make us free and fit for the Kingdom of God.

If Christ spent so much time healing, then the Church must be prepared to do likewise. The apostles certainly did so, as I have stated. Morton Kelsey, in a fascinating historical survey of the Church's ministry of healing, shows that the healing power did not evaporate from the Church for four or five hundred years. About the time of Gregory the Great, we begin to notice a change in outlook. When Aquinas gets a hold of Aristotle, Kelsey argues, he simply finds no room in the system for serious attention to healing. From that point on, there is scant awareness within the Church that it has a viable, practical, healing ministry.[4] In our own time, this ministry has been recovered on a scale not experienced since the thirteenth century. The recovery has neither been sectarian nor provincial, but catholic and worldwide. Yet, for many Christians, Lourdes, Guadalupe, Oral Roberts, and charismatic healing services have remained on the fringe of Christian experience, bizarre and confusing. There is little sense that healings are *meant* to be a normative part of a Christian's life.

Part of the problem is that the categories for dealing with healing have multiplied, and in our age we have a harder time keeping them straight. I distinguish three kinds of healing: charismatic healing (administered by those who have a supernatural gift of healing), medical healing and sacramental healing. (One could play around with the category of psychic healing, to see whether they overlap with charismatic healing.) Despite the blurring of the lines among these types, they function to describe our main experiences of healing. It is useful to me to separate "charismatic" from "sacramental" healings. The sacrament of healing is a normative part of the Church's life, distinct from an experience reserved for those who have a special gift for healing. In fact, I conclude that there is not a great deal of difference between these two approaches. I hold that the Sacrament of Unction (not extreme unction, the anointing of the dying, but the laying on of hands of the sick) is a development out of the primitive Church's experience with the less ordered gift of healing.

In exercising its power to heal, the Church is involved in all three kinds of healing. For most Christians this is not difficult, because we view God as the author of healing, no matter how it comes about. We need to understand some things about healing better than we presently do, however. Foremost among these is that the power of healing is given *to the entire body of believers*. Though there may be individuals with special gifts of healing, the healing power belonging to the Body is not to be ignored. Whether we are visiting in the hospital, laying on hands in a healing service, counseling the sick or the bereaved, praying with someone before an operation, or whatever, the power to heal *given to the Body* is present. Second, in its broadest sense, the Sacrament of Unction, while administered in some traditions by the clergy, is in its widest sense shared by all the people of God as we go about our total task of healing the sick of the Christian community and the world. Thus, the building of hospitals (as St. Basil understood), the war against malnutrition in the rural Carolinas, and the surgeon removing a tumor are all part of the Church's ministry of healing.

And this is where families come into the picture. There is no family that is not going to experience sickness and death sooner or later. When people get sick or when a family member dies, we have an enormously important opportunity to build faith in families. In preparing people and their families for death, in helping them to cope with sickness or bereavement, in our preaching and teaching about illness and the Church's vocation to heal, we have a host of rich occasions to help families grow. They cannot grow as well, however, if we keep the Church's ministry of healing a secret, or if we remain embarrassed by, distrustful of, and shy about Christ's power to heal through us. And families cannot be ministered to nearly so effectively by clergy alone as through whole congregations who are clear that their ministry includes supporting and shepherding the sick, the distressed and the bereaved.

SICKNESS

Virginia had called, one of the children said. I was to call her right back the minute I came in.

Members of the parish for several years, Virginia and her husband had scarcely been to church for the last twenty months or so. Their children had faithfully participated in choir and church school activities, while the parents had been working steadily to build and furnish a new home. It was almost complete. Gus had managed to put most of it up single-handedly, perhaps aided by some extra time he had during a long siege of unemployment. A new job for each of them seemed to ensure brighter days.

"What's up?" I asked. "The children said you seemed anxious to have me call."

"Can you maybe come over?" Virginia was shyer than I had come to expect. "Gus and I need to talk with you. I'd rather not go into it right now."

"Sure I can come. I don't mean for you to have to go into any detail now, but could you give me some idea as to what this is about, and when I should plan to come?"

She sighed deeply. "Well . . . Gus had some bad news from his doctor today. I hadn't mentioned anything about it, but he has been having some tests made. They came back with the news that he's got to have cancer surgery."

Sitting at their dining table, I listened to Gus and Virginia. They were dazed. Not crying, but confused, trying to make some sense

of what they should do. Should they get a second opinion? Who
among surgeons did I know? What could they expect from the local
hospital? Should they call an old doctor friend and get some
additional advice? We sorted through all the questions and alternatives. Then I asked them to tell me how the children were reacting
to all this. They seemed puzzled. Yes, they had mentioned to the
oldest of the three, but they had not brought it up with the other
two. It had not occurred to them to talk to the children much at
all, although all were between the ages of ten and fifteen. I
suggested that their first order of business was to talk together as
a family. I offered to come back in an evening or two to visit with
all of them.

By the time of my second visit, Gus and Virginia had had time
to talk a bit further with each other and with the children. All were
prepared for my coming. I brought Holy Communion with me,
as well as the Oil of the Sick for anointing Gus. Gathered in their
family room, we were all as informal as possible. The children were
clearly self-conscious, and the parents somewhat so, none of them
having done anything like this before. I tried to put them at ease
by saying why I had come, and what I hoped we would be able
to do during our time together that evening. We began with
communion, during which I read a passage about a healing, and
offered a brief commentary on it, emphasizing the necessity of
claiming and sharing our feelings with each other. After we had
received, I began a discussion by stating some things I had learned
from families who suddenly had to face illness. I invited them to
tell me what was going through their minds, especially giving the
children some space to vocalize their thoughts. We talked as frankly
as we could about what was scaring us, what was sad for us, what
our hopes were, what we were glad or thankful about. They opened
up. They surprised me and each other. When we wound down,
Virginia commented that that was their first such discussion as a
family. I expressed the hope that it would be the first of many.

Gus's illness was not long. He recovered from surgery rather
quickly, but began to lose strength rapidly. The family went on
that ever-familiar emotional roller coaster trying to cope in the
twilight between hope and acceptance, between father's getting
better and getting weaker. Therapy did its number on Gus's body.

Hospitalizations recurred. Home visits with Holy Communion and anointing continued. During all this, the team of lay pastoral caregivers from the parish swung into action. Some stayed in touch with Gus's family by phone. Others came by with an occasional casserole or a whole dinner. Many listened. We prayed daily for Gus, and remembered him at every eucharist. When he died, quite suddenly and when I least expected it, there was a whole community of love and support that had grown up around that family. A large part of the parish had found ways of ministering to them, and that ministry continues still.

The story of Gus and Virginia is one among many that illustrate both the use of the sacraments during a time of illness and the way unction becomes broadened to include as its ministers an entire community of faith. For me, it is a model story because it is one of those memorable times when a whole family was cared for by a parish. As Gus's illness progressed, and shortly after the funeral as well, parishioners took one or more of the children away for an afternoon. They were feeling the pressures of being in a house where sickness ruled the routine and needed a break. Some parishioners extended offers to finish up some of the work that Gus had not been able to do on the house. Clergy came and reflected with Gus on the various stages of his illness as he passed through them. There were some very difficult emotional turns to work through. My judgment is that this family grew tremendously during the last six months of Gus's life.

Certainly we all yearn for the kind of reflection that was possible here. It is not always like this. Some families simply cannot or will not deal with sickness together. I am amazed at the number of married couples in my memory who have been unable or unwilling to communicate openly about an illness of one of them. Yet, more often, we neglect opportunities for helping to bring this about. I now realize, after years of ministry, that it is up to the priest to suggest that the family get together and talk things over. I have learned to offer to help this happen, and to overrule my fears of awkwardness. A key to opening frank discussions, which has never failed me, is to ask people, "What runs through your mind when you think of N.'s illness?" If "I don't know" is the answer, I try gently but insistently to get them to say something, even if it's

"Things I'd rather not think about." That gives us an opening to talk about fears, facing what we do not know or understand, and perhaps even anger. Although I continue to respect my training not to be any more directive than necessary, I increasingly make statements about my own feelings or observations—such as that anger *is* often one of our responses to sickness—and invite others to react by telling me if they experience that feeling or thought.

The kind of response that parishioners made in this situation can become a standard part of the pastoral care of the parish. I pause to comment on the pastoral care evidenced here, because it is surprisingly singular among parishes today. It need not be exceptional. After some years of effort with an arm (commission) of the vestry (the "official board" in an Episcopal church) devoted to "ministry development," we became aware that nearly all the new ministries developed were either of the outreach or pastoral care variety. A pastoral care commission came into being, which subsequently organized itself into teams of 6-10 people each who swing into action when a need develops such as the one in Virginia and Gus's family. There are other groups whose task is to provide emergency support in the form of food, transportation, childcare, etc., and still other subgroups that perform a variety of supporting functions. A team continues to have contact with a family with serious illness or death until a year or more has passed.

Two exciting results have occurred. One is that these lay persons, doing pastoral ministries "on the front," have demanded—and received—the kind of continuing education needed to be good listeners, capable ministers, adept at assessing and responding to the needs of people in crisis situations. They themselves have arranged to have consultants and professionals come to train them in pastoral skills. Second, the ranks of the pastoral care teams have grown through the addition of people who, like Virginia, have themselves received help and support.

HEALING

Dealing with sickness is not the same thing as healing, however. (I resist the facile use of the word "healing" by Christians to cover any and every outcome of sickness. Of course, to die is for the person of faith to be "healed completely" in a sense; but we need to come clean about the possibility that, despite all attempts and all faith, some sickness is going to be fatal.) If the Church begins to recapture the centrality of healing in its life, then the first thing that will likely happen is that healing will become public. Services of public healing, including the laying on of hands with prayer for the sick, and anointing with oil blessed for that purpose in accordance with New Testament teaching,[5] will provide the context for teaching about healing.

Such teaching will need to cover the points raised in the first part of this chapter: the twin dangers of using healing to deny the reality of death, and ignoring the power of healing because we fear or misunderstand it. We need to give people adequate opportunity to reflect on the difficulties, as well as the joys of healing. One of the difficulties is confronting the fact that we do not always want to be healed. Jesus sometimes asked people, "Do you want to be healed?"[6] We would sometimes prefer to hang on to our illnesses— easier than making for ourselves a new life of health. Another problem is that we run the risk of not being healed. Like Paul, we may ask for the removal of a physical problem, and find to our dismay that we are left with it. A third problem is the relationship between faith and healing, and that between sin and sickness. In Chapter Two, I addressed the faith/healing relationship. Many Christians continue to see faith as a quantifiable thing: if you have enough of it, you can get well. Likewise, they view sin as somehow lying behind all sickness: "What did I do to deserve this?" Years of teaching about sickness, health and healing may begin to make a dent in reversing that kind of thinking.

If the service of public healing is in place, the logical next step to take (perhaps even *before* such a service is established) is to create a small group of people who will devote themselves to the study of scripture and other thought on the healing ministry. Groups like this evolve naturally into prayer groups, committed to interceding for those who are ill in any way. Such a group in the parish becomes not only a fount of healing concern, but potent support for clergy as they teach and preach on healing.

Within the confines of the small group, and within the public liturgy of healing, lay persons can join with the priest or minister in the laying on of hands.[7] Until we experience this kind of touch, we appreciate only minimally the touch with which Christ often healed. Moreover, once lay persons become comfortable with this sort of participation in the Sacrament of Unction, healing/intercessory teams become possible. Pairs or triads of laity can visit hospitals and homes, and can begin to pray with families.

Of course, many issues surface amid this kind of activity. My experience has been that lay people are terribly sensitive of being perceived as "holier-than-thou" or spiritually proud. The concern is warranted. Ground within a parish must be carefully cultivated before healing teams can be appreciated, received and understood. Perhaps the best approach is for clergy to be present at least for the first several visits to a parishioner or his family, to give "official sanction" to a healing ministry involving lay persons. This strategy can help to address another very real problem: what do healing teams *do* on such visits? They offer to gather around the sick person to pray and to lay on hands. No compulsory verbal prayer is required, though in most cases all on the healing team will wish to do so. Depending on the tradition of the parish, it might be helpful for this prayer to take place within the structure of a liturgy of communion, such as that provided by the Book of Common Prayer in the Ministration of the Sick.[8] In any event, for people who have never experienced Holy Unction, or who are unfamiliar with the healing ministry generally, it is helpful if Scripture precedes the laying on of hands and prayer, anchoring it in the Biblical tradition.

Some of my most powerful experiences of unction have happened as I administered it to children. Anointing children can be helpful not only as a means of healing, but as an occasion to raise and deal with issues of sickness: fear, hope, trust, danger, protection. If the custom and awareness of the parish facilitates the presence of a healing team with a sick child, that can be a very wonderfully supportive experience. I need not dwell on the harmful effects of gathering a group of strange adults around the bed of a sick child who has no idea of what is going on! The same caution is appropriate in dealing with ill adults.

Naturally, the direction in which to move with the healing ministry in families is to encourage family members themselves to pray openly with the sick person and to lay on hands, with or without the presence of the priest and lay healing team. I remember so well visiting a person who had had a series of heart attacks and was lying in a coma in the coronary care unit. When visiting periods would come, his wife, son and daughter-in-law would gather around his bed and talk to him, gently massaging his arms, hands, feet, legs. During one such time, I commented on how beautiful their presence was and said, "I think it's called the laying-on-of-hands."

DYING

Until present at a death, I was oblivious to the ambiguity separating living from dying. Watching an individual breathe more and more slowly, I was never sure whether a breath was the final one or if another would come. The end does not have to draw nearly so close, however, for the ambiguities of death to appear. As Elisabeth Kubler-Ross has often pointed out, she does not refer to people as terminally ill, because we do not in fact *know* that an illness is final. Recovery is always theoretically possible. What is more, all of us are "terminal." Still, there is a point, more visible at some times than at others, when we begin to discern that a person is in all probability not going to recover. Usually, the sick person is aware of the probability of oncoming death, and if we are engaging in frank conversations, can tell us so. When this point is reached, the ministry of healing takes a different turn.

Charles, a divorced parishioner in his mid-fifties, came to church one Sunday with a terribly swollen jaw. Though he barely could talk, he kidded about having a pretty bad toothache. Next day, I saw him in the hospital, where he soon learned that a malignant tumor had broken his jaw. A long and painful illness ensued. I visited him for the next six months until death finally relieved him of incredible suffering and pain. During the first weeks, I prayed fervently for Charles to be healed. As pain grew more intense, I prayed more for him to be sustained and supported by the Holy Spirit so that he could bear his pain. When for a time he returned home, I prayed with him that he would feel a sense of God's presence. Then, as it became clearer daily that he was dying, I prayed with him for the mercy of God to take him through death lovingly and gently. Prayer evolved from fervent pleas for healing to supplications for acceptance and mercy. I believe that such evolution, governed by the progress of an illness, is natural and inevitable. We do not fail God or the sick person by praying for death to come, when small hope for recovery becomes apparent. Charles aided honest prayer by his willingness to discuss openly his life and impending death. He gave me the cues that he was ready to face dying. I could respond. Anyone who ministers to the sick and the dying knows that such is not always the case.

Amazingly, we can often intuit the point when a person begins to head toward death. Obvious though it be, family members are often unwilling to accept and deal with it. Some people deeply believe that their duty is to keep believing and hoping "for a miracle" until the very end. I think it is appropriate for clergy and other pastoral caregivers to respect that belief. It is equally our ministry to encourage the sick person and the family to converse frankly about the possibility of death. Sometimes, through conversations with key family members, we can encourage this dialogue. Other times, we can deal more effectively with the patient, who can give permission to family members to talk frankly about death. In any case, the ministry of the church is to deal as openly as possible, taking special care to include children in conversations that focus on death. Though much has been written and said on this subject in the last decade, we are a long way from a cultural consensus that to talk freely about death is not a way of hastening it. Our biggest gift in the Christian community is our way of helping people deal with death. When we refuse to be forthright, we fail them and ourselves.

Andrew's family illustrates how kinfolk can be natural and helpful in dealing with death. During his long illness, Andrew rarely talked about the possibility that he would not recover. He seemed to believe that his task was to keep everyone around him hopeful and cheered. As he became weaker, he was less able to put forward a bright attitude. His pain was too great. A large family, including wife, children, grandchildren and many brothers, sisters, nieces and nephews all rallied around. They were able in varying degrees to tell that Andrew was dying, and some of them were able and willing to talk with me and each other about it. I am not aware that Andrew ever talked openly about death with his family. Yet family members exemplified the helpfulness of simple presence. Joan, Andrew's wife, could share her tears with in-laws and others. Julie, his daughter, never willing to believe her father would not recover, nursed him. Joe, able to see that his father would not live long, as often as possible made a long trip to be with Andrew, who grew too weak to tell who was near him. They came, sat, chatted, sometimes cried, often gathered around his bed and prayed.

On the day Andrew died, as many of this large family as could, gathered in his bedroom. We read Scripture lessons, psalms and prayed a litany for the dying. Never have I had such a powerful sense of family helping someone to die. Families praying together can often give more to their dying than open conversation.

After death, if not before, is the time to settle funeral plans. I will spare discussion of all details except a few of the most important. Whether cremation or burial is chosen, I urge the holding of a service in the church with body present, ashes present, or both absent. Strongly expected in some denominations, the church service has given way to funeral home services in many parts of the country, usually on the basis of the belief that "it's easier on the family." Baptized persons are properly buried from the church, where the community of faith can gather and make eucharist, sing hymns celebrating the resurrection, and hear the word of the Risen Lord proclaimed.

Funeral and burial customs vary widely in various parts of the United States, but in most cases visiting hours or a wake is observed, either at the funeral home or at the family home. A vigil allowing for family and friends to come together before the funeral can fittingly take place in the church. My experience with this has been very positive. If a burial will follow the next day, the body can be brought to the church and covered with a pall. Candles are lit, as family and friends gather for a vigil. In doing this, we state strongly that we and our dead are at home in the house of the Lord. Scriptures, psalms and prayers can be read at one or more points during the usual two-hour duration of a vigil. Many find this a satisfying alternative to the whisper-filled and stultifying atmosphere of a funeral home.

If there is a burial, either of a body or of ashes, it should take place in the context of a committal rite, provided by most denominations in their books of worship. Strangely, the purpose of this part of the burial rite has become obscure in this country. The reasons for going to a cemetery or other burial place is *to bury the dead*. Funeral directors, cemetery personnel and others have fostered the idea that such is unduly difficult on the family; so in many places, family and friends gather for what amounts to another mini-funeral, leaving the burial to cemetery stevedores. Through systematic teaching on death and funeral customs, clergy and church leaders need to try in every possible way to accustom people to the idea of burying their dead with love, with hope and with respect.

One Sunday morning between services, I was summoned to the hospital where a relatively young husband and father had quite suddenly died. The next days were hard as we tried to help four young children (the two youngest were in elementary school) to cope with their father's death. My belief in including children in the grieving process was severely tested by friends and relatives who did their best to "shield the children" from the inevitable. At the burial, which took place some distance away from home, the funeral director suggested that I take the children into the cemetery office while the gravediggers finished the actual burial. The children were straining at the window to see what was happening. None of them had ever been to a burial. I asked them if they would like to return to the gravesite to watch. Without hesitation they said yes. We all stood silently, watching while their father's coffin was lowered into the ground and the grave closed. The younger ones voiced questions, which the older ones answered as best they could. We shared observations and feelings. It was hard, but burial did not become wrapped in mystery, fear or shame. My hope is that they learned something about how the Christian faith affirms bodily death and burial, knowing that God keeps watch over the living and the dead.

GRIEVING

Grieving is healing. One woman recently told me that she knew she had to go ahead and grieve, or else she would have it to do later. It took me a while to discover that for myself. My grandmother, to whom I was devoted, died after a five-month illness. Her eighty-two years had been fulfilling, though she knew ample pain and sadness. As a twenty-five-year-old seminarian, I had the notion that I would betray my Christian faith by mourning her death, so I shed no tears.

Two years later, my wife and I were zipping down an interstate on our way to a conference. I began telling her of the dream about Grandma I had had the preceding night. For no reason I could discern, I began crying. The dream had not been particularly sad, but it had been a message that I needed to do some overdue grieving.

About the time that message came we had acquired Gretchen, a miniature dachshund. For the twelve years of her life, we referred to her as our first child. She was special. Animated when young, docile and wise when old, Gretchen was one of those dogs that was "human." She lived a dozen years, so we must have endured at least a dozen scares that Gretchen had contracted some new and fatal disease. Everything dachshunds are prone to have, Gretchen had. We grew accustomed to her medical complexity. One day we took her to the vet because she was seriously swollen. X-rays revealed a sizable, and probably inoperable, liver cancer. She would have surgery on Monday. We decided that she would be "put to sleep" if there was no hope for recovery. Meanwhile we had planned a family trip. The vet said to take her and enjoy her. We did.

Monday evening my wife told me that Gretchen was dead. I had known it was coming. In all those medical crises over the years, I had rehearsed what it would be like without Gretchen. Now I simply could not register that she was no more. I could not cry. I could not talk. I could not feel particularly sad. And I was surprised at my absence of pain.

Wipers smeared beads of early morning drizzle across the windshield as I drove to pick up her body. The veterinarian's assistant gave me a green garbage bag and her condolences. Hard, cold, the package I carried was Gretchen, I supposed, but never dared to check. I recall a big, gray blank between Dr. Silverlieb's and home.

Where does one dig a hole to contain twelve years of life, laughter and love? I more or less followed the shovel to the side yard, nearest the neighbor's where she used to sneak to pig-out on cat food in the late afternoon. Gretchen's happy hour, we had cracked. Put her where she could view it.

How absolutely stupid, sentimental, maudlin—all the things my finer taste hates! A dog, a pet, an animal; and I was carrying a corpse in green plastic as if I were a prissy old Parisienne and it my prize poodle. Well, confound it, it was my Gretchen. At last the tears got past my throat.

Barbara brought her old blanket. Chilled in the March rain, we wrapped Gretchen well and I lowered her into the pit I'd dug. The scene from Frost's "Home Burial" gelled in my head and ached behind my sobs. All the coffins of my past and of my future over which I might never weep came together in that muddy hole in the yard. And after I'd let my grief go, I got on with the job.

Does it cheapen grief to talk about a dog's death and burial? Surely a small thing beside the great tragedies of losing spouse, children, friends. But grief knows less logic than does repression. We sniffled and reminisced and bit our lips for the rest of the week. Sometime later Anne, then seven, gave us a book she had authored. On the front was a snapshot of Gretchen and inside was this:

> Gretchen was my favorite dog. But when my mom side Ga-ga had too get put to sleep I was raely sad. Maggie [the new puppy] had know one to play with. So we cried for 4 days. I feel sorry that she's gone. I'm glad she's not in pain. It's butter to be with god then to be in pain. so I'm glad she's with god. Maggie's sad that she's gone to and she's also lonely.

Beneath the last sentence of her "book" is a photograph of Anne hugging Gretchen.

Remembering what I had learned from Anne, I was a little more ready a year or two later when our neighbor's dog was hit by a car. Several children saw the accident and were convulsed with shock and grief. They buried McGregor under rhododendrons in the backyard. We gathered around, the neighborhood children moaning for real. Adults, doubtless recalling other deaths, sniffed too. I prayed for McGregor and for those who mourned. Maybe the children—and who knows, the adults—will remember some day that the Christian faith takes seriously all death, and all life, and that the providence of God is not reserved for *homo sapiens* alone.

Our faith can find a spot for all deaths in the saga of redemption. None of our grief need be lost. To sieze the moment of grief, and to sanctify it with reverence and prayer, is to use one of life's most durable materials for building faith within families.

LIVING

True treasure was lost when the Church in the tenth century allowed unction to become extreme unction, an anointing reserved for the dying. Unction, the grace of Jesus Christ to heal all sickness of body, mind and spirit, is for the living. By using this sacrament intelligently and consistently, church leaders can aid our people to open themselves to fuller, richer life. And, open to the Spirit of life and of power, we can face death, as Seward Hiltner has written, with the courage "that enables us . . . to trust in God through Jesus Christ, steadfast in the future as he has been in past and present."[9]

NINE

Confirmation: Maturing

To speak of confirmation as having anything to do with nurturing faith in families is to talk in contradictions. Or so it would seem. Confirmation is the sacrament of making a more or less mature affirmation of one's baptismal vows, and receiving, through the laying-on-of-hands, the strength of the Holy Spirit to live the life of baptism responsibly. It is, therefore, the point at which we might expect a young person to break away from depending on the family. Not to grasp this idea is to miss the whole point of confirmation. In my pastoral experience, churches, far and wide, are missing it still. Old ideas die hard; and though we have come some distance in the Church from the days when confirmation functioned as the passport to communion, we still have, in most parishes, a rite that looks like a far cry from entrance into adulthood or maturity. It goes without saying that Church educators have to be uncompromising in putting to rest the error that confirmation is in any sense "joining the Church." It does serve as a way of declaring oneself an adherent of one particular branch of the Church; but it can bestow no status of belonging to Christ's Body that baptism does not convey. Just as strongly, we have to insist that confirmation is not a last-ditch attempt to school children in basic Christian teaching. Far less is it a graduation from church school!

Indeed confirmation is appropriate for those who are, or who are soon going to be, adults. We are doubtless right in pursuing a higher age for confirmation carefully and gradually. We need to pursue it doggedly. As Augustus said, "Make haste slowly." Confirmation, however, should not be automatic at any age. I would nonetheless suggest a minimum age of fifteen. Sixteen might be even better. John Westerhoff thinks that either is about fifteen or twenty years too soon.[1] Yet acknowledging the transitional situation of most churches, I believe that an age that is recognizably adult, yet still within the time when most teenagers are at home and in high school, is a desirable place to be for a while.

ANTICIPATING ADULTHOOD

Someone once shocked me by saying that the goal of the nuclear family is to self-destruct. People already frightened by threats to family stability do not want to admit that, but it's true. A family is doing its job when children are reared to become self-sustaining adults. However, children are not leaving the nest; many finish high school and live at home while either continuing their education or working. A large factor in this trend is, of course, economic. Higher education is becoming discouragingly expensive. So is housing. Alternatives available a decade or two ago, such as renting an apartment or sharing one with friends, are in many parts of the country prohibitively costly. So kids stay home and reach maturity, or at least independence, more slowly.

There is nothing particularly wrong with all this. But it does stand in stark contrast to the situation of several centuries ago. In most of the Western world, children were put out of the family by age seven or eight. Many roamed the streets of Europe begging, stealing, sweeping chimneys and seeking their fortune—if they survived. Marriages took place often between people thirteen, fourteen, fifteen. When the role of a family was to be a work force scratching around for a living, there was some need to reduce the number of mouths to feed while keeping enough young persons at home to farm or to work. The situation is different now. Education is the great priority. How long young people stay at home is often dictated by whether they need to leave home to go to college.

In any event, the biological/sociological task of parents remains constant: to prepare children to survive on their own. The age when youth cut loose from the family will vary from culture to culture and from century to century. The methods for childrearing will change. The task of parents is the same.

So how do we do it? Ah, if we only knew! We do know a good bit more than sometimes we admit. We know that we cannot begin anticipating adulthood a few years before it is reached. We have to begin from Day One.

The basic principle is to teach children to accept responsibility for themselves and their actions. As children develop, responsibilities, which are limited during the earliest years, can expand. My wife and I made a decision early in childrearing to try to do nothing for our children that they could or should do for themselves. Of course, we have broken that principle countless times, and probably appropriately so. Yet, I still remember our children cleaning up spilt milk, even though a parent had to follow with a more thorough cleaning. The axiom: "The one who makes the mess cleans it up." All parents have to take care to insist that children accepting responsibility for their mistakes is never a matter of punishment. It is natural, right, sensible. Many parents are confused about this. Hence, they continually bail out a son or daughter in drug-related, financial or legal trouble, thinking that they are doing the loving thing. When parents become aware that these sorts of rescues contribute to their child's problem, they attempt to interrupt the cycle, only to feel guilty that they are being harsh and punitive.

Along with responsibility comes truth-telling. I am more and more impressed with the identification of Christ with Truth. The Holy Spirit is God leading us into all Truth, bearing witness to the Truth of the Crucified and Risen One. Our vocation as Christians is to tell the Truth, to point to the Truth, to witness to the Truth in Jesus Christ. Frankly, all that is bunk if we do not work at truthful living day in and day out. One of Jesus' most stinging sayings is, "He who is faithful in a very little is faithful also in much; and he who is dishonest in a very little is dishonest also in much."[2] There was a time when our society valued truth-telling as a basic element in right living. That time seems to have passed. "Honesty and openness" have become a hackneyed pair in our culture, and have about all the moral content as "bread and butter" or "salt and pepper." Honesty is more than verbalizing feelings. Openness includes allowing oneself to be changed, not simply to be aggressive. Christian families must place a high value upon confronting the truth about ourselves. As we came to see in discussing the Sacrament of Reconciliation, the truth about ourselves is not entirely negative. Though we are limited, confused, "far gone from original righteousness," we are also created in the image of God, and we are loved and gifted by God. Christ's life is in us through baptism. In a world where lies, distortion, exaggeration, evasion and propaganda are taken for granted, we need nothing more than for Christian parents to set a high standard for truth-telling, on all levels, about all things. That is a key preparation for our children's adulthood.

Discipline in another key. I do not advocate a Prussian regimen. Discipline is an ordering of life, giving coherence to all its facets and parts. Preparation for Christian adulthood includes developing a discipline of prayer. Nightly bedtime prayers can gradually extend to include a growing prayer life of intercession, thanksgiving, confession, adoration. Some form of disciplined spiritual reading is a *sine qua non* in preparing to be an adult. Simple Bible stories can give way to deeper reading. C.S. Lewis's *Chronicles of Narnia* and *Mere Christianity* should be required reading for serious children and adolescents (the latter is an adult book within reach of good adolescent readers). J.B. Phillips' *Your God is Too Small*, a classic, is excellent too. Recommend these to parents and youth.

Responsibility, truth-telling and discipline are foundational elements in anticipating adulthood. If they have never been in place before late childhood, or early adolescence, then assume it is not too late to begin planting seeds—though do not expect an overwhelming harvest. If they have been nurtured all along, the journey into adulthood will be considerably further along.

THE COMMUNITY'S ROLE

Too often, people think that the Church's business is to help parents prepare children for life in secular society—"in the world." More basic to the Church's identity is to assist young people to

take their places as adult members of Christ's Body. We have trouble
with that because we continue to see Christianity as one of those
tools that helps us get through life. It is, rather, a way of life. In
grooming children to be *adult believers,* we do not have to style
a "Christian" life as antisocial, otherworldly, or out of step with
the culture. But neither does the Church have to be the midwife
of cultural conformity.

The Christian assembly has its own agenda for the maturation
and development of its young. That agenda is clear. It is chiseled
into the baptismal covenant. Our task is to produce Christians who
will be committed to continuing in the apostles' teaching and
fellowship, in the breaking of bread, and in the prayers. Our agenda
is to produce Christian adults who will know how to repent, so that
they can keep turning Godward day by day. Our goal is to produce
Christian adults who will know the gospel of Christ inside and out,
and who will proclaim it in what they say and do. It is to produce
compassionate people, who are capable of getting beyond a life of
self-centeredness, defensiveness, narrowness and bigotry. It is to
produce adults who are committed to striving for justice and peace
for all people.

Of course we do not wait to address this agenda until youngsters
begin to approach adulthood. The baptismal covenant is the
backbone of all that the parish church does. It is the outline for
lifelong learning in the Christian way. Yet we do need to get into
high gear with youth of confirmation age.

We can move into high gear by fixing a point in the annual cycle
of congregational life at which to issue an invitation to prospective
confirmands and their parents. Invite them to a meeting to explore
the nature of confirmation preparation. Make plain to everyone
that the preparation for confirmation will take seriously the notion
that adulthood is arriving. Underscore the point that adulthood does
not appear automatically at a given age. Some youth will be ready
at age fifteen and others will not. Leaders of the preparation process
need to make clear that they will view confirmation as a healthy
breaking away—in some sense—from dependency upon family and
parents, and as marking entrance into a new phase of responsible
adult membership in the Christian community. (So long as Church
regulations make full voting membership contingent upon the age

of eighteen—or seventeen in some situations—it will be very difficult to speak convincingly of arrival at real adulthood before that age.)

Allow ample time between this initial meeting and the beginning of the preparation proper. During this interval, prospective confirmands might be prayed for during the Sunday liturgy and at daily morning and evening prayer. Encourage families to talk over the matter. What else is going on in family life? Is this a good time for the young person to be engaging in so demanding and exacting a preparation as that for confirmation? Is it merely a matter of peer group pressure; or is it a deeper personal conviction, or at least a search for convictions, that leads Jim or Jane to want to be confirmed? Parents should examine their own stance. Are they pushing confirmation as the acceptable convention, or are they fostering a sincere personal search on their young person's part?

Closely following this initial meeting, mentors should be selected. A mentor is an adult Christian in the congregation committed to living the Christian faith, and interested in sharing that faith informally and naturally with a young confirmand. I find it wise to keep a list of such people in the congregation. Records from year to year show which adults have been asked to be mentors and which ones seem best at it. Nearly every year, I invite someone to be a mentor who I think will do a superb job, and I find out that he or she has no talent for being a mentor. Prospective mentors receive a letter detailing the several things they are being asked to do: spend some time getting to know their confirmands; carry on some conversations about how he or she is doing in confirmation preparation; and talk a bit about Christian faith and life. Ideally, the parish sponsor a child had at baptism is the best person to be the mentor, but in our mobile society, that is often not possible. The important thing is to select people who will have a careful, sustained relationship with the confirmand. And, of course, the hope is that the friendship will continue long after Confirmation Day. To all this might be added some expectations that the mentor will be responsible for some of the catechesis (teaching) that will go on during the preparation.

A daylong retreat is a good way to launch confirmation preparation. Set aside time for prayer, silence, Bible study. Examine commitment and decision-making. Accent not so much learning about Church as learning about oneself, one's values, giving one's self away. The purpose of this day is to provide a serious opportunity to reflect on the meaning of, and requirements for, confirmation in an atmosphere of quiet (though not somber) reflection. At the end of the day, each person should be given the opportunity to signal his or her intention about participating in further preparation. The following Sunday's liturgy should include opportunity for enrollment in the process.

To enter the process of preparation for confirmation, each young person comes forward to the priest at the time of the Prayers of the People. The service in the *Book of Occasional Services* for Admission to the Adult Catechumenate can supply ideas for guidelines for this formal enrollment.[3] Mentors come forward as well, and the priest makes clear to the congregation that mentors are those who have been called forth, and have agreed, to have a special relationship with the confirmand *on behalf of the entire parish.* Prayers are offered, possibly including a brief blessing of each individual confirmand.

The congregation prays daily for the confirmands. A possibility for personalizing this process is to divide the list of names and encourage different families or individuals to pray for particular confirmands. Mentors can add a significant dimension to their relationship with the young persons by letting them know that they are praying for them daily.

It is not my intention at this point to offer a full outline of what confirmation preparation should include. My own belief is that it should stick to the basics. My experience with ready-made confirmation courses for young people is that not only are they geared to people much younger than fifteen or sixteen, but many attempt to summarize the history, tradition and lore of the Church. If the accent is to fall on any particular subject, it should be, I believe, on Scripture. In what appears to be an increasingly conservative religious climate, it is crucial for young persons to know how to handle the Bible intelligently. They need to know how to use it in prayer and meditation. They deserve to know that it has relevance for decision-making, but that it is not meant to be used as an oracle, to be flopped open willy-nilly to furnish particular advice.

Episcopalians can use as an outline for confirmation preparation either the baptismal covenant in the Prayer Book,[4] or some (perhaps all) of the sections of the catechism in the Prayer Book.[5] Each church has its own outline of the faith and can use that as a skeleton for basic Christian teaching.

In addition to Scripture, confirmation preparation ought to emphasize how to carry on a search for truth. Young people can get acquainted profitably with the Book of Job, Archibald MacLeish's *J.B.*, Goethe's *Faust*, St. Augustine's *Confessions,* and classical Christian documents that reflect deep searching for truth. Part of maturity—a large part—is recognizing that growth never ends. We need to equip our young people to keep growing and learning.

Standards should be high. Exceptions can be made for slow learners, the mentally handicapped, and those with other special problems. Or, the other way around: special demands and challenges for the gifted, the bright, the intelligent can augment a low standard. Let us not turn off our brightest young persons by asking too little of them. They are the ones most likely to be disenchanted by simplistic religion.

Maturing embraces more than the intellect, however. Confirmation is a time to bring to the fore both the reasons for Christian social ministry and ways to do it. It is unrealistic to expect average young people in middle-class environments to work for systemic change. But, at the very least, clergy and lay leaders of confirmation preparation ought to state (more than once) that Christians are at war with the evil powers of this world, against forces that corrupt and destroy God's creatures through social and environmental systems. We can stress that point through biographies of religious leaders such as Martin Luther King, Gandhi and Dorothy Day, who have combatted such systemic evils.

Some Christian social ministry is not directed towards systemic change. Youths need to know that there is also a time to do loving deeds of service: binding up wounds, taking care of the sick, feeding the hungry, visiting those in prison. Mother Teresa is known for her courageous witness in caring for the poor of Calcutta, not for her battles against corrupt authority. One of these forms of Christian social ministry is not superior to the other; both address different situations, and both are necessary.

Confirmands generally like helping others. Not unlike most of us, they crave seeing some concrete results of their faith. One way to involve them in significant social ministry is to have each person select one or more service projects they can do basically alone, under the supervision of (or with accountability to) the mentor. Another way is to involve the whole group in performing one or more pieces of social ministry. One of the most life-changing experiences I have ever witnessed was a group of teenagers cleaning up the wretched house of an elderly, mentally ill woman, giving her clean surroundings and a new lease on life. In any case, take the time to reflect on these things with the confirmands. We often err in assuming that the reason for doing social ministry in the name of Christ is self-evident. Young people are often not clear about the connection between "helping others" and "resurrection." If we do not explicity connect social ministry with our baptism and confirmation, we unwittingly signal that the Church is another well-meaning institution committed only to improving the quality of life in society. The Body of Christ is, rather, in the business of totally transforming persons and world. There is a difference.

Weave through all this preparation the theme of making decisions and commitments. Leaving home and kindred (Abraham), accepting the call to leadership (Moses), proclaiming the difficult truth, come what may and cost what it might (Jeremiah); these are some of the models of Christian maturity that can tie together readings, discussions and practice of doing Christian social ministry.

When the preparation comes to a close, take all the confirmands away on a weekend retreat. Make it interesting, fun, memorable. Don't go easy on the silence and prayer, however. Dramatize the importance of the decision to be confirmed. Meditate on the significance of the baptismal promises. Allow lots of room for reaction and comment. We are not trying to stamp out uniform Christians, but to produce thinking adult Christians. Give each person the opportunity to decide before the weekend ends whether to be confirmed. A simple service of worship can form the setting for this decision. In our parish, we have the custom of beginning and ending the weekend with such a service at the church. It is very effective to make this decision in familiar surroundings, with supporting parents and mentors present.

As much as a week might lapse between retreat and confirmation. A rehearsal the day before the service might include silent prayer for each candidate, Scripture readings and an exhortation or homily. We have each confirmand come forward (as they will do during the confirmation service) and kneel before the chair where the bishop will sit when confirming them the next day. In this way, they not only rehearse the service, but pray and are prayed for. Mentors and other presenters are standing nearby in prayer. Communities of other traditions can adapt that idea to make it congruent with their customs. There might follow a time of complete separation for each confirmand, to spend the night in fasting and prayer. Mentors and parish clergy might have a role during the night. Those who think another whole night is a bit much might try having such a period last until midnight. If it is to be effective, it should clearly presuppose that the confirmand will be separated from the family. If the group of confirmands spends all or part of the night at the parish church, calling them together for prayers and readings during the night can be very powerful. I would add that the group must be very carefully prepared for such an experience. Do it simply, and with utter seriousness (not necessarily humorlessness).

WHAT THE FAMILY CAN DO

During or shortly after the initial exploratory meeting of parents and confirmands, parents should be invited to discuss what they can do to enhance the preparation process at home. Households can offer daily prayers, probably at mealtime, remembering especially the confirmand. Since most parents will not have gone through any process of this sort themselves, encourage them to examine their own faith and commitment. Gently and firmly persuade those parents who will view all this as asking too much of their children or as being quite unrealistic in view of other commitments that they are wrong. Make the point again and again that now may not be the time to be confirmed, if too many things are getting in the way.

The confirmand can undertake new responsibilities in the family. Since confirmation is preparation for adult responsibilities, it is fitting to alter the household routine so that the young person can practice doing new, adult tasks. For example, if taking out the garbage, setting the table, and doing the dishes are children's tasks within the family, then parents might redistribute among other family members whichever of these the confirmand has been doing, and assign instead chores associated with adults. Making out menus, shopping for groceries, participating in major family decisions about money might be appropriate. Obviously, parents will need to commit time and energy themselves to supervise such tasks. Moreover, it is necessary to select these tasks with great discretion. Fifteen-year-olds, after all, have serious limitations of time, insight, attention and experience. Helped to do adult tasks, they can learn surprisingly much. Swamped with too much work to handle, or lacking adequate adult support, they can quickly become disenchanted, discouraged and frustrated.

Families can solidly support the confirmation preparation process. Parents can encourage their confirmands to take responsibility for leading family prayers. They may wish to delegate to confirmands the responsibility for overseeing the participation of younger siblings in family rituals. Above all, families can reinforce the kind of searching that the Church is training confirmands to do in the confirmation classes. Parents have no greater obligation than to be present for the key events of the confirmation process, including the decision-making liturgy described above.

CUTTING THE STRINGS

Every time I baptize an infant, like many clergy I hand the child to one of the godparents when the rite is complete. It is a simple way of underscoring the fact that the Christian community claims the child as its own. The godparents, or sponsors, represent the whole assembly. Yet, it is *in the family* that the infant normally grows to adulthood. Not until marriage will the break with the family of origin be relatively complete. Moreover, the break from the family will be gradual. All the little departures—entering school, summer camp, first date, driver's license—will prepare the way for the ultimate departure from home. Socially, confirmation is not such a time. Status of the newly confirmed person within the family remains virtually unchanged by confirmation. Ties will remain intact.

Much parental concern in the Christian household revolves around the spoken or assumed issue of whether the children will remain actively involved in church, especially through high school and the years following. Indeed, one of the reasons that many of us simply cannot let go of adolescent confirmation is the fear that "we'll lose 'em" if our youth are not confirmed some considerable time before high-school graduation. The pull of the nonreligious culture is strong, and they will be many whom it will suck out of Christian community. In other words, ties may be cut all too soon and all too cleanly.

My own upbringing does not illustrate this kind, but another sort of cutting ties. I remember one day when I was wrestling with the issue of whether to be confirmed. Though I was ten years beyond fifteen, I was still very much an adolescent, and I carried around with me precious notions of my own identity. For me, confirmation meant leaving the tradition in which I had grown up. To espouse another church, however attractive the prospect, was frightening. Something at my very core kept telling me, "You can't! You can't turn your back on what you are. You can't leave kindred and past and roots."

With all this running through my head, I stood in the university store, flipping through greeting cards. "And how are you, my boy?" came a familiar voice on the other side of the rack. It was a professor of mine of whom I was greatly fond. He had been in succession a Roman Catholic Benedictine, a French Huguenot, a Presbyterian and finally Russian Orthodox. If anyone knew what it meant to convert—I mused—he did.

"I'm not doing so well, Dr. Barrois," I mumbled. He wanted to know what was the matter.

"The matter is that I'm thinking about becoming an Anglican, but I don't find it easy to leave my Methodist background. There are just so many ties. Ties to family, to the past . . . And so many obstacles."

"Take it from me," he chuckled under his heavy French accent, "Follow where your heart leads you. And those obstacles—those ties—they will melt as the snow in the spring sun."

His was a *Word* to me. It was a moment of Truth. I knew then that there was something in me deeper than ties that was straining to express itself.

I am certain that no failure on the part of the church community in which I came to adulthood caused me to leave it and to seek another. I have come to see in recent years that instead of repudiating the faith in which I had been nurtured, I simply sought new ground in which it could flower.

My experience, personal and pastoral, tells me that we have no formula that guarantees to make faithful Christians, or, for that matter, active church members out of our youth. We have no "magic" that will ensure where they will come out, or even *that* they will come out. Christians are not born. Neither are they made by successful educational programs or by nurture. We have to be transformed—converted—into the image of Christ, and that involves a life-long process. True conversion means, I believe, that we do not become something opposed to our deepest and truest selves, but that we become more nearly the full and free selves we are created to be. No community of faith can control the process. The most it can do is to offer families the best help possible in preparing youth to be believing adults. If that help is given in a positive and growth-producing way, chances are that something will take root in the soul, and will produce the fruits of faith in adulthood.

Despite all our efforts, some—even many—young people will drop away. Some will rebel against the Church out of a need to repudiate the family's values, standards and beliefs. Others will repudiate the faith because they honestly cannot find a way to accept Christian believing as a way of life. Still others will drop out because they will not grasp the basic message of the gospel, or grasping it, will find it so threatening as to evoke denial. I contend that we need not worry so much about all this. The truth is that even the most faithful adults have to go through a period of rejecting certain tenets of childhood faith in order to affirm a mature, personally believed, Christianity.

One of the big jobs of the Church, through its lay and ordained leaders, is to help families—both parents and youth—understand that. Where we are today is no indication of where we shall be tomorrow. Youth are no exception. Many will cut the strings not only from family but from community of fáith as well. Don't agonize about it! The task of Christian parents and of the Church is the same task of Christians always and everywhere: to bear witness to the good news of God in Jesus Christ. We do that to and with our children and youth. Then we get out of the way. We let them respond as the Holy Spirit leads them.

When I think of these things, I always remember an elderly woman in one of my parishes. Ann was unquestionably faithful. When I knew her, she could not walk without help. Several men of the parish would assist her in getting to the communion rail each Sunday. And she was there without fail, taking pains, literally, to get to the altar each week. Once, when I was visiting her, I asked her to tell me her story—of how she became such a committed Christian. She told me of growing up in the Church, of reaching adulthood, of becoming a social worker. To Ann, the "organized Church" tasted stale and flat. Her absence from Christian community stretched to forty years. One Sunday morning she awoke and said to herself, "I wonder what they're saying in church these days. I think I'll go find out." She went and heard a sermon on the topic, "God is love." That was it. I think she would agree that she was "converted" then.

Whether or not our children remain involved in the Church, and whether or not they become on some level "converted" to the truth of Christ, there will come a day when the strings will be cut— must be cut—so growth can continue. The point of confirmation is to ensure that when that day comes, young persons will have absorbed enough of the Christian faith that their lives will truly reflect Christ.

PART THREE

THE CORNERSTONE

TEN

Holding the Spiritual House Together

Placing the sacraments at the center of pastoral ministry profoundly transforms parish life. Liturgy emerges as the community's way of celebrating its growing union with God. Sacraments themselves evoke our trust as power-releasing events bringing us into contact with the divine life of Christ. We no longer see the church's pastoral task as the hand-holding of individuals through tough times. We recognize the life crises through which we pass as integral phases of the spiritual journey into the very Self of God. Indeed, Christians stop seeing the parish as guardian of society's moral investments, and instead come to church to hammer out the meaning of that journey. Christian education, it follows, becomes increasingly vital, providing occasions for reflecting theologically on all our experiences. Parents no longer expect the church school primarily to furnish religious rhetoric that youth can apply "later on in life."

The preceding chapters have detailed a systematic plan for using the sacraments as the spine of all parochial activity. I contend that, if we are doing an adequate job preparing people for receiving sacraments that are "rightly and duly administered," the bases of pastoral care will be more than sufficiently covered. Moreover, parents and church leaders will integrate the tasks of childrearing and individual nurture into the larger work of the Christian community: shepherding persons into deeper life with God. Family and parish will yoke themselves together in an alliance whose vision is to form in individuals the Image of Christ, persons whole and free, at peace with God, with one another and with the whole world.

Using the sacraments in pastoral ministry can become, however, just another program promising cures for all the church's ills, and those of the family, too. This will be far less likely to happen if we remember that the aim of the whole Church is to be truly the Body of Christ, vivified with his life, and given completely to his ministry of reconciliation. The house of faith, for families and for the churches, will crumble unless Christ is its cornerstone.

There is no way to build faith in families if that faith is not linked inseparably with the life of the Church. And the faith at the heart of the Church's life is faith in Christ Jesus, the Incarnate, Crucified and Risen Son of God. Pastoral ministry of families continually happens against the background of believing that everything we do is directed towards living out that reality. Living through all the crises of human life has only one point: that we discover on each occasion what it means to be children in the Family of God, bringing the whole creation to know, to love and to glorify him.

BRINGING THE SACRAMENTS FRONT AND CENTER

It takes years to fashion the kind of parish community in which everything coheres around a single vision. Especially in a society as flexible and mobile as ours, the turnover in membership is so great in many places that the job is never finished. New people keep introducing new ideas, and bringing different sets of expectations for what the parish should be and do. How do we go about building a core group of people who understand and appreciate the centrality of the sacraments, who comprehend ministry as the process of bringing all life into contact with the Spirit of the Most High God?

Without offering a glib set of answers to that, I believe that we can indeed set down some necessary, or at least helpful, steps. The following guidelines, adaptable to local situations, have proven workable under a variety of conditions.

Use a coherent language in talking about parish life. I stumbled upon the importance of this principle quite by accident. Years ago, attending a summer conference on Christian education, I mused for a week about how it was possible to get people to engage in activities and to appreciate experiences in a conference/camp setting that they would find strange or objectionable back home. Of course, the reasons are many, but one thing kept grabbing my attention. The leaders of this particular conference consistently used a set of terms (jargon, but not too esoteric) to convey their conception of Christian education. Conferees participated in practically everything together. As the week went by, conferencewide jokes, cryptic references to skits, repeated phrases from keynoters' addresses, helped to build a sense of shared experience. In short, we at the conference enjoyed a common symbol-system. It became obvious to me that that kind of experience is not possible on just any Sunday morning in the parish, because the "life together" simply does not exist in that depth.

Whatever I learned from that conference I shelved until later. When I became rector of my first parish, I did my best to use a consistent set of images of what we were and what we (I believed) were called to become. Indeed, the very phrase "called to become" was a major term in my vocabulary: we were on the road somewhere, we were not in a simple holding pattern. I tried to use the word "liturgy" wherever possible to replace "church service" and its relative "worship service." We began to speak about "community" rather than "congregation," and about the "parish family" rather than the "membership." Perhaps most important of all, I stopped speaking of "programs" entirely; we talked of "ministries" instead. What could not be called a ministry without exaggeration became suspect in my own mind. One day, after about two years of my rectorship, we had an orientation for newcomers. I asked the senior warden if he would comment briefly on his view of the parish's purpose and character. To my amazement, he talked in these terms I had been using. And, what is more, they were clearly *his* language. He knew the language, and he meant what he said; so he said it convincingly. I remembered what I had previously learned at that conference about a shared language. It takes longer than a week, but a parish can discover itself through its rhetoric.

Language shapes us. Church leaders have in words the most powerful tool possible for fashioning a parish's life according to the Word. Don't underestimate it! Talk about community, reconciliation, sacraments, lifelong sanctification. People will catch on. In a striking passage in her novel *I Heard the Owl Call My Name*, Margaret Craven shows Mark, young missionary to an Indian tribe, one day recognizing that the jabber of a Kwakwala conversation was about him. When he began to absorb the language, the people had become his and he theirs.[1]

Develop one or more central symbols. Some parishes are rich in symbols. Others hardly pay any attention at all to symbols. The symbol-surfeited church is not necessarily peopled with those who know what the symbols mean, and the church without *visual* symbols is not necessarily without symbols altogether. I mean something broader and more primary than visual symbols, though they have their place. I am talking about the key images from the common language. "Community," or "liturgy," or "call" are such central symbols. Certainly "God," "God's people" and "God's family" are central symbols. The symbol must be worked into consciousness in as many ways as possible. Through logos, in the weekly bulletin, in the parish newsletter, in art, banners, mottoes on the church letterhead; the central symbol(s) can be ubiquitous. One of the best examples of this symbol development is the phrase from St. Paul's Episcopal Church, Darien, Connecticut: "To know Christ and to make him known." This phrase captures the identity of that congregation.

Certainly altar and font need to become more than furnishings in a parish that seeks to build its life around the sacraments. If at all possible, the font (or baptistery) should be located in a prominent place. I prefer the very entrance to the church, so that we nearly fall into it on our way into church, to remind ourselves that our life in Christ began at baptism, and that all life since then is a living out of the baptismal covenant. At the center of the congregation's life is the family meal. So it is fitting for the family table to occupy a prominent place, indicating its centrality.

With great care we need to avoid putting "family" into too dominant a place within the life of the parish, particularly if family is not carefully defined to include more than the nuclear two-parent family. Yet, the church should not apologize for family ministry. In as many ways as possible, we need to let the evidence show that we are building faith in families as we build it in the entire congregation. The baptismal tree, mentioned in Chapter Four, is one such visual symbol of that. The occasional display of banners families make in connection with first communion preparation is another. Granting a prominent liturgical place to occasions like the Thanksgiving for the Birth of a Child is a third.

Accord Holy Baptism and Holy Eucharist the highest priority in the church's liturgy and teaching. In many places, baptism is still, regrettably, administered as a private rite after the Sunday service, or in a living room. And many churches find that pondering a weekly Sunday eucharist is totally bizarre. If either of those situations prevails, begin by using every opportunity to teach about these two sacraments. What do they mean? Why are they central? How does our life begin in the waters of the font? And how do the bread and wine of Holy Eucharist nurture us? In some places, it is desirable to make sure that every parish educational effort is overtly tied to either baptism or to eucharist. (If we are doing anything that cannot be legitimately connected to one of these, why are we doing it?) Programs on world peace are connected to our baptismal responsibility. Give to a Lenten series on depression or grief a title like, "Coping with Grief in the Eucharistic Community" —and then proceed to show how the eucharist, as thanksgiving, does not militate against depression or grief, but addresses and redeems them. Above all, demonstrate through the program that the eucharist, including unction, is a resource for the depressed and the bereaved.

Call forth and train laity to be caregivers. So long as clergy are perceived as the *only* pastors in the congregation, lay people will have no sense of ownership and responsibility for pastoral ministry. It is obvious from this book that using the sacraments in the pastoral care of families presupposes that the whole parish community gets involved in the process. Otherwise, clergy will wear themselves out. A strong group (even a strong small group) of people who are growing in their understanding of the church's pastoral ministry will, with clergy, discern what steps need to be taken to build faith in the community and its families.

In Chapter Eight, I described the work of pastoral care teams who support families in times of crisis. This kind of pastoral ministry is indispensable. It does not require adding another parish activity or group, however. It might make sense to start with an already existing group. In past generations, women's groups did many of the kinds of ministry pastoral care teams do. In parishes where there are active women's groups, propose to one or two circles the possibility of training in hospital visiting or supportive listening. Men's groups, likewise, are often searching for a project. Perhaps they can sponsor an event to train laity to support the unemployed, or to work with retirees.

Giving pastoral care will come to mean more than being helpful in rough situations, especially when we explicitly help baptismal sponsors, confirmation mentors and marriage sponsors to realize that they are pastors. Once these ministries are in place, convene a number of people engaged in one or more of them. Let them talk about what they have learned in their roles. Invite them to identify what they need to be more effective pastors. "Show and tell" sessions invariably work wonders! Let them swap stories about their experiences. Train them in pastoral arts, like listening.

View families as the major clients of parish education. I do not mean that everything we offer in Christian education should be family-oriented in the narrow sense; but build a tradition of bringing in parents to help plan the learning activities of their children. Start with one or two classes. Always look for opportunities to include parents in education activities designed for children and youth. If families, even a few, can be sold on the worthiness of a parish family weekend, or a series of intergenerational programs during a season in the church year, do it. Others will join in, if careful planning allots a place for everyone. Pepper adult education with a good measure of "how to rear your children" events. Always seek chances to knit the sacramental life of the church into such contexts, explaining the connection of baptism, eucharist and the other sacraments to the family's life and concerns.

Design bold, challenging marriage preparation. Traditionally, premarital instruction has been exclusively the province of clergy. I do not defend that view; but I do suggest accepting it as *carte blanche* for clergy to put some teeth into what they offer premarital counselees. My experience over the years is that, if people are serious about getting married in church, they are very likely to do what the church asks them. Capitalize on that! With all the diplomacy you can muster, sell them on what the church offers in the Sacrament of Holy Matrimony. Let us not be intimidated by mothers of brides who think that preparation for Christian marriage takes too much time from wedding planning.

Inaugurate changes through "pilot groups." This advice is particularly directed to those who think that "our people would never agree to that." Few congregations are full of people who get unanimously excited about anything. But they will respond to good sense when they are told that, for a year a certain approach to baptismal instructions or confirmation preparation has been tried, and it has worked well enough to continue. Before my parish embarked on the prebaptismal instruction model outlined in Chapter Four, we selected one or two couples who would experiment with us. They became valuable witnesses to the effectiveness of the model, and shared their enthusiasm with others.

Print and distribute widely an attractive, readable outline of the Church's sacramental ministry. Most parishes, however small, have some means of listing programs and emphases. A well-designed photocopied brochure might suffice, though spending a few extra dollars for a nicely produced printed piece may prove its worth. List the sacraments, and tell how the church cares for its families through the use of them. Show how the whole congregation gets involved through baptismal preparation, being mentors to confirmands, ministering the church's gift of healing, and so on. Tell the good news: the Church is the community to which people can look for a unique, sacrament-centered framework for their whole lives.

FAMILY LIFE AS SACRAMENTAL

In advocating ministry to families, the temptation is ever present to view families as more important than they are. The Church does not exist to serve families, but it can and should "serve them" in its major task of reconciling the world to God. The truth is that its own families are the best allies the Church has in that process.

Throughout this book, I have argued that to build faith in families is to strengthen faith within the Church itself.

Having claimed that the Church is primary, I am ready to argue that the Christian family is more than a constellation of kin relationships. It is a subgroup within the Church, bound together not only through ties of flesh and blood, but by Water and the Spirit in Christ. In one of his sermons, St. John Chrysostom taught his hearers to let their houses become "a church at night." He advocated getting up in the middle of the night to offer prayers, and to watch for the coming of the Lord with power and great glory.[2] The family can indeed become a church within a home—not because they are sealed off on some private tangent from the larger community of faith, but because they know themselves to be more closely related to each other through Christ than in any other way. Not only at bedtime, or in the middle of the night, but at mealtime and at playtime and at work, families can appreciate and celebrate their oneness in Christ.

And, because as Christians their life together is an extension of Christ's incarnation, that shared life becomes, like his, sacramental. Family, like church, is sacramental in at least two senses: because it hosts the unseen reality of God's Life, and because it displays to the rest of the world what it is like to be a community of faith, peace and love.

Church leaders face an urgent task to help all Christians, especially those squeezed by the pressures of contemporary family life, to know that all our moments, our decisions, our crises matter enormously. For every stitch of our lives, from birth-cry to final breath, shows the world what it is to live within the Family of God, children of a Father who touches everything about us making us holy, and whole.

Notes

INTRODUCTION

1. *The Book of Common Prayer*, p. 456. (Hereafter abbreviated as *BCP*.)

ONE—DOES THE CHURCH CARE?

1. John H. Westerhoff, III, *Will Our Children Have Faith?*, pp. 3-10.
2. Mark 3:31-35.
3. Mark 10:28.
4. Balthasar Fischer, "Common Prayer of the Congregation and Family in the Ancient Church," *Studia Liturgica*, 10:3-4 (1974), 118.
5. Edward H. Shorter, *The Making of the Modern Family*, pp. 63, 64.

TWO—FAMILIES NEED GRACE

1. Romans 5:2-5.
2. Genesis 1:3-4.
3. Bede Griffiths, *The Marriage of East and West*, p. 103.
4. John 1:2.
5. Genesis 1:28.
6. Psalm 145:15-16.
7. *The Hymnal 1982*, 409.
8. Gerard Manley Hopkins, "God's Grandeur," in *Chief Modern Poets of England and America*, p. 60-I.

9. Genesis 3:7.

10. Exodus 4:24.

11. Revelation 22:2.

12. Griffiths, *op. cit.*, p. 88.

13. Wayne Oates, *The Psychology of Religion*, p. 209.

14. Genesis 3:8.

15. Genesis 4:23-24.

16. Genesis 6:5-7.

17. Romans 4:14.

18. Galatians 4:22-26, 28, 31.

19. Galatians 5:21.

20. Genesis 3:6.

21. Philippians 2:8.

22. Romans 5:18-19.

23. Ephesians 2:14-15.

24. *BCP* p. 855.

25. 2 Corinthians 5:16-21.

26. Mark 8:34 and parallels.

27. Galatians 5:19-21.

28. *The Methodist Hymnal (1939)*, 137.

29. *BCP*, p. 837.

30. George Herbert, "The Elixir," in *George Herbert—The Country Parson, The Temple*, p. 311.

31. *The Hymnal 1982*, 313.

32. *Ibid.*

33. Bartlett, *Familiar Quotations*, p. 189.

34. *BCP*, p. 302.

35. Ephesians 6:12.

36. Ann Belford Ulanov, *The Feminine in Jungian Psychology and Christian Theology*, p. 261.

37. *BCP*, p. 309.

38. Gail Sheehy, *Passages*.

39. Theodore Lidz, *The Person*.

40. Daniel Levinson *et al*, *The Seasons of a Man's Life*.

41. Shorter, *op. cit.*, p. 159.

42. *BCP*, p. 420.

43. In traditions other than Roman Catholic, Orthodox, and Anglican, confession is often heard by a pastor or a group of (lay) peers.

44. Rudolf Otto, *The Idea of the Holy.*
45. *BCP*, p. 861.
46. Shorter, *op. cit.*, pp. 220-230 *passim.*
47. *Ibid.*, p. 237.
48. *Ibid.*, pp. 129; 227-228.
49. Matthew 5:15.

THREE—HOLY MATRIMONY: BEGINNING

1. Mark 10:9.
2. John 4:16-18.
3. Mark 7:23.
4. Hosea 1-3.
5. Mark 2:18-20.
6. Matthew 22:1-10; Luke 14:16-24.
7. Matthew 25:1-13.
8. Matthew 22:11-14.
9. Ephesians 5:21 (New English Bible).
10. Ephesians 5:31 (NEB).
11. *Ibid.*
12. Ephesians 5:26 (NEB).
13. Ephesians 5:27 (NEB).
14. Revelation 21:2-4.
15. Ezekiel 37:27.
16. *BCP*, p. 423.
17. *Ibid.*, p. 429.
18. *Ibid.*
19. Mark 8:34.
20. Marion Hatchett, *Commentary on the American Prayer Book*, pp. 427-430.
21. *BCP*, p. 423.

FOUR—HOLY BAPTISM: GROWING

1. *The Book of Occasional Services*, p. 142. (Hereafter *BOS*.)
2. *BCP*, p. 303.
3. *Ibid.*, pp. 304-5.

FIVE—HOLY EUCHARIST: RITUALIZING

1. Matthew 22:1-14; Luke 14:16-24; Matthew 25:1-13; Luke 12:35-36.
2. Luke 7:36-50.
3. Luke 14:7-11.
4. Exodus 24:9-11 (cf. 18:12).
5. Revelation 19:9.
6. 1 Corinthians 11:27-32.
7. *BCP*, p. 334.
8. When I speak of first communion, I refer to a situation in which it is normal for children to begin *receiving* communion at age six or seven. Catechesis for first communion also includes those children who began receiving at baptism or at some age between infancy and school age.
9. *We Celebrate the Eucharist* (Morristown, N.J.: Silver Burdett Co., 1985).
10. Erik Erikson, "The Development of Ritualization" in Cutler, Donald R., ed. *The Religious Situation: 1968*, p. 724.
11. *BCP*, p. 109.
12. *BOS*, pp. 8-14.
13. *BCP*, p. 832.
14. *Ibid.*, p. 111.
15. *Ibid.*, p. 124.

SIX—RECONCILIATION: SHAPING THE SOUL

1. Psalm 139:1-6, 23-24, Coverdale (1928 *BCP*).
2. 1 John 1:8-10.
3. Martin L. Smith, *Reconciliation: Preparing for Confession in the Episcopal Church*, pp. 113-115.
4. 1 Corinthians 5.
5. Smith, *op. cit.*, p. 115.
6. "Auricular," meaning "heard," is the term applied to personal confession of a penitent to a priest.
7. Edward H. Shorter, *The Making of the Modern Family*, p. 238.
8. John Updike, *Rabbit Run*, p. 185.
9. *Ibid.*, p. 282.
10. *Ibid.*, p. 283.
11. *Ibid.*, p. 102.

12. *Ibid.*, p. 101.

13. Family Service Association, *The Future of the Family*, pp. 78-9.

14. Shorter, *op. cit.*, pp. 276-7.

15. Family Service Association, *op. cit.*, p. 81.

16. John E. Corrigan, *Growing up Christian*, pp. 59-60.

17. Evelyn Duvall, *Faith in Families*, p. 27.

18. May McNeer and Lynd Ward, *John Wesley*, p. 11.

19. Corrigan, *op. cit.*, pp. 63ff.

20. Anthony F. Bullen, *Parents, Children, and God*, p. 127.

21. Herbert Otto, *Use of Family Strengths Concepts . . .* , pp. 4-11.

22. Wayne Oates, *The Psychology of Religion*, p. 204.

23. Wayne G. Rollins, *Jung and the Bible*, p. 36. See also p. 135.

24. *Ibid.*, p. 26.

25. Ann Belford Ulanov, *The Feminine in Jungian Psychology and in Christian Theology*, p. 71.

26. *Ibid.*

27. Rollins, *op. cit.*, pp. 39-40. See also p. 135.

28. *Ibid.*, p. 40.

29. *BCP*, p. 305.

SEVEN—WORKING

1. "Education for Ministry: Prospectus," pp. 1-3.

2. *BCP*, p. 305.

3. *The Hymnal 1940*, 510.

4. James Glasse, *Putting It Together in the Parish*.

5. Jackie McMakin, "How to Prevent Lay Leader Burnout," *Alban Institute Action Information*, 8 (Jan.-Feb., 1982), 1-4.

6. Wayne Oates, *Confessions of a Workaholic*, p. 106.

7. John Westerhoff and William Willimon, *Liturgy and Learning Through the Life Cycle*, pp. 149-152.

8. *BCP*, p. 420.

9. The Monday, Tuesday and Wednesday prior to Ascension Day, traditionally connected to agricultural rites and, by extension, to economic and ecological concerns.

EIGHT—HOLY UNCTION: FACING OUR MORTALITY

1. Ursula Le Guin, *The Farthest Shore*, pp. 1-4, 178-185.

2. Luke 9:24.

3. Norman O. Brown, *Life against Death*, p. 322.

4. Morton Kelsey, *Healing and Christianity*, pp. 213-230.

5. James 5:14-16; Mark 6:12-13.

6. John 5:6.

7. *BOS*, p. 151.

8. *BCP*, p. 453.

9. Seward Hiltner, *Theological Dynamics*, p. 165.

NINE—CONFIRMATION: MATURING

1. Gwen Kennedy Neville and John H. Westerhoff, III, *Learning through Liturgy*, p. 180.

2. Luke 16:10.

3. *BOS*, p. 115.

4. *BCP*, pp. 304-5.

5. *Ibid.*, pp. 844ff.

TEN—HOLDING THE SPIRITUAL HOUSE TOGETHER

1. Margaret Craven, *I Heard the Owl Call My Name*, p. 79.

2. Balthasar Fischer, "Common Prayer of Congregation and Family in the Ancient Church," *Studia Liturgica*, 10:3-4 (1974), 121.

Bibliography

Ackerman, Nathan Ward. *The Psychodynamics of Family Life.* New York: Basic Books, 1958.

Anderson, Herbert E. *Christian Baptism and the Human Life Cycle.* Ann Arbor: University Microfilms, 1970.

Bartlett, John *Familiar Quotations,* fourteenth edition. Boston: Little, Brown, & Company, 1968.

Bell, Norman W. and Ezra F. Vogel. *A Modern Introduction to the Family.* Glencoe, Ill.: Free Press, 1960.

The Book of Common Prayer and Administration of the Sacraments and Other Rites and Ceremonies of the Church. New York: Church Hymnal Corporation, 1979.

The Book of Occasional Services. New York: Church Hymnal Corporation, 1979.

Bossard, J.H.S. and E.S. Boll. *Ritual in Family Living.* Philadelphia: University of Pennsylvania Press, 1950.

Brown, John. *New Ways in Worship for Youth.* Valley Forge: Judson Press, 1969.

Brown, Norman O. *Life against Death: the Psychoanalytical Meaning of History.* Middletown, Ct.: Wesleyan University Press, 1970.

Bullen, Anthony Francis. *Parents, Children, and God.* London: Collins, 1962.

Cahaniss, Jane Allen. *Liturgy and Literature.* [n. p.]: University of
    Alabama Press, 1970.
Carr, Jo and Imogene Sorley. *The Intentional Family.* Nashville:
    Abingdon, 1971.
Chaplin, Dora P. *Children and Religion,* revised edition. New York:
    Charles Scribner's Sons, 1961.
Christenson, Laurence. *The Christian Family.* Minneapolis: Bethany
    Fellowship, 1970.
Corrigan, John E. *Growing Up Christian: Penance and the Moral
    Development of Children.* Dayton: Pflaum, 1970.
Craven, Margaret. *I Heard the Owl Call My Name.* Garden City:
    Doubleday & Co., 1973.
Crook, R.H. *The Christian Family in Conflict.* Nashville: Broadman, 1970.
Curry, Louise H. *Worship Services Using the Arts.* Philadelphia: West-
    minster Press, 1963.
Cutler, Donald R., ed. *The Religious Situation: 1968.* Boston: Beacon Press,
    1968.
Denton, Wallace. *What's Happening to Our Families?* Philadelphia:
    Westminster Press, 1963.
Duvall, Evelyn Ruth. *Faith in Families.* Chicago: Rand McNally, 1970.
Edwards, Tilden. *Spiritual Friend.* Ramsey, N.J.: Paulist Press, 1980.
Epstein, Morris. *All about Jewish Holidays and Customs,* revised edition.
    [n. p.]: Ktav Publishing House, Inc., 1970.
Family Service Association of America. *The Future of the Family.* New
    York: Family Service Association, 1969.
Ferre, Nels F.S. "A Christian Theology of Family Life." *Religion in Life,*
    1 (Winter, 1963-64), 90-98.
Fischer, Balthasar. "Common Prayer of Congregation and Family in the
    Ancient Church." *Studia Liturgica,* 10 (March-April, 1974),
    106-124.
Frieman, Donald G. *Milestones in the Life of the Jew: A Basic Guide to
    Belief and Ritual.* New York: Block, 1965.
Furnish, Dorothy Jean. *Exploring the Bible with Children.* Nashville:
    Abingdon, 1975.
Gangel, Kenneth O. and Elizabeth Gangel. *Between Christian Parent
    and Child.* Grand Rapids: Baker Book House, 1974.
Glasse, James D. *Putting It Together in the Parish.* Nashville: Abingdon,
    1972.

Gordon, Lawrence. *People Types and Tiger Stripes.* [n. p.]: Center for Application of Psychological Type, 1982.

Griffiths, Bede. *The Marriage of East and West.* Springfield, Illinois: Templegate Publishers, 1982.

Hatchett, Marion. *Commentary on the American Prayer Book.* New York: Seabury Press, 1981.

Herbert, George. *The Country Parson, The Temple,* ed. with and intro. by John R. Wall, Jr. Ramsey, N.J.: Paulist Press (Classics of Western Spirituality), 1974.

Hiltner, Seward. *Theological Dynamics.* Nashville: Abingdon, 1972.

Holmes, Urban T. III. *Young Children and the Eucharist.* New York: Seabury, 1972.

Hovda, Robert W. *There's No Place like People: Planning Small Group Liturgies.* Chicago: Argus Communications, 1971.

Hubbard, David Allen. *Is the Family Here to Stay?* Waco, Tex.: Word Books, 1971.

Huffman, John A. *Becoming a Whole Family.* Waco, Tex.: Word Books, 1975.

Huxley, Julian, ed. "Report of Symposium on 'Ritual Behavior in Animals and Man.' " *The Philosophical Transactions of the Royal Society of London,* Series B, 77, vol. 251 (December 1966).

The Hymnal 1940. New York: The Church Hymnal Corporation, 1940.

The Hymnal 1982. New York: The Church Hymnal Corporation, 1982.

Israel, Martin. *Healing as Sacrament.* Cambridge: Cowley Publications, 1984.

Johnson, Frederick Ernest. *Religious Symbolism.* New York: Institute for Religion and Social Studies, 1955.

Jones, Paul D. *Rediscovering Ritual.* New York: Newman Press, 1973.

Jones, W.T. *A History of Western Philosophy.* New York: Harcourt, Brace, & World, 1952.

Kelsey, Morton. *Healing and Christianity.* San Francisco: Harper & Row, 1973.

Kiley, Daniel. *The Peter Pan Syndrome.* New York: Dodd, Mead, & Company, 1983.

Lee, Roy Stuart. *Your Growing Child and Religion.* New York: Macmillan, 1963.

Leech, Kenneth. *Soul Friend.* San Francisco: Harper & Row, 1977.

LeGuin, Ursula K. *The Farthest Shore.* New York: Bantam Books, 1972.

Levinson, Daniel J., *et al. The Seasons of a Man's Life.* New York: Ballantine Books, 1978.

Lidz, Theodore. *The Person: His Development Throughout the Life Cycle.* New York: Basic Books, 1968.

Liturgical Conference, Inc., The. *Children's Liturgies.* Washington: Liturgical Conference, [n. d.].

_____. *Parishes and Families.* Washington: Liturgical Conference, [n. d.].

Luschen, Gunther, *et al.* "Family, Ritual, and Secularization." *Social Compass,* 19:4 (1972), 519-536.

_____. "Family Organization, Interaction, and Ritual." *Journal of Marriage and Family,* 33 (February, 1971), 228-234.

MacGregor, Geddes. *The Rhythm of God.* New York: Seabury, 1974.

McCullough, Colleen. *An Indecent Obsession.* New York: Harper & Row, 1981.

McMakin, Jackie. "How to Prevent Lay Leader Burnout." *Alban Institute Action Information,* 8:3 (January-February, 1982), 1-4.

McNeer, May, and Lynd Ward. *John Wesley.* Nashville: Abingdon Press, 1951.

The Methodist Hymnal. Nashville: The Methodist Publishing House, 1939.

Miller, Randolph Crump. *Your Child's Religion.* Garden City: Doubleday, 1962.

Moses, L.E. *Home Celebrations.* Ramsey, N.J.: Paulist/Newman, 1970.

Moyer, P.N. "The ABC's of the Christian Family." *Pastoral Psychology,* 22 (May, 1971), 46-53.

Myers, Isabel Briggs. *Gifts Differing.* Palo Alto: Consulting Psychologists Press, 1980.

Neville, Gwen Kennedy, and John H. Westerhoff, III. *Learning through Liturgy.* New York: Seabury, 1978.

Neville, Joyce. *How to Share Your Faith Without Being Offensive.* Minneapolis: Winston Press, 1983.

Oates, Wayne E. *Confessions of a Workaholic.* New York: World Publishing Company, 1970.

_____. *The Psychology of Religion.* Waco, Tex.: Word Books, 1973.

Oesterley, William Oscar Emil. *The Jewish Background of the Christian Liturgy.* Gloucester, Mass.: P. Smith, 1965.

Otto, Herbert A., ed. *The Family in Search of a Future.* New York: Appleton-Century-Crofts, 1970.

_____. *Marriage and Family Enrichment: New Perspectives and Programs.* Nashville: Abingdon, 1976.

_____. *The Use of Family Strength Concepts and Methods in Family Life Education.* Beverly Hills: The Holistic Press, 1975.

Otto, Rudolf. *The Idea of the Holy,* second edition. London: Oxford, 1970.

Pregnall, William S. *Laity and Liturgy.* New York: Seabury, 1975.

Reilly, Terry and Mimi. *Family Nights Throughout the Year.* St. Meinrad, Ind.: Abbey Press, 1978.

Rollins, Wayne G. *Jung and the Bible.* Atlanta: John Knox Press, 1983.

Sanders, Gerald DeWitt; John Herbert Nelson; and M.L. Rosenthal, eds. *Chief Modern Poets of England and America,* fourth edition. New York: Macmillan, 1965.

Satir, Virginia M. *Conjoint Family Therapy.* Palo Alto: Science & Behavior Books, 1964.

_____. *Peoplemaking.* Palo Alto: Science & Behavior Books, 1972.

Sawin, Margaret. "Overall View of the Family Cluster Experience." *Religious Educator,* 69 (March-April, 1974), 184-92.

Seward, Rudy Ray. "Colonial Family in America: Toward a Socio-historical Restoration of its Structure." *Journal of Marriage and Family,* 35 (February, 1973), 58-70.

Sheehy, Gail. *Passages: Predictable Crises of Adult Life.* New York: E.P. Dutton & Co., 1974.

Shorter, Edward H. *The Making of the Modern Family.* New York: Basic Books, 1975.

Skolnick, Arlene S. and Jerome H. Skolnick. *Family in Transition.* second edition. Boston: Little, Brown, & Co., 1977.

_____. *Intimacy, Family, and Society.* Boston: Little, Brown, & Co., 1974.

Smith, Martin L. *Reconciliation: Preparing for Confession in the Episcopal Church.* Cambridge: Cowley Publications, 1985.

Smith, Leon. *Family Ministry: an Educational Resource for the Local Church.* Nashville: Discipleship Resources, 1975.

Tatford, Frederick A. *The Festivals of Israel.* Upper Gardens, Eastbourne, Sussex: Prophetic Witness Publishing House, 1971.

Terkel, Studs. *Working.* New York: Avon Books, 1974.

Thamm, Robert. *Beyond Marriage and the Nuclear Family.* San Francisco: Canfield Press, 1975.

Ulanov, Ann Belford. *The Feminine in Jungian Psychology and Christian Theology*. Evanston: Northwestern University Press, 1983.

Updike, John. *Rabbit, Run*. New York: Fawcett Crest, 1960.

Weisenberg, David H. *The Jewish Way*. N. Quincy, Mass.: Christopher Publishing House, 1969.

Westerhoff, John H. III. *Bringing Up Children in the Christian Faith*. Minneapolis: Winston Press, 1980.

_____. *Values for Tomorrow's Children*. Philadelphia: Pilgrim Press, 1970.

_____. *Will Our Children Have Faith?* New York: Seabury, 1976.

_____ and Gwen Kennedy Neville. *Generation to Generation*. Philadelphia: United Church Press, 1974.

_____ and William H. Willimon. *Liturgy and Learning Through the Life Cycle*. Minneapolis: Seabury-Winston, 1980.

Wicks, Robert Russell. *One Generation and Another: Handing On a Family Tradition*. New York: Charles Scribner's Sons, 1939.

Winter, Gibson. "Ritual and Worship in Family Life." *Pastoral Psychology*, 11 (March, 1960), 29-34.

Wolf, Arnold Jacob. "Toward a Theology of Family." *Journal of Religion and Health*, 6 (October, 1967), 280-89.

Index